Chambers
Paperback
Reference
Books

CHAMBERS

atlas of world history

First published in *Chambers Paperback Reference Books* 1975

The original edition was prepared by Oddvar Bjørkland, Haakon Holmboe and Anders Rohr with maps by Berit Lie.

The publishers of this edition wish to record their gratitude to Haakon and Lotte Holmboe for their assistance in the revision and preparation, and also to many teachers and lecturers in history who gave advice.

ISBN 0 550 18006 0

Printed in the Netherlands by the Ysel Press, Deventer

Introduction

Chambers *Atlas of World History* has been designed with two kinds of reader in mind.

First, students who require a handbook which is more convenient for easy reference than the existing standard, expensive works. Second, the growing number of people who are simply interested in history and wish to add more meaning to their reading and viewing.

The maps are reliable and informative but the use of colour and the careful selection of place names make it attractively clear and easy to use.

The obvious aim is to illustrate history with the help of maps. But the editors have tried to do more than simply localise past events geographically. They have aimed to show the movement and progress of history—the migration of races and nations; the encroachment of conquerors and the course of wars; the shifting of national boundaries; the growth and decline of empires; the fluctuating influence of nations and religions; the fortunes of political and cultural movements.

Here, then, are not only the details but also the broad sweep of history projected in maps, forming a useful and interesting background to word and picture.

Contents

Ancient Times

From the dawn of civilization to the time of the Roman emperors

Maps 1 to 31

1 The spread of civilization to A.D. 200
2 Ancient Egypt
3 The Pyramids at Giza
4 The Temple of Amon at Karnak
5 The Necropolis at Thebes
6 The Near East *c.* 1400 B.C.
7 The East *c.* 600 B.C.
8 Mesopotamia at the time of Hammurabi
9 Israel and Phoenicia 860 B.C.
10 The Persian Empire *c.* 500 B.C.
11 Greek and Phoenician colonies in the Mediterranean area
12 Ancient Crete
13 The Acropolis of Athens from Mycenaean times to 470 B.C.
14 Ancient Greece
15 Central Greece
16 Greek and Carthaginian colonization of Sicily and southern Italy
17 The Acropolis of Athens in the Classical period
18 Olympia in Classical times
19 The Sanctuary of Apollo at Delphi
20 Greece during the Persian Wars
21 Greece during the Peloponnesian War
22 The Empire of Alexander the Great
23 Italy before the First Punic War 264 B.C.
24 The Retreat of the Ten Thousand 401-399 B.C.
25 The Punic Wars 264-146 B.C.
26 Asia Minor in 189 B.C.
27 Gaul in Caesar's time
28 The Roman Republic at the death of Caesar 44 B.C.
29 The Roman Empire at the death of Trajan A.D. 117
30 Rome *c.* 100 B.C.
31 The Imperial Fora in Rome

Contents

The Middle Ages

From the Barbarian migrations to the great voyages of discovery

Maps 32 to 55

32 The Barbarian migrations and kingdoms A.D. 526
33 The expansion of Islam and the Empire of Charlemagne in 814
34 The Lombard Kingdom before its conquest by Charlemagne in 774
35 Expansion of the Papal States 756-817
36 Division of Charlemagne's Empire at Verdun in 843
37 Viking raids 800-1000, and the political division of Europe *c.* 900
38 The Holy Roman Empire and the Norman Kingdom in south Italy
39 Europe in 1100
40 The Crusades and the political situation *c.* 1230
41 Crusader states *c.* 1140
42 Asia *c.* 1300 and the Empires of Genghis Khan and Tamerlane
43 European civilization in the Middle Ages
44 The Hanseatic League and the political situation in northern Europe after the Peace of Stralsund in 1370
45 Renaissance Italy
46 Activities of the Medici and Fuggers in western and central Europe *c.* 1500
47 The Great Schism 1378-1417
48 The Swiss Confederation 1536
49 The organization of the Church in western and central Europe *c.* 1500
50 France in the Middle Ages 1180-1453
51 England and France in 1429
52 The Byzantine Empire 1265
53 The Byzantine and Ottoman Empires 1355
54 The Iberian Peninsula 900-1180
55 The Iberian Peninsula towards the end of the 15th century (1476)

Contents

Recent Times

From Charles V to Bismarck

Maps 56 to 93

56 The Aztec, Maya and Inca Empires
57 Europe in 1556. The Habsburg Dominions
58 The exploration of the world to *c*. 1600
59 The exploration of North America 1518-1844
60 The expansion of the Ottoman Empire 1355-1680
61 The Netherlands War of Independence
62 France during the Huguenot Wars 1562-92
63 The religious situation in Europe 1560
64 Germany during the Thirty Years' War 1618-48
65 England, Scotland and Ireland in the mid-17th century
66 London *c*. 1600
67 The Holy Roman Empire after the Peace of Westphalia 1648
68 The Netherlands after the Peace of Westphalia 1648
69 French conquests in the 17th century
70 Northeastern Europe in 1660;
Expansion of Sweden in 17th century
71 Europe at the outbreak of the War of the Spanish Succession 1701
72 The expansion of Russia from 1300 to 1825
73 Campaign of Charles XII 1700-09
74 Lithuania and Poland, 13th-14th centuries
75 European colonial powers and their territories *c*. 1750
76 Europe in 1721
77 The expansion of North America 1650-1763
78 The United States of America in 1783
79 The development of India 1600-1780
80 India 1858
81 Brandenburg-Prussia 1415-1797
82 Central Europe during the Seven Years' War 1756-63
83 Paris during the French Revolution 1789
84 The three Partitions of Poland 1772, 1793, 1795
85 Italy *c*. 1800
86 Europe in Napoleon's time
87 Europe after the Congress of Vienna 1815
88 South America 1810-1914
89 Northern Italy 1859
90 The Kingdom of Sardinia
91 The unification of Germany 1865-71
92 The United States of America 1783-1912: The Civil War 1861-65
93 The Balkans after the Congress of Berlin 1878

Contents

The Twentieth Century

From the Boer War to the present day

Maps 94 to 108

94 The Balkans after the wars of 1912-13
95 South Africa 1899-1910
96 Africa 1914
97 Asia 1914
98 Europe during the First World War 1914-18
99 The Western Front 1914-18
100 Eastern Front 1914-18
101 Europe 1919-35
102 Conquests of Hitler, Mussolini and Franco
103 Europe during the Second World War, Sept. 1939-June 1941
104 Europe during the Second World War, Oct. 1942-May 1945
105 The Far East, Dec. 1941-Aug. 1942
106 The Far East, Aug. 1942-Aug. 1945
107 Europe today
108 Africa and Asia today

Abbreviations

AB.	Archbishopric
A.D.	Archduchy
B.	Bishopric
C.	County
c.	*circa*
D.	Duchy
Dsp.	Despotate
EL.	Electorate
exp.	expedition
G.D.	Grand Duchy
I., Is.	Island(s)
K.	Kingdom
LG.	Landgraviate
MG.	Margraviate
mod	modern name
Mt., Mts.	Mount, Mountain(s)
Pr.	Principality
Prov.	Province
Rep.	Republic

Index follows Map 108

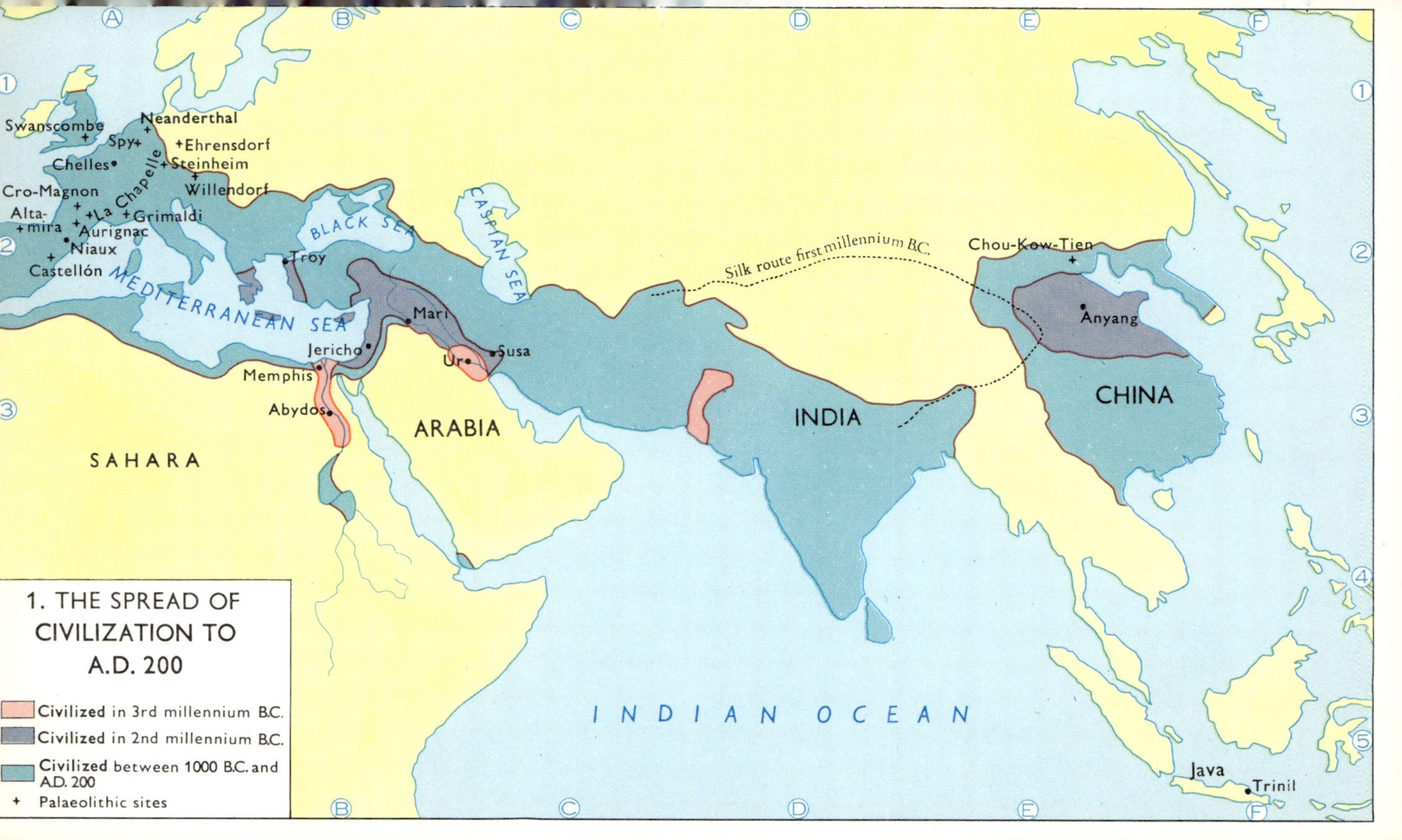
1. THE SPREAD OF CIVILIZATION TO A.D. 200
Civilized in 3rd millennium B.C.
Civilized in 2nd millennium B.C.
Civilized between 1000 B.C. and A.D. 200
+ Palaeolithic sites
Swanscombe
Neanderthal
Spy
Ehrensdorf
Chelles
Steinheim
Willendorf
Cro-Magnon
La Chapelle
Grimaldi
Alta-mira
Aurignac
Niaux
Castellón
MEDITERRANEAN SEA
BLACK SEA
CASPIAN SEA
Troy
Mari
Jericho
Susa
Ur
Memphis
Abydos
SAHARA
ARABIA
INDIA
Silk route first millennium B.C.
Chou-Kow-Tien
Anyang
CHINA
INDIAN OCEAN
Java
Trinil

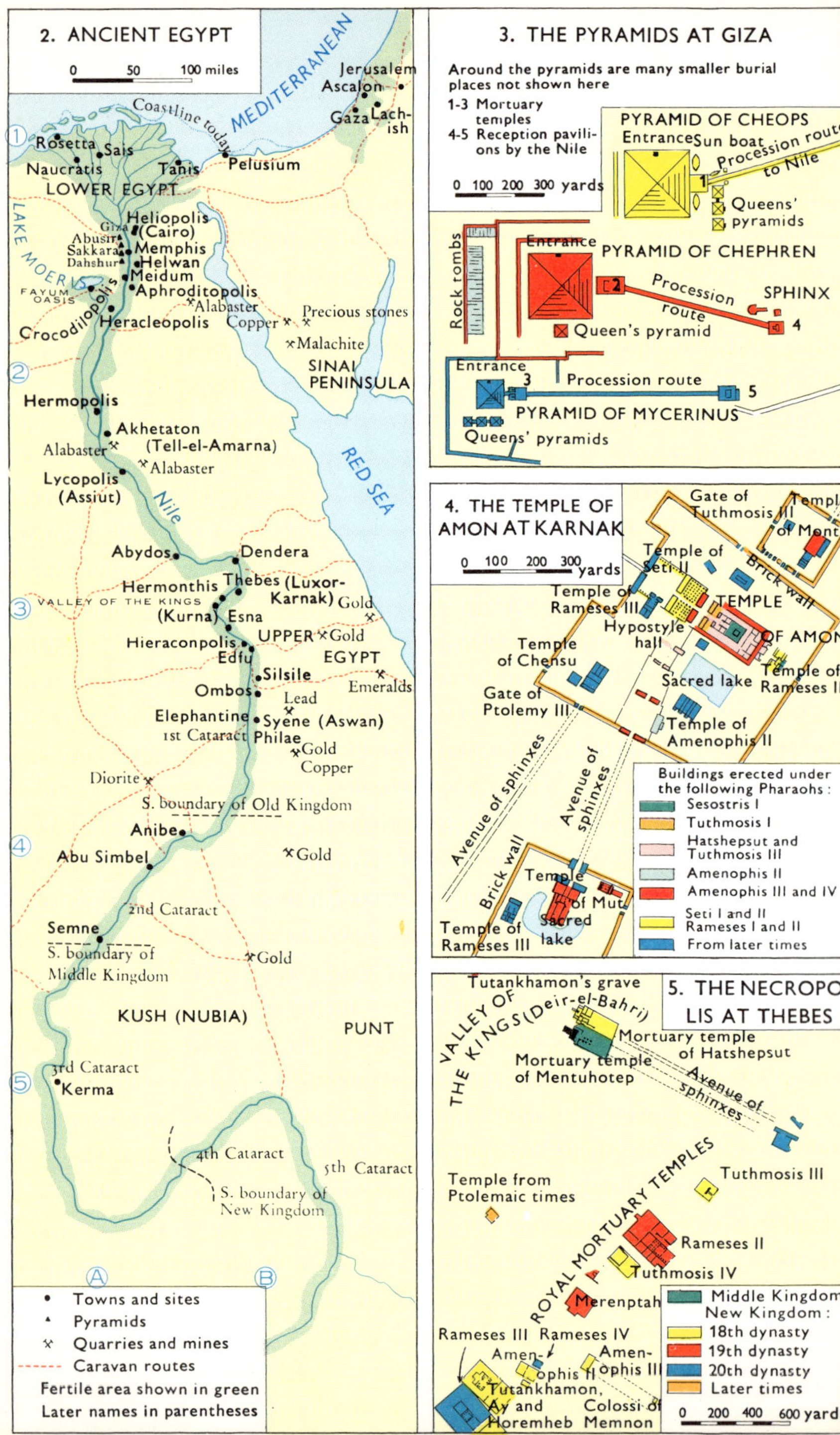

2. ANCIENT EGYPT
0 50 100 miles
MEDITERRANEAN
Coastline today
Jerusalem
Ascalon
Gaza
Lach-ish
Rosetta
Sais
Naucratis
Tanis
Pelusium
LOWER EGYPT
LAKE MOERIS
Heliopolis (Cairo)
Giza
Abusir
Sakkara
Dahshur
Memphis
Helwan
Meidum
FAYUM OASIS
Aphroditopolis
Alabaster
Crocodilopolis
Heracleopolis
Copper
Precious stones
Malachite
SINAI PENINSULA
Hermopolis
Akhetaton (Tell-el-Amarna)
Alabaster
Alabaster
Lycopolis (Assiut)
Nile
RED SEA
Abydos
Dendera
Hermonthis
Thebes (Luxor-Karnak)
Gold
VALLEY OF THE KINGS
(Kurna)
Esna
Hieraconpolis
UPPER EGYPT
Gold
Edfu
Silsile
Ombos
Emeralds
Lead
Elephantine
Syene (Aswan)
1st Cataract
Philae
Gold
Copper
Diorite
S. boundary of Old Kingdom
Anibe
Abu Simbel
Gold
2nd Cataract
Semne
S. boundary of Middle Kingdom
Gold
KUSH (NUBIA)
PUNT
3rd Cataract
Kerma
4th Cataract
5th Cataract
S. boundary of New Kingdom
Towns and sites
Pyramids
Quarries and mines
Caravan routes
Fertile area shown in green
Later names in parentheses
3. THE PYRAMIDS AT GIZA
Around the pyramids are many smaller burial places not shown here
1-3 Mortuary temples
4-5 Reception pavilions by the Nile
0 100 200 300 yards
PYRAMID OF CHEOPS
Entrance
Sun boat
Procession route to Nile
Queens' pyramids
Rock tombs
Entrance
PYRAMID OF CHEPHREN
Procession route
SPHINX
Queen's pyramid
Entrance
Procession route
PYRAMID OF MYCERINUS
Queens' pyramids
4. THE TEMPLE OF AMON AT KARNAK
0 100 200 300 yards
Gate of Tuthmosis III
Temple of Montu
Temple of Seti II
Brick wall
Temple of Rameses III
TEMPLE OF AMON
Hypostyle hall
Temple of Chensu
Sacred lake
Temple of Rameses II
Gate of Ptolemy III
Temple of Amenophis II
Avenue of sphinxes
Avenue of sphinxes
Brick wall
Temple of Mut
Sacred lake
Temple of Rameses III
Buildings erected under the following Pharaohs:
Sesostris I
Tuthmosis I
Hatshepsut and Tuthmosis III
Amenophis II
Amenophis III and IV
Seti I and II
Rameses I and II
From later times
5. THE NECROPOLIS AT THEBES
Tutankhamon's grave
THE VALLEY OF KINGS
(Deir-el-Bahri)
Mortuary temple of Hatshepsut
Mortuary temple of Mentuhotep
Avenue of sphinxes
Tuthmosis III
Temple from Ptolemaic times
ROYAL MORTUARY TEMPLES
Rameses II
Tuthmosis IV
Merenptah
Rameses III
Rameses IV
Amenophis II
Amenophis III
Tutankhamon, Ay and Horemheb
Colossi of Memnon
Middle Kingdom
New Kingdom:
18th dynasty
19th dynasty
20th dynasty
Later times
0 200 400 600 yards

6. THE NEAR EAST
c. 1400 B.C.
Later names are in parentheses
0 100 200 300 miles
BLACK SEA
COLCHIS
CAUCASUS
Ararat
SEA OF MARMARA
Troy
PHRYGIA
Halys
(Alaça Hüyük)
Hattushash (Bogaz-Köy)
HITTITE EMPIRE
Sardes
Kanesh
(Malatya)
(Maras)
(Zincirli)
Sakjegözü
Tarsus
AMQ
Amanus
Carchemish
MITANNI
ASSYRIA
Nineveh
Arbela
Great Zab
Little Zab
Ashur
KASSITES
Rhodes
MINOAN-MYCENAEAN TERRITORY
Alalakh (Atchana)
Haleb (Aleppo)
Ugarit (Ras Shamra)
Orontes
Cyprus
Qatna
Kadesh
MESOPOTAMIA
Mari
Euphrates
Tigris
Byblos
Sidon
Tyre
Damascus
MEDITERRANEAN SEA
Megiddo
Ascalon
Jerusalem
Lachish
EGYPTIAN EMPIRE
Sippar
Babylon
Kish
Nippur
Lagash
Urek
Larsa
Ur
ELAM
BABYLONIA
SYRIAN DESERT
Memphis
LAKE MOERIS
FAYUM
SINAI
ARABIA
(Tell-el-Amarna)
RED SEA
Nile
Thebes
7. THE EAST
c. 600 B.C.
Lydian Kingdom
Median Kingdom
Neo-Babylonian Empire
Greatest extent of Assyrian Empire c. 700 B.C.
0 200 400 miles
BLACK SEA
CAUCASUS
CASPIAN SEA
LYDIA
Sardes
Miletus
PISIDIA
ARMENIA
Cyrus
CILICIA
ASSYRIA
MEDIA
Tigris
Rhodes
Cyprus
SYRIA
MESOPOTAMIA
Euphrates
PARTHIA
BACTRIA
MEDITERRANEAN SEA
Sidon
Tyre
Damascus
Ecbatana
ARIA
ARACHOSIA
Sais
Gaza
Babylon
BABYLONIA
Susa
GOSHEN
Memphis
Nile
EGYPT
Indus
PERSIA
Thebes
RED SEA
ARABIA
PERSIAN GULF
GEDROSIA

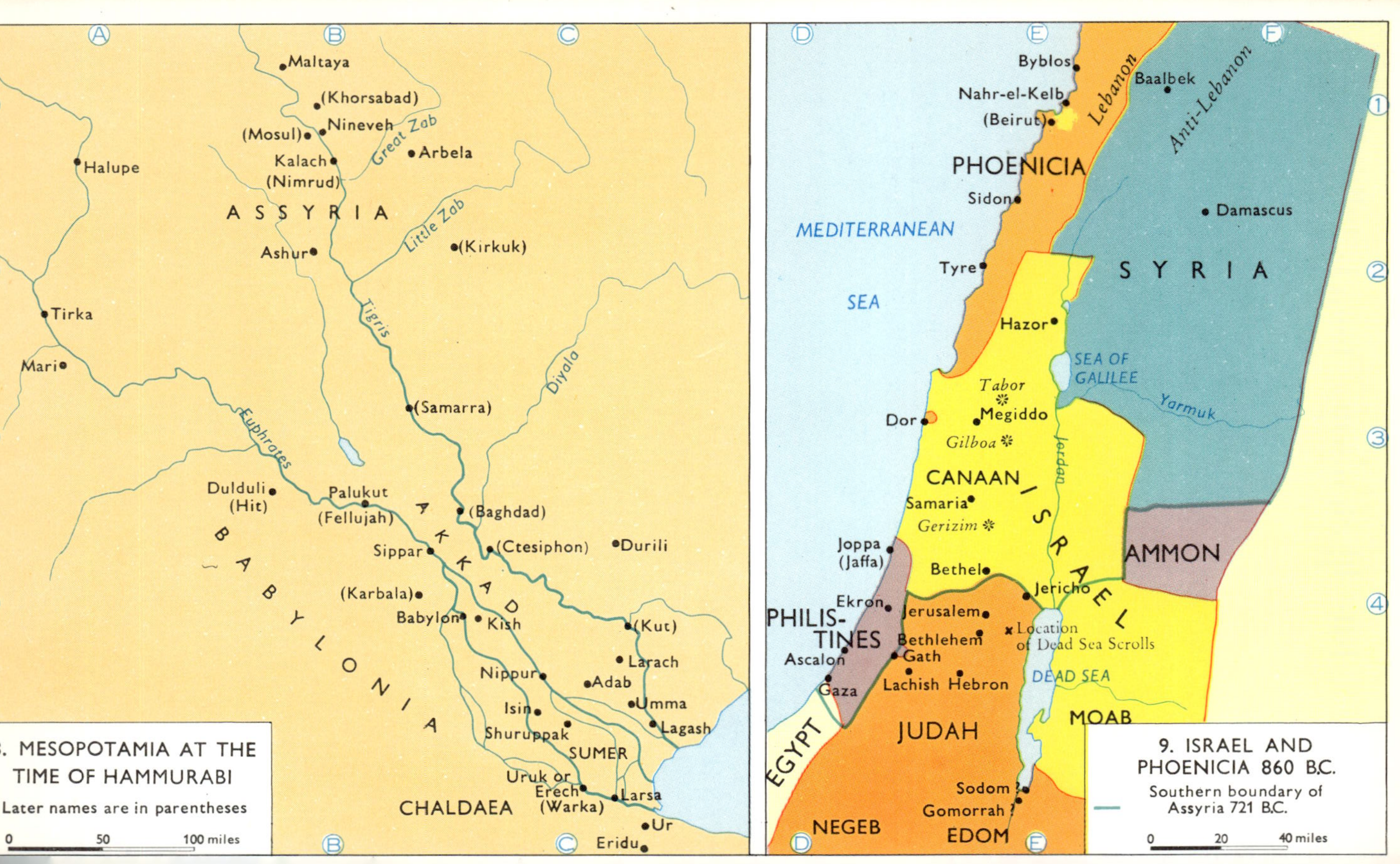

8. MESOPOTAMIA AT THE TIME OF HAMMURABI

Later names are in parentheses

9. ISRAEL AND PHOENICIA 860 B.C.

10. THE PERSIAN EMPIRE c. 500 B.C.
King's road between Susa and Sardes
0 200 400 600 miles
SCYTHIANS
MACEDONIA
THRACE
BLACK SEA
GREECE
Delphi
AEGEAN SEA
Athens
Sparta
PHRYGIA
Gordium
Sardes
Miletus
LYDIA
CAPPADOCIA
Halys
Taurus
COLCHIS
Caucasus
Cyrus
Araxes
CASPIAN SEA
ARAL SEA
Jaxartes
Oxus
SOGDIANA
BACTRIA
Crete
Rhodes
CILICIA
Tarsus
Carchemish
Tigris
Gaugamela
Nineveh
Arbela
Ashur
Cyprus
MEDITERRANEAN SEA
SYRIA
Sidon
Tyre
Damascus
Euphrates
ASSYRIA
MEDIA
PARTHIA
Ecbatana
Behistun
ARIA
LIBYA
PHOENICIA
ISRAEL
Samaria
Jerusalem
Ctesiphon
Babylon
Susa
SYRIAN DESERT
LIBYAN DESERT
Sais
Pithom
JUDAH
BABYLONIA
Oracle of Amon
Memphis
Nile
Pasargadae
Persepolis
Indus
EGYPT
PERSIA
PERSIAN GULF
RED SEA
Thebes
ARABIA
GEDROSIA

11. GREEK AND PHOENICIAN COLONIES IN THE MEDITERRANEAN AREA

12. ANCIENT CRETE

13. THE ACROPOLIS OF ATHENS FROM MYCENAEAN TIMES TO 470 B.C.

14. ANCIENT GREECE
Greek peoples:
Ionians
Dorians
Aeolians
Northwest Greeks (North Dorians)
Arcadians
0 20 40 60 miles
ILLYRIA
MACEDONIA
EPIRUS
THESSALY
THRACE
CHALCIDICE
CHERSONESUS
Axius
Pella
Amphipolis
Philippi
Abdera
Thessalonica
Thasos
Samothrace
Pydna
Olynthus
Potidaea
Mt. Athos
Imbros
Abydos
HELLES PONT
Troy (Ilium)
Tenedos
Lemnos
Haliacmon
Mt. Olympus
Heracleum
Vale of Tempe
Peneus
Europus
Ossa
Larisa
Dodona
Pindus
Pelion
Pharsalus
Ambracia
THRACIAN SEA
AEGEAN SEA
Lesbos
Mytilene
Peparethos
Scyros
Phocaea
Chios
Actium
Achelous
Lamia
Mt. Oeta
Thermopylae
Leucas
ACARNANIA
AETOLIA
Parnassus
LOCRIS
PHOCIS
Euboea
Chalcis
Eretria
Ithaca
Naupactus
Delphi
BOEOTIA
Tanagra
Leuctra
Thebes
Cephallenia
GULF OF CORINTH
ACHAEA
Marathon
ATTICA
Carystus
Megara
Athens
Andros
Samos
Elis
Clitor
Corinth
Zacynthus
ELIS
Mycenae
Epidaurus
CAPE SUNIUM
Ceos
Tenos
Icaria
ARCADIA
Olympia
Tiryns
ARGOLIS
Calauria
Alpheus
Syros
Myconos
Cyclades
Delos
Patmos
Cythnos
PELOPONNESUS
Hydra
IONIAN SEA
MESSENIA
Sparta
Taygetus
Seriphos
Paros
Naxos
Pylus
Vaphio
Siphnos
Amorgos
Sphacteria
LACONIA
Melos
Sicinos
Ios
Thera
Cythera
SEA OF CRETE
Heracleum (Candia)
Cnossus
Crete
Phaestus
15. CENTRAL GREECE
0 10 20 miles
Mt. Parnassus
Orchomenus
Euboea
Aegitium
Delphi
Chaeronea
L. COPAIS
Chalcis
Polis
PHOCIS
Aulis
Eretria
Coronea
BOEOTIA
Thebes
Mt. Helicon
Thespiae
Tanagra
GULF OF CORINTH
Aegium
Ascra
Leuctra
Plataea
ACHAEA
Aegira
Decelea
Marathon
Eleusis
ATTICA
Sicyon
Megara
Athens
Carystus
Salamis
Salamis
Piraeus
Mt. Hymettus
Clitor
Stymphalus
Corinth
Andros
Prasiae
Nemea
GULF OF SAROS
ARCADIA
ARGOLIS
Aegina
Aegina
Mycenae
Midea (Dendra)
Argos
Tiryns
Epidaurus
CAPE SUNIUM
Ceos
Mantinea
Lerna
Asine

16. GREEK AND CARTHAGINIAN COLONIZATION OF SICILY AND SOUTHERN ITALY
Panormus: Carthaginian colony
Syracuse: Greek colony
Boundary of Carthaginian territory
0 20 40 60 80 miles
TYRRHENIAN SEA
MAGNA GRAECIA
IONIAN SEA
MEDITERRANEAN SEA
Laus
Cerilli
Sybaris (destroyed 510 B.C.)
Thurii
Consentia
Croton
Hipponium
Scyllecium
Liparaeae Is.
Lipara
Metaurum
Caulonia
Scyllaeum
Messana
Locri
Mylae
Tyndaris
Rhegium
Strait of Messina
Panormus
Solus
Drepanum
Segesta
Himera
Mytistratum
Lilybaeum
Hypsus
Tauromenium
Naxus
Etna
Mazara
Selinus
Symaithus
Catana
Heraclea Minoa
Halycus
Himera
Gelas
Eryces
Leontini
Acragas (Agrigentum)
Megara
Anapus
Syracuse
Gela
Acrae
Camarina
17. THE ACROPOLIS OF ATHENS IN THE CLASSICAL PERIOD
Buildings from before 450 B.C.
Buildings from the time of Pericles
Buildings from the Hellenistic period
Buildings from the time of the Roman emperors
0 20 40 60 80 100 yards
Wall of Themistocles
Stoa
Clepsydra
Erechtheum
Altar of Athena
Temple of Zeus
Pinacothek
Statue of Athena
Old Temple of Athena
Propylaea
Temple of Roma and Augustus
Temple of Artemis of Brauron
Parthenon
Pantheon
Temple of Nike
Chalcotheke
Supporting wall
Wall of Cimon
Odeum of Herodes
Temple of Asclepius
Theatre of Dionysus
Stoa of Eumenes

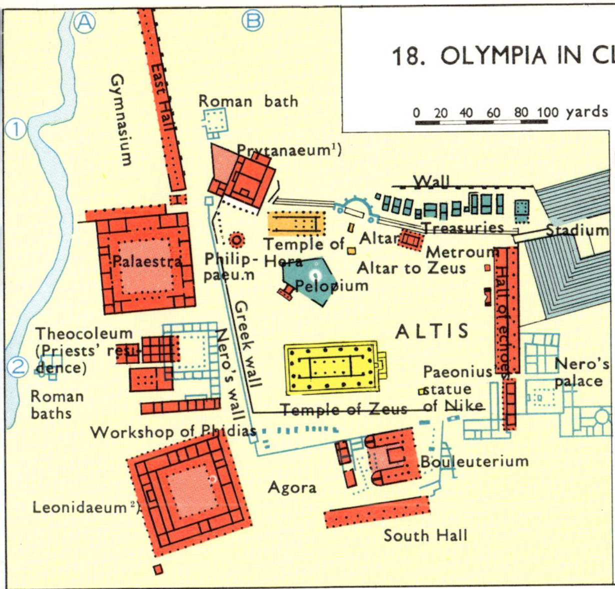

18. OLYMPIA IN CLASSICAL TIMES

0 20 40 60 80 100 yards

Buildings from:
- 7th century B.C.
- 6th century B.C.
- Middle of 5th cent. B.C.
- 4th and 3rd cent. B.C.
- Time of Nero

A B 1 2
Gymnasium
East Hall
Roman bath
Prytanaeum[1])
Wall
Treasuries
Stadium
Temple of Hera
Altar
Metroum
Altar to Zeus
Palaestra
Philippaeum
Pelopium
Hall of echoes
ALTIS
Theocoleum (Priests' residence)
Roman baths
Greek wall
Nero's wall
Nero's palace
Paeonius statue of Nike
Temple of Zeus
Workshop of Phidias
Bouleuterium
Agora
Leonidaeum[2])
South Hall

[1]) In the Prytanaeum stood an altar to Hestia where the sacred fire of Olympia burned and a hall where banquets were held for the victors.

[2]) The Leonidaeum was built by the Elean Leonidas. It was later rebuilt to serve as a residence for the Roman governor.

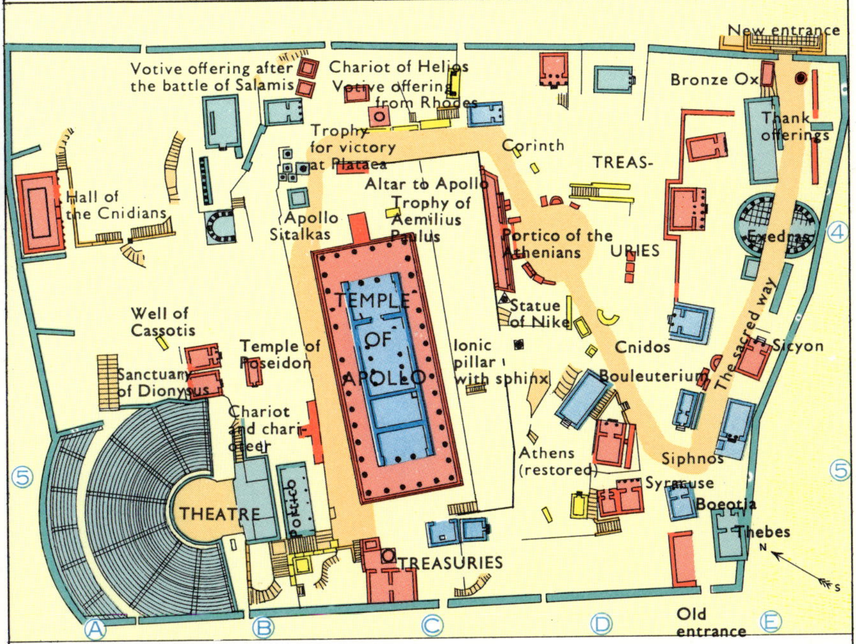

New entrance
Votive offering after the battle of Salamis
Chariot of Helios
Votive offering from Rhodes
Bronze Ox
Thank offerings
Trophy for victory at Plataea
Corinth
TREAS-
URIES
Hall of the Cnidians
Altar to Apollo
Trophy of Aemilius Paulus
Apollo Sitalkas
Portico of the Athenians
Exedras
4
TEMPLE OF APOLLO
Statue of Nike
Well of Cassotis
Ionic pillar with sphinx
Cnidos
Sicyon
Temple of Poseidon
The sacred way
Sanctuary of Dionysus
Bouleuterium
Chariot and charioteer
Athens (restored)
Siphnos
5
Syracuse
Boeotia
THEATRE
Portico
Thebes
N
S
TREASURIES
Old entrance
A B C D E

19. THE SANCTUARY OF APOLLO AT DELPHI

- Buildings and monuments from before 525 B.C.
- Buildings and monuments from 525-448 B.C.
- Buildings and monuments from 423-321 B.C.
- Buildings and monuments from the period after 321 B.C.

THE TEMPLE OF APOLLO

Destroyed by fire in 548 B.C. Rebuilt magnificently from c. 515 B.C. by the Alcmaeonids. Destroyed by an earthquake in 373 B.C. Rebuilt once more 370-330 B.C.

0 10 20 30 40 50 yards

ILLYRIA
MACEDONIA
THRACE
BLACK SEA
EPIRUS
Corcyra (Corfu)
Dodona
THESSALY
Castanea
Xerxes' canal
Thasos
Samothrace
Mt. Athos
Lemnos
Ambracia
Leucas
Thermopylae
Artemisium
AEGEAN
SEA
Scyros
PHOCIS
Delphi
LOCRIS
BOEOTIA
Thebes
Euboea
Eretria
Plataea
Marathon
Athens
ATTICA
Salamis
Aegina
Corinth
ACHAEA
ARGOS
PELOPONNESUS
Sparta
LACONIA
Cythera
Cephallenia
Zacynthus
IONIAN SEA
Andros
Delos
Paros
Naxos
Cyclades
Melos
Icaria
Mt. Mycale
Chios
Lesbos
Samos
Rhodes
Byzantium
Nicomedia
SEA OF MARMARA
Cyzicus
Abydos
Troy (Ilium)
BITHYNIA
PHRYGIA
Sangarius
THE PERSIAN EMPIRE
MYSIA
Pergamum
LYDIA
Hermus
Sardes
The Persian royal road to Susa
Eumenia
Antiochia
Smyrna
IONIA
Colophon
Ephesus
Maeander
Priene
Miletus
CARIA
Colossae
Halicarnassus
PAMPHYLIA
LYCIA
20. GREECE DURING THE PERSIAN WARS
Ionian rebels
Greek allies
Neutral states
Persia
0
50
100 miles
PERSIAN CAMPAIGNS AGAINST GREECE
Route of fleet under Mardonius 492 B.C.
Route of fleet under Datis 490 B.C.
Route of army under Xerxes 480 B.C.
Route of fleet under Xerxes 480 B.C.

21. GREECE DURING THE PELOPONNESIAN WAR

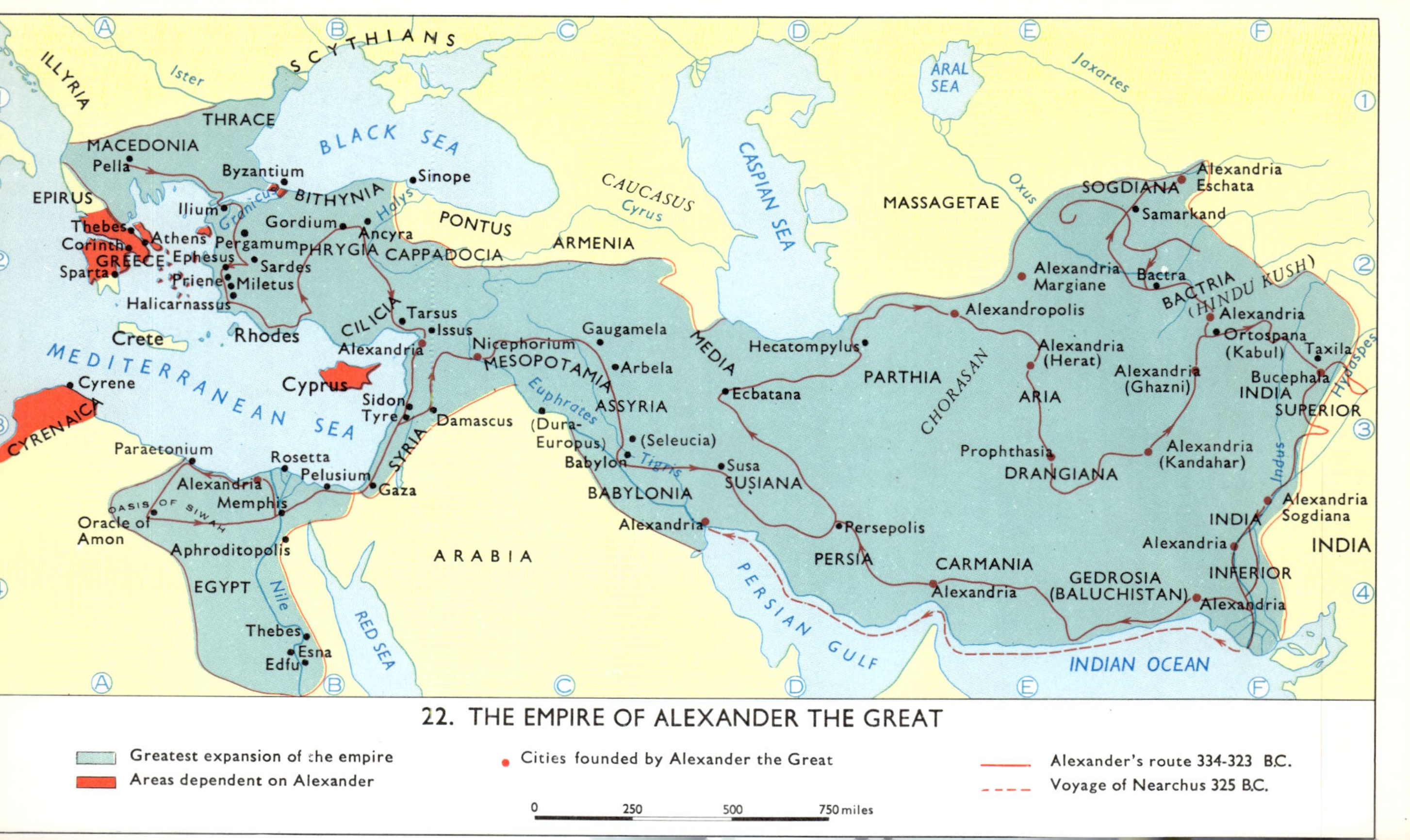

22. THE EMPIRE OF ALEXANDER THE GREAT

23. ITALY BEFORE THE FIRST PUNIC WAR 264 B.C.
Etruscans
Greek colonies
Carthaginian dominions
Italians
Other peoples
Gallic territory
Southern and northern boundaries of Roman territory 264 B.C.
Important Roman roads and roads built after 264 B.C.
0 50 100 150 miles
GALLIA TRANSPADANA
Mediolanum
Vercellae
Augusta Taurinorum
Verona
Mantua
VENETIA
Patavium
Cremona
Placentia
Padus
Pola
Parma
Mutina
Bononia
GALLIA CISPADANA
Via Aemilia
LIGURIA
Genua
Via Aemilia Scauri
Ravenna
Ariminum
Rubico
Nicaea
Pisa
Arnus
Florentia
Sena
Ancona
Arretium
UMBRIA
ETRURIA
Perusia
Camerinum
PICENUM
Asculum
Via Flaminia
Via Aurelia
Tiberis
Ilva
CORSICA
Aleria
Vulci
Tarquinii
Veii
SABINI
Via Salaria
Via Valeria
AEQUI
Caere
Fidenae
Corfinium
Ostia
Rome
Praeneste
LATIUM
VOLSCI
SAMNIUM
APULIA
Cannae
Terracina
Capua
Beneventum
Via Appia
Neapolis
Vesuvius
Pithecussa
Pompeii
Puteoli
Herculaneum
CAMPANIA
Paestum
Brundisium
Tarentum
CALABRIA
LUCANIA
Heraclea
SARDINIA
Neapolis
Carales
TYRRHENIAN SEA
Sybaris
Croton
BRUTTIUM
Liparaeae Is.
IONIAN SEA
Aegates Is.
Panormus
Messana
Rhegium
Segesta
Lilybaeum
SICILY
Etna
Catana (Catania)
Agrigentum (Acragas)
Gela
Syracuse
Utica
AFRICA
Carthage
A
B
C
1
2
3
24. THE RETREAT OF THE TEN THOUSAND 401-399 B.C.
Route followed by the Greeks, first under the leadership of Cyrus, later under Xenophon
0 100 200 miles
Byzantium (399 B.C.)
Heraclea
Sinope
Cerasus
Cotyora
Trapezus
CAUCASUS
Abydos
PONTUS
CAPPADOCIA
Pergamum
ARMENIA
Araxes
LYDIA
Sardes
PHRYGIA
Halys
(400 B.C.)
(401 B.C.)
PERSIAN EMPIRE
Ephesus
Priene
Miletus
Iconium
Tyana
MEDIA
(KURDISTAN)
CILICIA
Tarsus
ASSYRIA
Myriandrus
Mespila (Nineveh)
Rhodes
Tigris
Thapsacus
MESOPOTAMIA
Cyprus
Euphrates
MEDITERRANEAN SEA
Sidon
Damascus
Cunaxa (401 B.C.)
Sittace
Babylon
Jerusalem
BABYLONIA
ARABIA
C
D
E
5
6

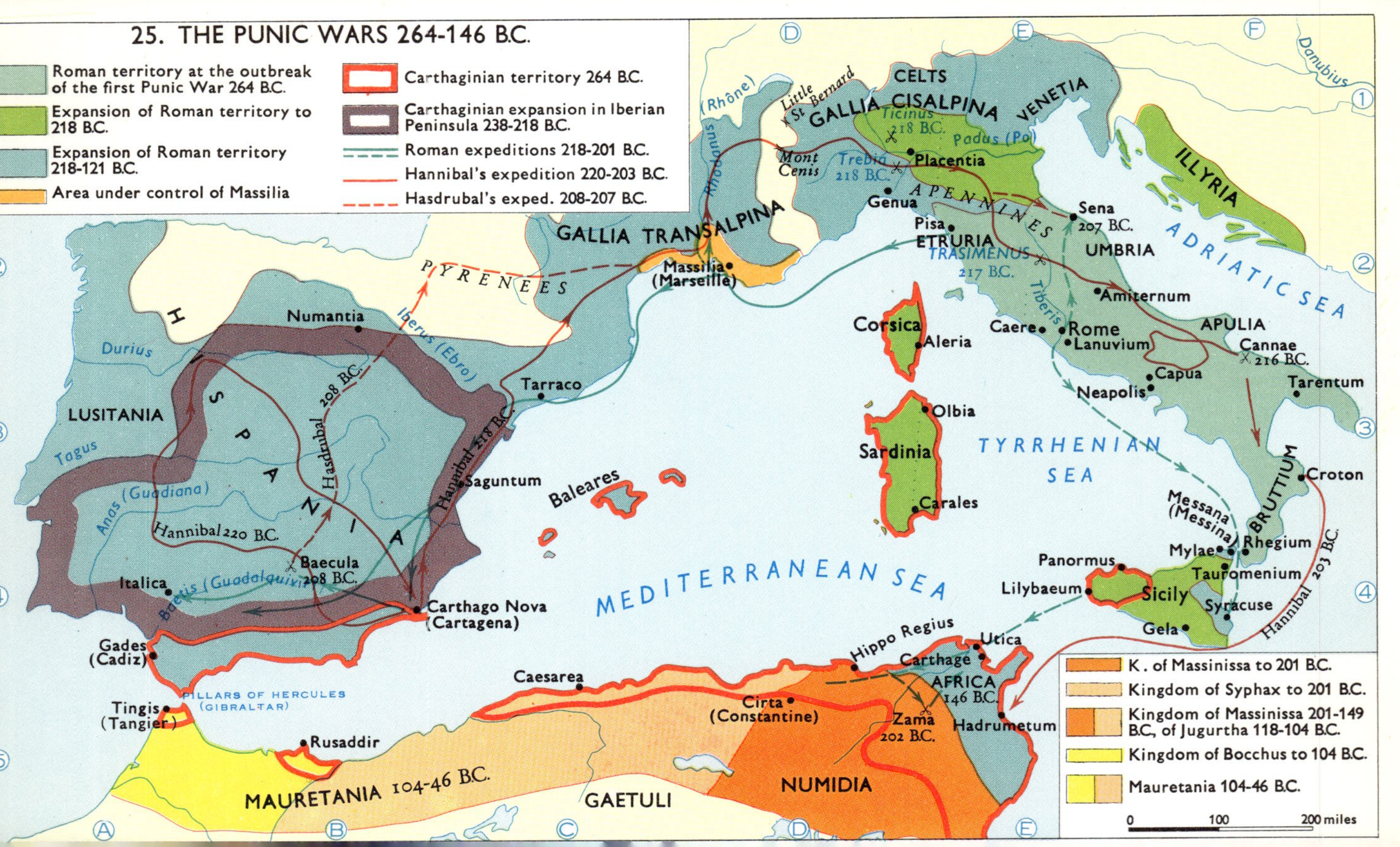

25. THE PUNIC WARS 264-146 B.C.
Roman territory at the outbreak of the first Punic War 264 B.C.
Expansion of Roman territory to 218 B.C.
Expansion of Roman territory 218-121 B.C.
Area under control of Massilia
Carthaginian territory 264 B.C.
Carthaginian expansion in Iberian Peninsula 238-218 B.C.
Roman expeditions 218-201 B.C.
Hannibal's expedition 220-203 B.C.
Hasdrubal's exped. 208-207 B.C.
K. of Massinissa to 201 B.C.
Kingdom of Syphax to 201 B.C.
Kingdom of Massinissa 201-149 B.C., of Jugurtha 118-104 B.C.
Kingdom of Bocchus to 104 B.C.
Mauretania 104-46 B.C.
0
100
200 miles
Danubius
CELTS
GALLIA CISALPINA
VENETIA
ILLYRIA
Little St Bernard
Mont Cenis
Ticinus 218 B.C.
Padus (Po)
Trebia 218 B.C.
Placentia
Genua
APENNINES
Sena 207 B.C.
Rhodanus
(Rhône)
GALLIA TRANSALPINA
Massilia (Marseille)
Pisa
ETRURIA
TRASIMENUS 217 B.C.
UMBRIA
ADRIATIC SEA
PYRENEES
Amiternum
Tiberis
Caere
Rome
Lanuvium
APULIA
Cannae 216 B.C.
Capua
Tarentum
Neapolis
HISPANIA
Numantia
Iberus (Ebro)
Durius
LUSITANIA
Tagus
Anas (Guadiana)
Hasdrubal 208 B.C.
Hannibal 218 B.C.
Hannibal 220 B.C.
Tarraco
Saguntum
Baecula 208 B.C.
Italica
Baetis (Guadalquivir)
Carthago Nova (Cartagena)
Gades (Cadiz)
Corsica
Aleria
Sardinia
Olbia
Carales
Baleares
TYRRHENIAN SEA
BRUTTIUM
Croton
Messana (Messina)
Mylae
Rhegium
Tauromenium
Panormus
Lilybaeum
Sicily
Syracuse
Gela
Hannibal 203 B.C.
MEDITERRANEAN SEA
Hippo Regius
Utica
Carthage
AFRICA 146 B.C.
Hadrumetum
Zama 202 B.C.
Cirta (Constantine)
Caesarea
PILLARS OF HERCULES (GIBRALTAR)
Tingis (Tangier)
Rusaddir
MAURETANIA 104-46 B.C.
GAETULI
NUMIDIA
A
B
C
D
E
F
1
2
3
4
5

26. ASIA MINOR IN 189 B.C.
Pergamum before 218 B.C.
Pergamum 218-189 B.C.
Pergamum 189 B.C.
Seleucid Kingdom
Free Greek states
Area periodically under Pergamum
0 100 200 miles
THRACIA
BLACK SEA
SEA OF MARMARA
Byzantium
Chalcedon
Heraclea
Sinope
Amisus
PONTUS
Amasia
Zela
BITHYNIA
Sangarius
PAPHLAGONIA
Gangra
Ancyra
Gordium
GALATIA
Abydos
Cyzicus
Ilium
MYSIA
Lesbos
Pergamum
Cyme
LYDIA
Hermus
Chios
Smyrna
Sardes
Ephesus
Maeander
Samos
Priene
Miletus
K. OF PERGAMUM
Ipsus
Apamea
PISIDIA
Iconium
Halys
Mazaca
(Caesarea)
CAPPADOCIA
Sarus
CARIA
Cibyra
Cos
Cnidus
Patara
Rhodes
LYCIA
Attalia
Side
CILICIA
Tarsus
Antioch
Orontes
MEDITERRANEAN SEA
Cyprus
(under Ptolemies)
SYRIA
Damascus
Tyre
27. GAUL IN CAESAR'S TIME
Roman provinces before 58 B.C.
Caesar's conquests 58-51 B.C.
Under control of Massilia to 49 B.C.
0 50 100 150 miles
Battlefields with year of battle
Invasions of Germania and Britannia
BRITANNIA
Londinium
BELGAE
FRETUM GALLICUM
Portus Gesoriacus
GERMANIA
Aduatuca
54 B.C.
Rhenus
GALLIA BELGICA
Samarobriva
Mosa
Mosella
Rotomagus
Durocortorum
Lutetia
Sequana
Matrona
VOSEGUS MONS
GALLIA
Cenabum
52 B.C.
Agedincum
52 B.C.
Raurici
58 B.C.
Portus
Namnetum
Alesia
52 B.C.
Liger
Avaricum
52 B.C.
Vesontio
58 B.C.
Limonum
Bibracte
58 B.C.
CELTICA
Ambarri
58 B.C.
Genava
Lugdunum
Gergovia
52 B.C.
Rhodanus
ALPES MONTES
Burdigala
Garumna
Duranius
Uxellodunum
51 B.C.
GALLIA NARBONENSIS
Arausio
Nemausus
GALLIA CISALPINA
AQUITANIA
Tolosa
Arelate
Aquae
Sextiae
Nicaea
Massilia
PYRENAEI MONTES
Narbo
Martius
HISPANIA
MARE INTERNUM

28. THE ROMAN REPUBLIC AT THE DEATH OF CAESAR 44 B.C.

29. THE ROMAN EMPIRE AT THE DEATH OF TRAJAN A.D.117

SOME ROMAN PLACE-NAMES AND THEIR MODERN EQUIVALENTS

Roman	Modern	Roman	Modern
Aquincum	Budapest	Eburacum	York
Arelate	Arles	Gades	Cadiz
Argentoratum	Strasbourg	Hierosolyma	Jerusalem
Ariminum	Rimini	Lugdunum	Lyon
Augusta Treverorum	Trier	Lutetia	Paris
Burdigala	Bordeaux	Massilia	Marseille
Carthago Nova	Cartagena	Mediolanum	Milan
Colonia Agrippinensis	Cologne	Moguntiacum	Mainz
		Rotomagus	Rouen
		Vindobona	Vienna

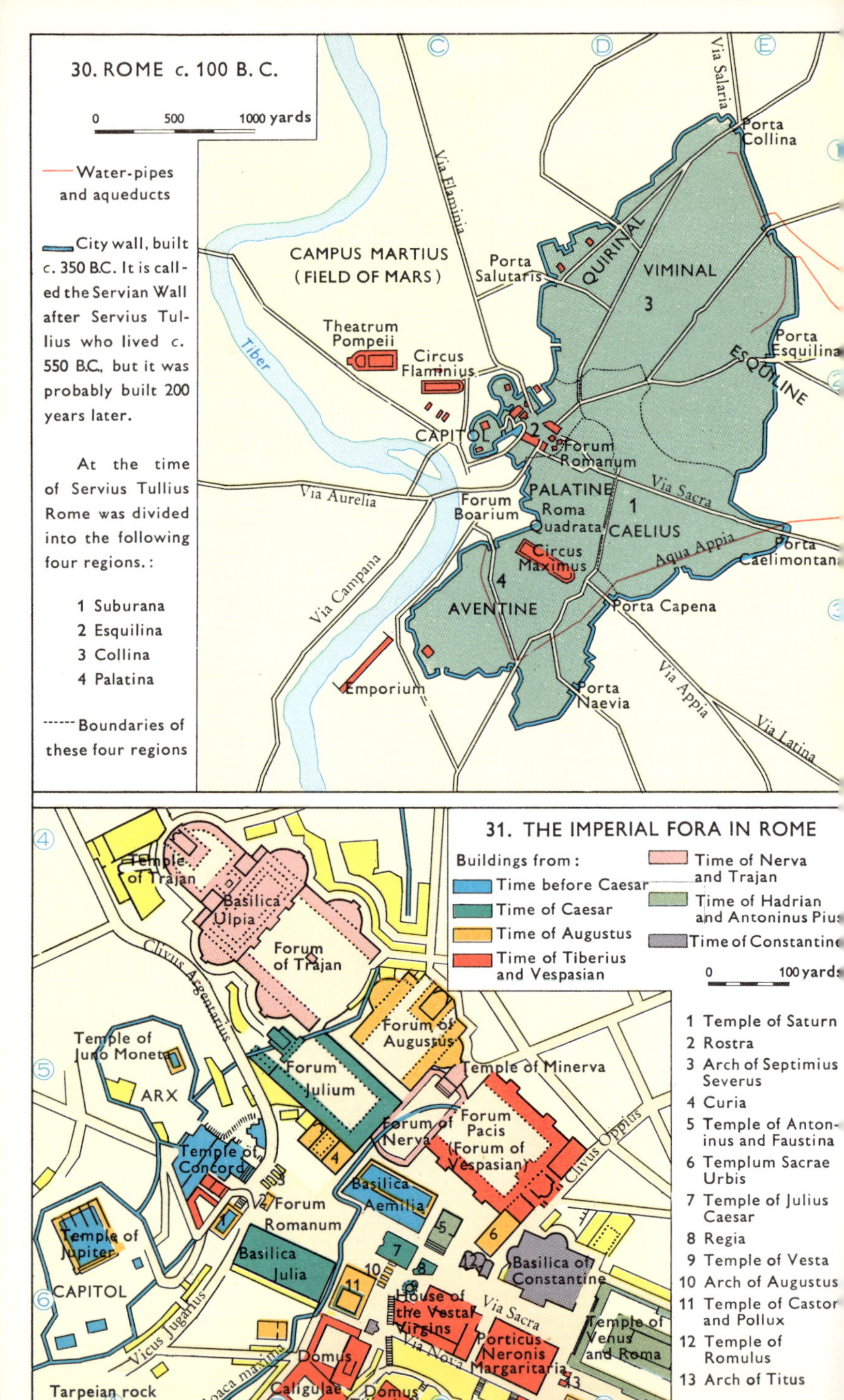
30. ROME c. 100 B. C.
0 500 1000 yards
Water-pipes and aqueducts
City wall, built c. 350 B.C. It is called the Servian Wall after Servius Tullius who lived c. 550 B.C., but it was probably built 200 years later.
At the time of Servius Tullius Rome was divided into the following four regions.:
1 Suburana
2 Esquilina
3 Collina
4 Palatina
Boundaries of these four regions
Via Salaria
Porta Collina
Via Flaminia
CAMPUS MARTIUS (FIELD OF MARS)
Porta Salutaris
QUIRINAL
VIMINAL
Theatrum Pompeii
Circus Flaminius
Tiber
Porta Esquilina
ESQUILINE
CAPITOL
Forum Romanum
Via Aurelia
Forum Boarium
PALATINE
Roma Quadrata
CAELIUS
Via Sacra
Circus Maximus
Aqua Appia
Porta Caelimontana
Via Campana
AVENTINE
Porta Capena
Emporium
Porta Naevia
Via Appia
Via Latina
31. THE IMPERIAL FORA IN ROME
Buildings from:
Time before Caesar
Time of Caesar
Time of Augustus
Time of Tiberius and Vespasian
Time of Nerva and Trajan
Time of Hadrian and Antoninus Pius
Time of Constantine
0 100 yards
1 Temple of Saturn
2 Rostra
3 Arch of Septimius Severus
4 Curia
5 Temple of Antoninus and Faustina
6 Templum Sacrae Urbis
7 Temple of Julius Caesar
8 Regia
9 Temple of Vesta
10 Arch of Augustus
11 Temple of Castor and Pollux
12 Temple of Romulus
13 Arch of Titus
Temple of Trajan
Basilica Ulpia
Forum of Trajan
Clivus Argentarius
Temple of Juno Moneta
ARX
Forum of Augustus
Temple of Minerva
Forum Julium
Forum of Nerva
Forum Pacis (Forum of Vespasian)
Clivus Oppius
Temple of Concord
Basilica Aemilia
Forum Romanum
Temple of Jupiter
Basilica Julia
Basilica of Constantine
CAPITOL
House of the Vestal Virgins
Via Sacra
Temple of Venus and Roma
Vicus Jugarius
Porticus Neronis Margaritaria
Via Nova
Domus Caligulae
Domus Tiberiana
Cloaca maxima
Tarpeian rock

32. THE BARBARIAN MIGRATIONS AND KINGDOMS A.D. 526
Vandals
Goths
Ostrogoths
Kingdom of Attila c. 450
Visigoths
Huns
Franks
Bugundians
Jutes, Angles and Saxons
Britons
The dates on the routes are those of the Barbarian migrations.
0 200 400 miles
ATLANTIC OCEAN
NORTH SEA
BALTIC SEA
BLACK SEA
MEDITERRANEAN SEA
ADRIATIC SEA
NORWAY
PICTS
SCOTS
c. 350
BRITISH (CELTIC) KINGDOMS
WALES
CORNWALL
WESSEX
SUSSEX
KENT
ESSEX
SUFFOLK
NORFOLK
ANGLO-SAXON KINGDOMS
Whitby
York
Sutton Hoo
Jutes
Angles
Saxons
449
BRITTANY (BRITANNIA MINOR)
HOMELAND OF THE FRANKS
FRANKISH KINGDOM
Paris
Orleans
Catalaunian Plain
451
Trier
Worms
BURGUNDIAN KINGDOM
443
ALAMANS
Lyon
Loire
Rhône
Bordeaux
Toulouse
413
Visigoths
Marseille
Narbonne
BASQUES
409
KINGDOM OF THE SUEVI
Duero
Vandals
Ebro
Tagus
Toledo
Zaragoza
VISIGOTHIC KINGDOM
Guadiana
Almendralejo
GOTHALUNIA (CATALONIA)
Balearic Is.
(V)ANDALUSIA
Cadiz
Tarifa
Malaga
Cartagena
429
Oran
460
430
Hippo
Carthage
VANDAL KINGDOM
Corsica
Sardinia
456
Genseric 435
440
455
Sicily
Malta
GOTHS
Gotland
Bornholm
BALTS
Burgundians
Oder
Elbe
Weser
c. 150
Vistula
Vandals c. 170
Goths c. 150-200
THURINGIANS
SLAVONIC PEOPLES
LOMBARDS
401
Danube
OSTROGOTHIC KINGDOM
Milan
Pavia
Verona
Aquileia
Cividale
Ostrogoths 454
Po
Pollentia
402
Genoa
412
Ravenna
410
Rome
Monte Cassino
Naples
Vesuvius
Cosenza
Rhegium
Drava
Sava
CROATS
397-401
Residence of Attila (434-453)
KINGDOM OF THE GEPIDES
Ostrogoths 200
OSTROGOTHS
Dnieper
Don
Huns 375
Huns 373
CRIMEA
VISIGOTHS
Visigoths 376
DOBRUJA
446
SERBS
BULGARS
Marcianople
Adrianople
378
Naissus (Nish)
447
ILLYRIA
Alaric 395
Thessalonica (Salonica)
Constantinople
Nicaea
Ancyra
Halys
EASTERN ROMAN EMPIRE (BYZANTINE EMPIRE)
Athens
Sparta
Crete
Rhodes
Cyprus
Antioch
A B C D E F
1 2 3 4 5

33. THE EXPANSION OF ISLAM AND THE EMPIRE OF CHARLEMAGNE IN 814
Conquests of Mohammed to 632
Expansion of Islam to 656
Extent of Islamic Empire in 814 (by this time the most northerly part of Spain had been lost)
Expansion of Islam under the Ommayads
Moslem silver mines
The Byzantine Empire
Frankish Kingdom at the death of Charlemagne in 814
New conquests of Charlemagne
States dependent on the Frankish Kingdom
0
400
800 miles
IRELAND
ANGLO-SAXON KINGDOMS
London
Cologne
Aachen
Paris
NEUSTRIA
BRITTANY
Tours
Poitiers (732)
Lyon
BURGUNDY
AQUITANIA
Toulouse
Roncesvalles
ASTURIAS
SPANISH MARCH
Zaragoza
Barcelona
SPANISH EMIRATE
Toledo
Seville
Cordoba
Granada
Jerez de la Frontera (616)
Gibraltar (Jebel Tarik)
Tangier
Tlemcen
Fez
EMIRATE OF MOROCCO
Marrakesh
BERBERS
ATLANTIC OCEAN
Balearic Is.
Elbe
Magdeburg
SAXONY
AUSTRASIA
BOHEMIA
Regensburg
MORAVIA
Vienna
MARCH OF PANNONIA
Vistula
Dniester
Dnieper
MAGYARS
SLOVAKS
AVARS
Danube
BULGARS
SERBIA
Milan
Venice
Ravenna
Nice
Avignon
PAPAL STATES
Rome
Corsica
Naples
D. OF BENEVENTO
Salerno
Sardinia
Palermo
Syracuse
Carthage
Tunis
Kairouan
EMIRATE OF TUNIS
Tripoli
FEZZAN
SAHARA
CRIMEA
BLACK SEA
Constantinople
Ancyra (Ankara)
Smyrna
Athens
Crete
Rhodes
Cyprus
THE BYZANTINE EMPIRE
MEDITERRANEAN SEA
Alexandria
LIBYA
El Fustat (Cairo)
Nile
EGYPT
SYRIA
Edessa
Antioch
Emesa
Damascus
Yarmuk (636)
Jerusalem
Tiflis
ARMENIA
MESOPOTAMIA
Mosul
Samarra
Baghdad
Karbela
Kadesia
Babylon
Kufa
Basra
Hamadan (Ecbatana)
Ispahan
SASSANID KINGDOM
Shiraz
PERSIAN GULF
OMAN
ARABIA
HEJAZ
Medina
Mecca
RED SEA
YEMEN
HADRAMAUT
ARABIAN SEA
Ural
Volga
CASPIAN SEA
ARAL SEA
Jaxartes
Oxus
SOGDIANA
Bokhara
Samarkand
Kabul
CHORASAN
AFGHANISTAN
Indus
SIND
TURAN

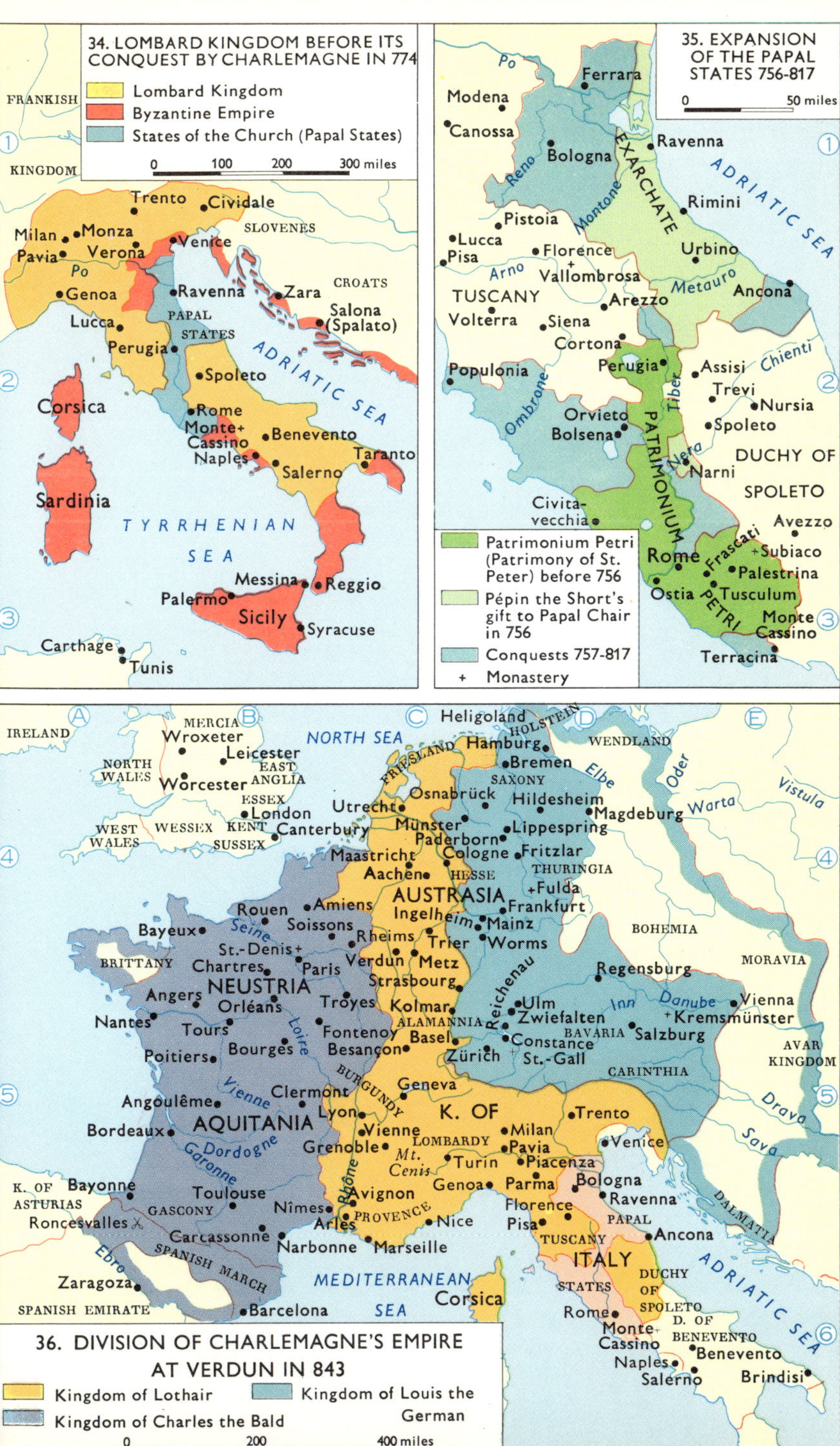
34. LOMBARD KINGDOM BEFORE ITS CONQUEST BY CHARLEMAGNE IN 774
Lombard Kingdom
Byzantine Empire
States of the Church (Papal States)
0 100 200 300 miles
FRANKISH KINGDOM
Trento
Cividale
Milan
Monza
Pavia
Verona
Venice
SLOVENES
Po
Genoa
Ravenna
Zara
CROATS
Salona (Spalato)
Lucca
PAPAL STATES
Perugia
ADRIATIC SEA
Spoleto
Corsica
Rome
Monte Cassino
Benevento
Naples
Salerno
Taranto
Sardinia
TYRRHENIAN SEA
Messina
Reggio
Palermo
Sicily
Syracuse
Carthage
Tunis
35. EXPANSION OF THE PAPAL STATES 756-817
0 50 miles
Po
Ferrara
Modena
Canossa
Ravenna
Bologna
Reno
EXARCHATE
ADRIATIC SEA
Rimini
Montone
Pistoia
Lucca
Pisa
Florence
Vallombrosa
Urbino
Arno
Metauro
Ancona
TUSCANY
Arezzo
Volterra
Siena
Cortona
Assisi
Chienti
Populonia
Perugia
Tiber
Trevi
Nursia
Ombrone
Orvieto
Spoleto
Bolsena
PATRIMONIUM
DUCHY OF SPOLETO
Nera
Narni
Civita-vecchia
Avezzo
Rome
Frascati
Subiaco
Palestrina
Ostia
PETRI
Tusculum
Monte Cassino
Terracina
Patrimonium Petri (Patrimony of St. Peter) before 756
Pépin the Short's gift to Papal Chair in 756
Conquests 757-817
+ Monastery
IRELAND
MERCIA
Wroxeter
Leicester
NORTH SEA
Heligoland
HOLSTEIN
WENDLAND
NORTH WALES
EAST ANGLIA
Worcester
FRIESLAND
Hamburg
Bremen
Elbe
Oder
Vistula
SAXONY
ESSEX
London
Utrecht
Osnabrück
Hildesheim
Magdeburg
Warta
WEST WALES
WESSEX
KENT
Canterbury
Münster
Lippespring
SUSSEX
Paderborn
Maastricht
Cologne
Fritzlar
Aachen
HESSE
THURINGIA
AUSTRASIA
Fulda
Amiens
Rouen
Frankfurt
Ingelheim
Soissons
Mainz
BOHEMIA
Bayeux
Seine
Rheims
Trier
Worms
St.-Denis
BRITTANY
Chartres
Paris
Verdun
Metz
Reichenau
MORAVIA
Regensburg
NEUSTRIA
Strasbourg
Angers
Orléans
Troyes
Kolmar
Ulm
Inn
Danube
Vienna
Nantes
ALAMANNIA
Zwiefalten
Kremsmünster
Tours
Loire
Fontenoy
Basel
BAVARIA
Salzburg
Bourges
Besançon
Constance
AVAR KINGDOM
Poitiers
Zürich
St.-Gall
BURGUNDY
CARINTHIA
Geneva
Vienne
Clermont
Drava
Angoulême
Lyon
K. OF
Trento
AQUITANIA
Vienne
Milan
Bordeaux
Dordogne
LOMBARDY
Pavia
Venice
Sava
Grenoble
Mt. Cenis
Turin
Piacenza
Garonne
Rhône
Genoa
Parma
Bologna
K. OF ASTURIAS
Bayonne
Toulouse
Avignon
Ravenna
DALMATIA
GASCONY
Nîmes
PROVENCE
Florence
PAPAL
Roncesvalles
Arles
Nice
Pisa
Ancona
Carcassonne
TUSCANY
Narbonne
Marseille
ITALY
Ebro
SPANISH MARCH
DUCHY OF SPOLETO
ADRIATIC SEA
Zaragoza
MEDITERRANEAN SEA
Corsica
STATES
SPANISH EMIRATE
Barcelona
Rome
D. OF BENEVENTO
Monte Cassino
Benevento
Naples
Salerno
Brindisi
36. DIVISION OF CHARLEMAGNE'S EMPIRE AT VERDUN IN 843
Kingdom of Lothair
Kingdom of Louis the German
Kingdom of Charles the Bald
0 200 400 miles

37. VIKING RAIDS 800-1000 AND THE POLITICAL DIVISION OF EUROPE c. 900

38. THE HOLY ROMAN EMPIRE AND THE NORMAN KINGDOM IN SOUTH ITALY

A B C
K. C
1
K. OF SCOTLAND
NORTH SEA
Edinburgh
IRELAND
Dublin (Danish)
Man
K. OF ENGLAND
Durham
Lancaster
York
Stamford
2
Cork
Waterford
WALES
Sherwood Forest
Norwich
Bremen
SAXONY
Worcester
Cardiff
Oxford
Windsor
London
Utrecht
Rhine
Exeter
Canterbury
Münster
Wight
Hastings
Maas
C. OF FLANDERS
Cologne
ATLANTIC OCEAN
1066
Bouvines
Aachen
LORRAINE
D. OF NORMANDY
Bayeux
Rouen
Amiens
Gelnhausen
3
Seine
C. OF Soissons
Rüdesheim
Worms
D. OF BRITTANY
Château-Gaillard
Rheims
Trifels
FRA
Paris
Weinsberg
Chartres
CHAMPAGNE
C. OF MAINE
Sens
Strasbourg
Waiblingen
C. OF ANJOU
Loire
Orléans
Clairvaux
KINGDOM OF FRANCE
D. OF BURGUNDY
SWABIA
C. OF POITOU
Poitiers
Cluny
K. OF BURGUNDY
D. OF AQUITAINE
Geneva
Clermont
Lyon
Rhône
4
Bordeaux
Legnano
Milan
Garonne
Pavia
Piacenza
K. OF LEON
Roncaglia
D. OF GASCONY
C. OF TOULOUSE
Avignon
Genoa
Toulouse
PROVENCE
K. OF CASTILE
K. OF NAVARRE
Oporto
Burgos
Arles
Nice
C. OF PORTUGAL
K. OF ARAGON
Carcassonne
Marseille
Duero
Ebro
C. OF CATALONIA (BARCELONA)
Zaragoza
Lerida
Corsica
Tagus
Madrid
Barcelona
5
Toledo
Merida
Guadiana
Valencia
Balearic Is.
Sardinia
Cordoba
Seville
Guadalquivir
Alicante
Granada
Cartagena
MEDITERRA
Cadiz
CALIPHATE OF CORDOBA
DOMINIONS OF THE ALMORAVIDES
Tangier
Ceuta
6
Tunis
Oran
A B C

39. EUROPE IN 1100
The Holy Roman Empire
Kingdom of Canute 1028-35
William the Conqueror's invasion of England in 1066
For English possessions in France, see Map 50
0
100
200 miles
D
E
F
2
3
4
5
6
ORWAY
slo
Uppsala
K. OF
SWEDEN
Dagö
Ösel
ESTONIA
Dvina
Gotland
Kalmar
Öland
BALTIC SEA
LITHUANIA
Memel
Lund
NMARK
Bornholm
STEIN
MECKLENBURG
POMERANIA
PRUSSIA
RUSSIAN PRINCIPALITIES
Lüneburg
Elbe
Brandenburg
Warta
Vistula
Brunswick
Kyffhäuser
Vartburg
Erfurt
K. OF POLAND
Breslau
Oder
Krakow
Dnieper
Main
Prague
BOHEMIA
MORAVIA
Dniester
Bug
HOLY
Dürnstein
BAVARIA
Inn
Vienna
Pressburg
Theiss
Prut
Lechfeld
Salzburg
Buda
Pest
CUMANS
(Turks)
ROMAN
KINGDOM OF HUNGARY
TRANSYLVANIA
Merano
EMPIRE
Venice
VENICE
Drava
Sava
Danube
Bologna
CROATIA
Belgrade
Ravenna
Zara
BLACK SEA
Florence
SERBIA
Spalato
BULGARS
ITALY
ADRIATIC SEA
Ragusa
Maritsa
Spoleto
Tiber
Adrianople
BOSPORUS
Rome
Constantinople
Nicaea
Albano
Aquino
Vardar
D. OF APULIA
Durazzo
Bari
Thessalonica
Naples
Salerno
Brindisi
Amalfi
Taranto
EPIRUS
BYZANTINE EMPIRE
Lesbos
NORMAN
AEGEAN SEA
Cotrone
Ephesus
Athens
Messina
Corinth
Palermo
C. OF SICILY
KINGDOM
Rhodes
Syracuse
Crete

40. THE CRUSADES AND THE POLITICAL SITUATION c. 1230

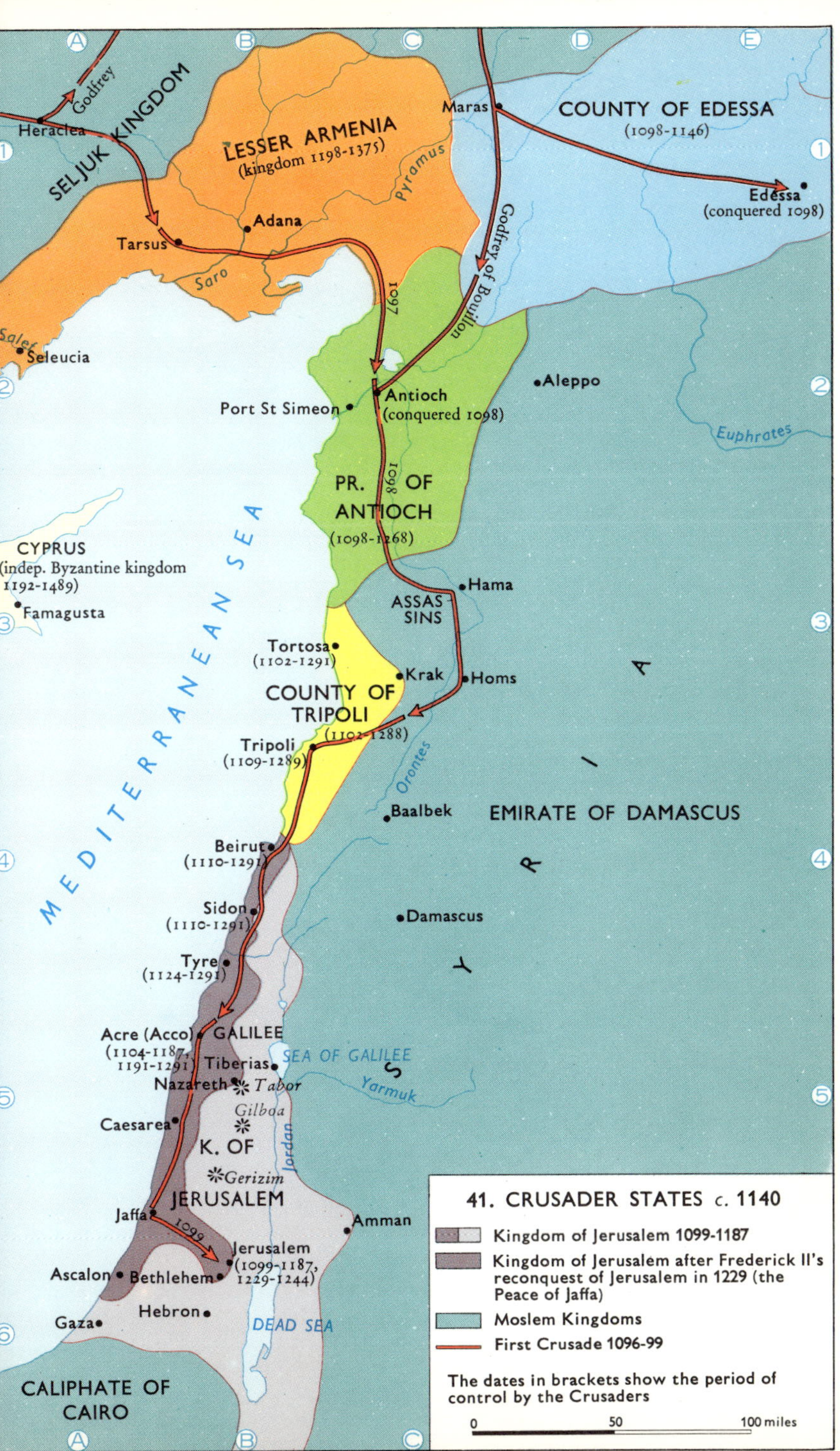

41. CRUSADER STATES c. 1140
Kingdom of Jerusalem 1099-1187
Kingdom of Jerusalem after Frederick II's reconquest of Jerusalem in 1229 (the Peace of Jaffa)
Moslem Kingdoms
First Crusade 1096-99
The dates in brackets show the period of control by the Crusaders
0
50
100 miles
SELJUK KINGDOM
Godfrey
Heraclea
LESSER ARMENIA
(kingdom 1198-1375)
Pyramus
Adana
Tarsus
Saro
Salef
Seleucia
Maras
COUNTY OF EDESSA
(1098-1146)
Edessa
(conquered 1098)
Godfrey of Bouillon
1097
Antioch
(conquered 1098)
Port St Simeon
Aleppo
Euphrates
PR. OF ANTIOCH
(1098-1268)
1098
CYPRUS
(indep. Byzantine kingdom 1192-1489)
Famagusta
MEDITERRANEAN SEA
Hama
ASSASSINS
Tortosa
(1102-1291)
Krak
Homs
COUNTY OF TRIPOLI
(1102-1288)
Tripoli
(1109-1289)
Orontes
Baalbek
EMIRATE OF DAMASCUS
SYRIA
Beirut
(1110-1291)
Sidon
(1110-1291)
Damascus
Tyre
(1124-1291)
Acre (Acco)
(1104-1187, 1191-1291)
GALILEE
Tiberias
SEA OF GALILEE
Nazareth
Tabor
Yarmuk
Gilboa
Caesarea
K. OF JERUSALEM
Jordan
Gerizim
Jaffa
1099
Jerusalem
(1099-1187, 1229-1244)
Amman
Ascalon
Bethlehem
Hebron
Gaza
DEAD SEA
CALIPHATE OF CAIRO

HUNGARY
GOLDEN HORDE
EMPIRE OF JAGATAI
EMPIRE OF THE GREAT KHAN
ILKHAN EMPIRE
MONGOLIA
TURKESTAN
PERSIA
TIBET
CHINA
KOREA
JAPAN
INDIA
SIAM
MAMELUKES
HIMALAYAS
GOBI
The Great Wall
PACIFIC OCEAN
YELLOW SEA
BAY OF BENGAL
RED SEA
PERSIAN GULF
BLACK SEA
CASPIAN SEA
ARAL SEA
LAKE BALKHASH
LAKE BAIKAL
Danube
Dnieper
Volga
Ural
Ob
Yenisei
Amur
Tigris
Euphrates
Indus
Ganges
Brahmaputra
Hwang-ho
Yangtse-kiang
Mekong
Moscow
Kiev
Bulgar
Kalka
Kaffa
Sarai
Astrakhan
Constantinople
Angora (Ankara)
Tiflis
Cyprus
Tabriz
Damascus
Jerusalem
Hamadan
Baghdad
Ispahan
Basra
Medina
Mecca
Ormuz
Bokhara
Samarkand
Merv
Balkh
Herat
Kabul
Kandahar
Kashgar
Delhi
Goa
Calicut
Karakorum
Peking
Nanking
Kinsai (Hangchow)
Zaiton
Canton
Lhasa
Ava
Hainan
Formosa
Philippines
1224
1223
1395
1402
1403
1393
1400/01
1220
1391
1219
1375
1218
1221
1398
1211/15
1226/27
42. ASIA c. 1300 AND THE EMPIRES OF GENGHIS KHAN AND TAMERLANE
Empire of Genghis Khan in 1227
Important campaigns of Genghis Khan
Empire of Tamerlane in 1405
Important campaigns of Tamerlane
0
500
1000 miles

43. EUROPEAN CIVILIZATION IN THE MIDDLE AGES

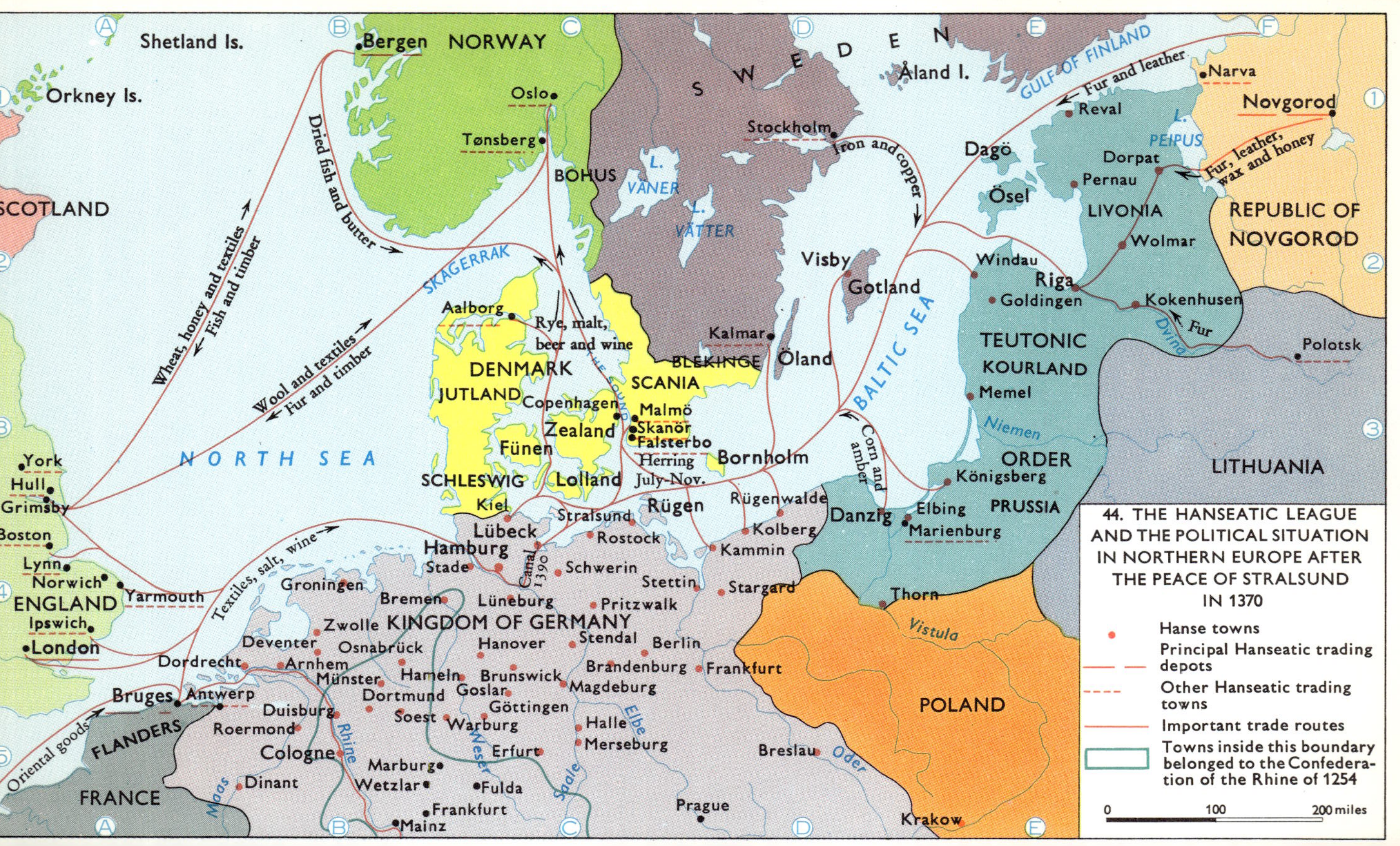

Shetland Is.
Orkney Is.
SCOTLAND
ENGLAND
York
Hull
Grimsby
Boston
Lynn
Norwich
Yarmouth
Ipswich
London
Bergen
NORWAY
Oslo
Tønsberg
BOHUS
SWEDEN
Åland I.
Stockholm
L. VÄNER
L. VÄTTER
Kalmar
Öland
Visby
Gotland
Dagö
Ösel
GULF OF FINLAND
Reval
Narva
Novgorod
L. PEIPUS
Dorpat
Pernau
LIVONIA
Wolmar
REPUBLIC OF NOVGOROD
Windau
Riga
Goldingen
Kokenhusen
Dvina
Polotsk
TEUTONIC KOURLAND
ORDER
Memel
Niemen
Königsberg
PRUSSIA
LITHUANIA
Elbing
Marienburg
Danzig
Thorn
Vistula
POLAND
Krakow
Breslau
Oder
Prague
SKAGERRAK
NORTH SEA
BALTIC SEA
Aalborg
DENMARK
JUTLAND
SCHLESWIG
Kiel
Fünen
Zealand
Lolland
Copenhagen
THE SOUND
SCANIA
BLEKINGE
Malmö
Skanör
Falsterbo
Herring July-Nov.
Bornholm
Rügen
Rügenwalde
Kolberg
Kammin
Stargard
Stettin
Stralsund
Rostock
Lübeck
Hamburg
Stade
Canal 1390
Schwerin
Lüneburg
Pritzwalk
Bremen
Groningen
Zwolle
KINGDOM OF GERMANY
Deventer
Osnabrück
Hanover
Stendal
Berlin
Dordrecht
Arnhem
Münster
Hameln
Brunswick
Brandenburg
Frankfurt
Magdeburg
Bruges
Antwerp
Dortmund
Goslar
Duisburg
Soest
Göttingen
Halle
Elbe
Roermond
Warburg
Weser
Erfurt
Merseburg
Cologne
Rhine
Marburg
Wetzlar
Fulda
Saale
Maas
Dinant
Frankfurt
Mainz
FLANDERS
FRANCE
Oriental goods
Textiles, salt, wine
Wheat, honey and textiles
Fish and timber
Dried fish and butter
Wool and textiles
Fur and timber
Rye, malt, beer and wine
Iron and copper
Corn and amber
Fur and leather
Fur, leather, wax and honey
Fur
44. THE HANSEATIC LEAGUE AND THE POLITICAL SITUATION IN NORTHERN EUROPE AFTER THE PEACE OF STRALSUND IN 1370
Hanse towns
Principal Hanseatic trading depots
Other Hanseatic trading towns
Important trade routes
Towns inside this boundary belonged to the Confederation of the Rhine of 1254
0
100
200 miles

45. RENAISSANCE ITALY
Boundaries after the Peace of Lodi, 1454
0 50 100 miles
DUCHY OF SAVOY
DUCHY OF MILAN
REP. OF VENICE
MONT- FERRAT
REP. OF GENOA
DUCHY OF MODENA
DUCHY OF FERRARA
MANTUA
LUCCA
REP. OF FLORENCE
REP. OF SIENA
DUCHY OF PIOMBINO
PAPAL STATES
KINGDOM OF NAPLES (Aragon)
Corsica (Genoa)
Elba
(to Savoy)
ROMAGNA
UMBRIA
ABRUZZI
ADRIATIC SEA
TYRRHENIAN SEA
LAKE MAGGIORE
LAKE GARDA
Rhône
Adda
Po
Piave
Arno
Tiber
Garigliano
Pieve di Cadore
Trent
Feltre
Trieste
Pirano
Como
Bergamo
Bicocca
Brescia
Castelfranco
Vicenza
Milan
Crema
Verona
Padua
Venice
Turin
Casale
Pavia
Lodi
Este
Piacenza
Cremona
Mantua
Asti
Gonzaga
Mirandola
Ferrara
Pola
Parma
Reggio
Correggio
Modena
Berceto
Genoa
Bologna
Ravenna
Faenza
Rimini
Pesaro
Lucca
Prato
Fiesole
Pisa
Vinci
Florence
San Miniato
Urbino
Sinigaglia
Caprese
Anghiari
Arezzo
Ancona
Siena
Perugia
Assisi
Fermo
Chiusi
Ascoli
Grosseto
Orvieto
Spoleto
Pitigliano
Bolsena
Atri
Corneto
Tivoli
Rome
Ostia
Palestrina
Aquino
Fossanova
Capua
Naples
46. ACTIVITIES OF THE MEDICI AND FUGGERS IN WESTERN AND CENTRAL EUROPE c. 1500
The Medici city (Florence) and branches
The Fugger city (Augsburg) and branches
Fugger mines and iron-works
Most important commercial routes of the Medici
Most important commercial routes of the Fuggers
ATLANTIC OCEAN
MEDITERRANEAN SEA
K. OF FRANCE
K. OF HUNGARY
OTTOMAN EMPIRE
K. OF SPAIN
K. OF PORTUGAL
London
Antwerp
Bruges
Leipzig
Breslau
Erfurt
Krakow
Cologne
Teschen
Frankfurt
Nuremberg
Vienna
Augsburg
Buda (Ofen)
Salzburg
Innsbruck
Geneva
Lyon
Milan
Venice
Genoa
Avignon
Pisa
Florence
Marseille
Rome
Barcelona
Naples
Madrid
Lisbon
Almaden
Guadalcanal
Seville

47. THE GREAT SCHISM 1378-1417
Adherents of the Pope in Avignon
Adherents of the Pope in Rome
Areas of undecided allegiance
0 200 miles
K. OF SCOTLAND
NORTH SEA
K. OF NORWAY
K. OF SWEDEN
Ireland
K. OF DENMARK
LITHUANIA
K. OF ENGLAND
Oxford
London
Canterbury
Danzig
TEUTONIC ORDER
FRIESLAND
HOLLAND
BRANDENBURG
K. OF POLAND
FLANDERS
HOLY ROMAN EMPIRE
Leipzig
Mainz
K. OF BOHEMIA
Prague
Paris
MORAVIA
BAVARIA
AUSTRIA
K. OF HUNGARY
ATLANTIC OCEAN
K. OF FRANCE
Constance
STYRIA
CARINTHIA
CARNIOLA
Lyon
Vienne
SAVOY
ITALY
K. OF NAVARRE
Avignon
Marseille
Lucca
Bologna
Pisa
Siena
Perugia
K. OF PORTUGAL
K. OF ARAGON
K. OF CASTILE
Corsica
Rome
Greek Orthodox area
Balearic Is.
K. OF NAPLES
Naples
Sardinia
K. OF GRANADA
MEDITERRANEAN SEA
K. OF SICILY
MOSLEM STATES
48. THE SWISS CONFEDERATION 1536
Original cantons 1315
Expansion of the Confederation to 1481
Areas belonging to the Confederation in 1536
Areas under the protection of the Confederation
Areas subject to one or more cantons
0 20 40 60 miles
MÜLHAUSEN
Schaffhausen
Constance
BODENSEE
Rhine
THURGAU
Basel
Baden
Winterthur
Habsburg
Zürich
St Gallen
APPENZELL
ARGAU
BURGUNDY
Solothurn
Aare
LUZERN
Kappel
Wildhaus
Sempach
ZUG
Einsiedeln
C. OF TYROL
Luzern
Morgarten
NEUCHÂTEL
Schwyz
SCHWYZ
Bern
Stans
GLARUS
UNTERWALDEN
Rütli
Chur
BERN
Altdorf
Freiburg
URI
Rhine
Zwing-Uri
VAUD
Morges
Lausanne
St Gotthard
GRAUBÜNDEN
L. OF GENEVA
CHABLAIS
Rhône
Geneva
VALAIS
D. OF MILAN
D. OF SAVOY
REP. OF VENICE
St Bernard

49. THE ORGANIZATION OF THE CHURCH IN WESTERN AND CENTRAL EUROPE c. 1500

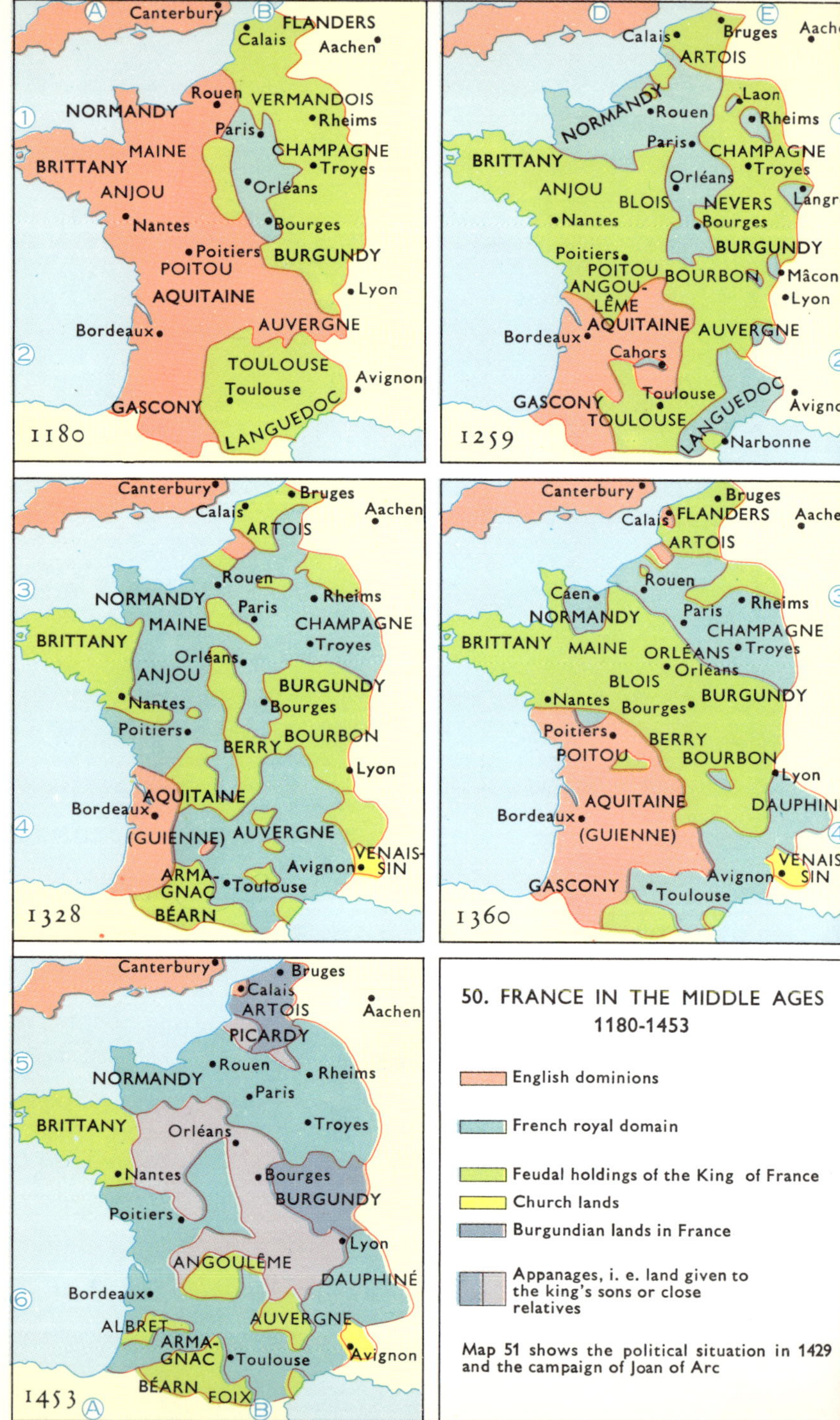

50. FRANCE IN THE MIDDLE AGES 1180-1453

51. ENGLAND AND FRANCE IN 1429
English possessions
Lands of the French crown
Feudal holdings of the French crown
Church lands
Burgundian lands
Joan of Arc's campaign
0 50 100 150 200 miles
K. OF SCOTLAND
ULSTER
IRELAND
Dublin
Man
NORTHUMBERLAND
Carlisle
CUMBERLAND
Richmond
Lancaster
LANCASTER
YORKSHIRE
York
Towton
Wakefield
LINCOLN
Conway
K. OF ENGLAND
NORTH SEA
Shrewsbury
WALES
NOTTINGHAM
Nottingham
LEICESTER
Bosworth
NORFOLK
WARWICK
WOR-CESTER
Kenilworth
Warwick
Ely
HEREFORD
GLOU-CESTER
Gloucester
Berkeley
BED-FORD
Cambridge
SUFFOLK
HERTFORD
Bristol
Oxford
ESSEX
Bath
Windsor
London
SOMERSET
WILT-SHIRE
SURREY
KENT
Canterbury
CORNWALL
DEVON
DORSET
HAMPSHIRE
SUSSEX
HOLLAND
ZEELAND
Rhine
Maas
Blankenberghe
Sluys
Bruges
FLANDERS
BRABANT
Calais
Ypres
Ghent
ARTOIS
Lille
Brussels
Cologne
ENGLISH CHANNEL
Agincourt
Arras
Liège
LIM-BURG
Crécy
HAINAULT
Namur
Limburg
PICARDY
Cherbourg
Amiens
Péronne
LUXEMBOURG
Harfleur
Caen
Rouen
Laon
NORMANDY
Beauvais
VALOIS
RETHEL
Compiègne
Soissons
ILE-DE-FRANCE
Marne
Rheims
BRITTANY
St Denis
Paris
Châlons
MAINE
CHAMPAGNE
Seine
Chartres
Brétigny
Nancy
Montereau
Domrémy
LORRAINE
Patay
ORLÉANS
Sens
Troyes
ANJOU
Orléans
Nantes
Blois
Plessis
Tours
Loire
Auxerre
Amboise
Chinon
Dijon
Bourges
BERRY
NEVERS
Nevers
Besançon
POITOU
Poitiers
Vienne
BURGUNDY
FRANCHE-COMTÉ
La Rochelle
BOURBON
BAY OF BISCAY
Limoges
Geneva
Clermont
DUCHY OF SAVOY
Lyon
Blaye
Vienne
AQUITAINE
Dordogne
Bordeaux
(GUIENNE)
AUVERGNE
Le Puy
DAUPHINÉ
Cahors
Rodez
Garonne
Rhône
GASCONY
Albi
VENAISSIN
Bayonne
ARMAGNAC
Castres
Avignon
Ebro
Toulouse
BÉARN
LANGUEDOC
PROVENCE
K. OF NAVARRE
Marseille
Narbonne
K. OF CASTILE
Toulon
K. OF ARAGON
MEDITERRANEAN SEA

52. THE BYZANTINE EMPIRE 1265

53. THE BYZANTINE AND OTTOMAN EMPIRES 1355

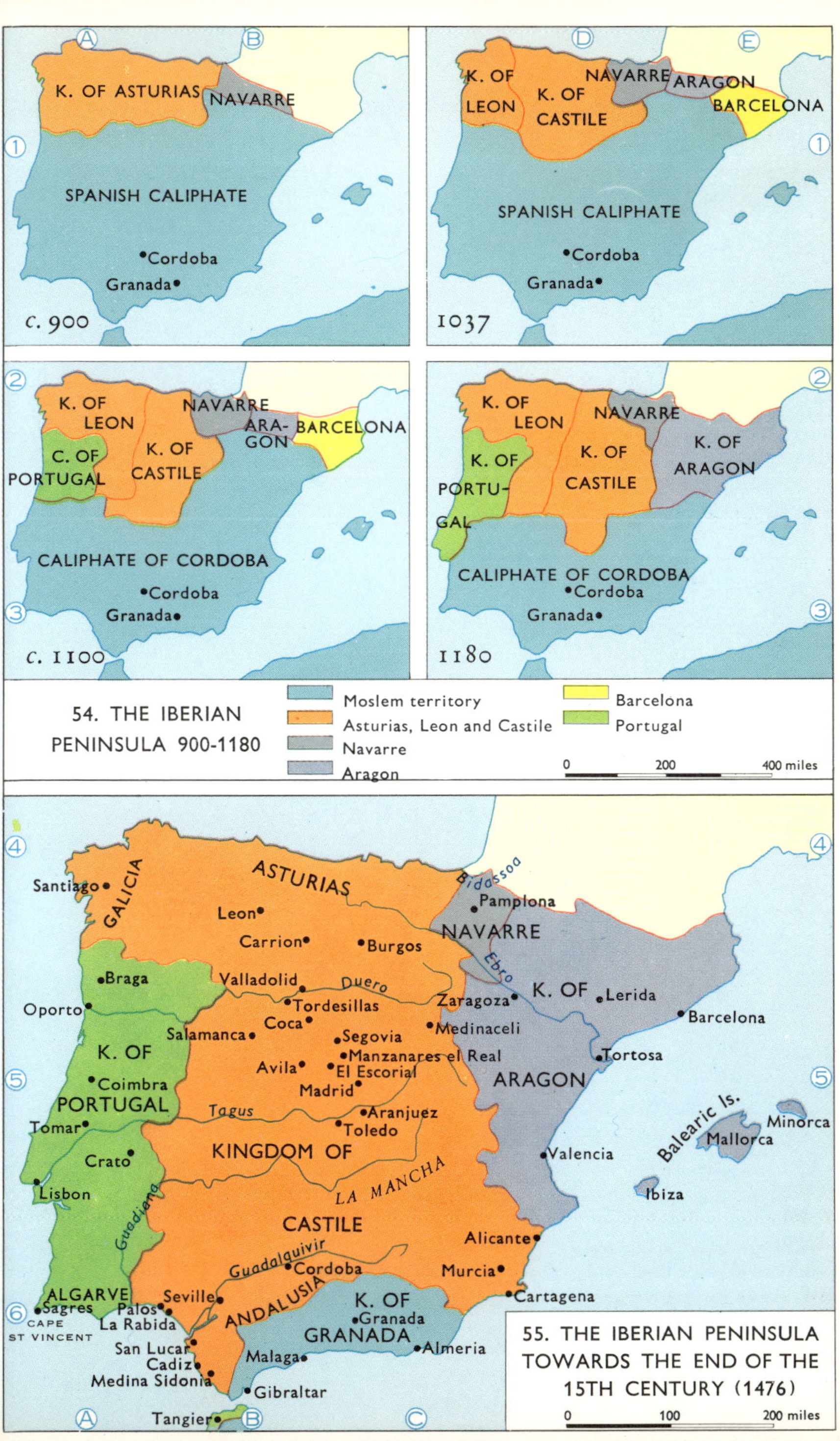

54. THE IBERIAN PENINSULA 900-1180

55. THE IBERIAN PENINSULA TOWARDS THE END OF THE 15TH CENTURY (1476)

56. THE AZTEC, MAYA AND INCA EMPIRES

- Aztec Empire 1486
- Aztec Empire 1519
- Maya Empire in 7th century
- Maya Empire 1520
- Inca Empire in 11th century
- Inca Empire 1533

Modern names of states are included for the purpose of orientation

0 500 1000 miles

57. EUROPE IN 1556. THE HABSBURG DOMINIONS

58. THE EXPLORATION OF THE WORLD TO *c.* 1600

- Portugal and Portuguese territory
- Spain and Spanish territory
- England and English territory
- France and French territory
- Portuguese routes of exploration
- First voyage of Columbus 1492
- Fourth voyage of Columbus 1502-4
- Other Spanish routes of exploration
- English voyages of discovery
- Voyage of William Barents 1596
- Voyage of Jacques Cartier 1534
- Route of Marco Polo 1271-95

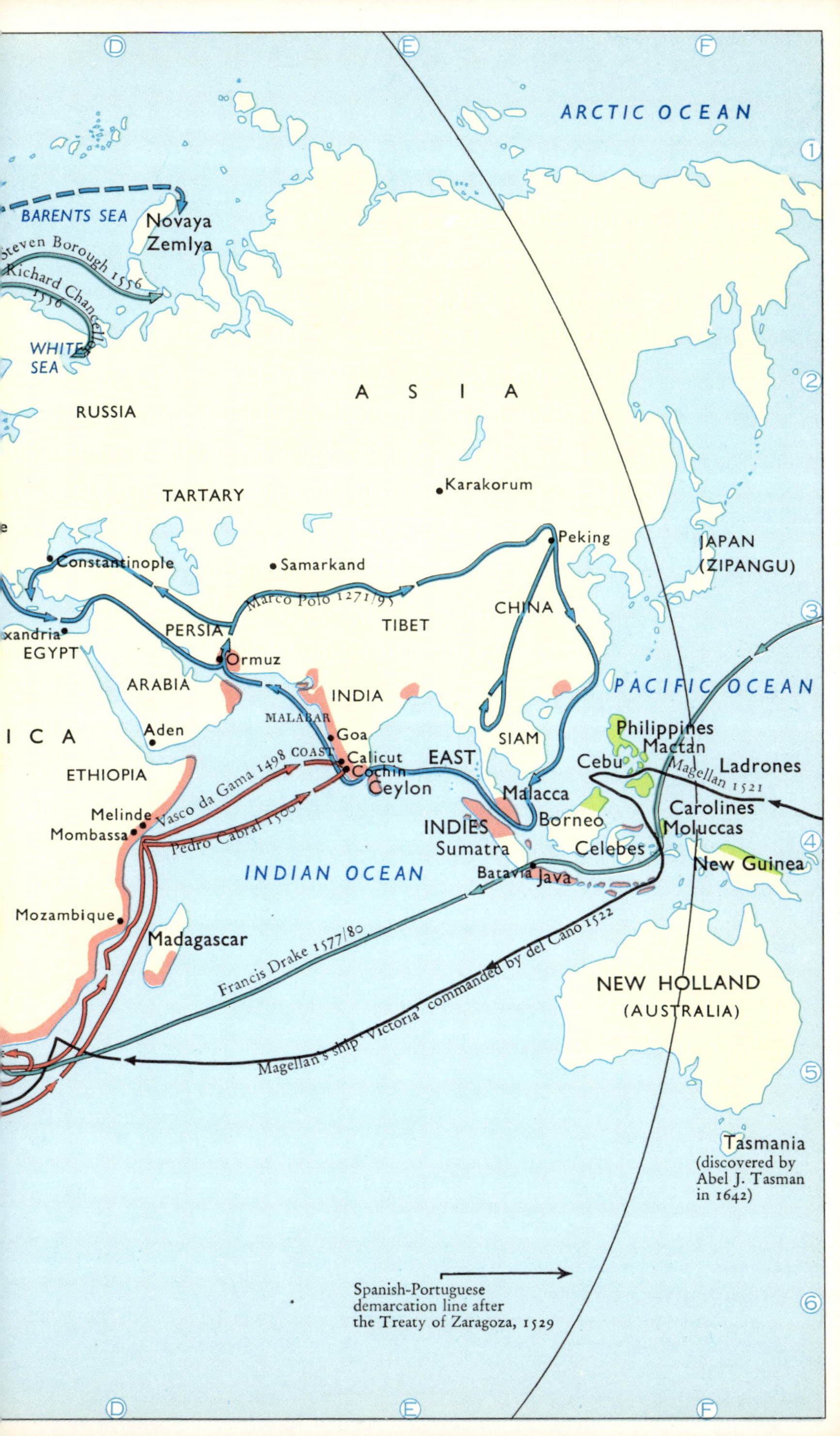

ARCTIC OCEAN
BARENTS SEA
Novaya
Zemlya
Steven Borough 1556
Richard Chancellor 1556
WHITE SEA
RUSSIA
A S I A
TARTARY
Karakorum
Peking
JAPAN
(ZIPANGU)
Constantinople
Samarkand
Marco Polo 1271/95
CHINA
TIBET
PERSIA
xandria
EGYPT
Ormuz
ARABIA
INDIA
PACIFIC OCEAN
MALABAR
COAST
Goa
Calicut
Cochin
Ceylon
Aden
I C A
ETHIOPIA
EAST
INDIES
SIAM
Philippines
Mactan
Cebu
Ladrones
Magellan 1521
Malacca
Borneo
Carolines
Moluccas
Melinde
Mombassa
Vasco da Gama 1498
Pedro Cabral 1500
Sumatra
Celebes
New Guinea
INDIAN OCEAN
Batavia
Java
Mozambique
Madagascar
Francis Drake 1577/80
Magellan's ship 'Victoria' commanded by del Cano 1522
NEW HOLLAND
(AUSTRALIA)
Tasmania
(discovered by
Abel J. Tasman
in 1642)
Spanish-Portuguese
demarcation line after
the Treaty of Zaragoza, 1529

59. THE EXPLORATION OF NORTH AMERICA 1518-1844

APACHE Indian tribes at time of white settlement

Battlefields of Indian wars

16th century exploration

17th century exploration

18th century exploration

19th century exploration

0 200 400 600 800 1000 miles

60. THE EXPANSION OF THE OTTOMAN EMPIRE 1355-1680
Extent of Empire in 1355
Conquests before fall of Constantinople in 1453
Expansion 1453- c. 1520
Expansion c. 1520-1680
Turkish penetration into Europe
0
200
400 miles
POLAND
RUSSIA
Kiev
Poltava
Dnieper
Dniester
Bug
Don
Geneva
Innsbruck
Salzburg
Vienna
1529
Pressburg
Buda
Pest
1526
Milan
Turin
Trento
Drava
Graz
Sava
Theiss
HUNGARY
Mohacs
1526
Zenta
CROATIA
Venice
Genoa
Nice
Florence
TRANSYLVANIA
Jassy
Bender
MOLDAVIA
Hermannstadt
Azov
SEA OF AZOV
KUBAN
Crimea
BOSNIA
Belgrade
WALLACHIA
Danube
Bucharest
Corsica
Rome
Sardinia
ADRIATIC SEA
HERZE-GOVINA
SERBIA
Ragusa
Nish
Nicopolis
Sofia
BULGARIA
Varna
MONTE-NEGRO
Durazzo
Philippopolis
Adrianople
Naples
Salerno
Bari
Brindisi
MACEDONIA
Thessalonica
Constantinople
Gallipoli
Brussa
BLACK SEA
CAUCASUS
Tiflis
GEORGIA
Baku
CASPIAN SEA
Sinope
Trebizond
ARMENIA
Aras
Nakwitchevan
AZER-BAIJAN
Tabriz
Palermo
Messina
Sicily
Syracuse
TUNIS
Janina
Lepanto
Lesbos
Ankara
Halys
Athens
MOREA
Smyrna
ANATOLIA
Konya
KURDISTAN
Adalia
TAURUS
Mosul
Teheran
PERSIA
MEDITERRANEAN SEA
Rhodes
Crete
Aleppo
Antioch
Euphrates
MESOPOTAMIA
Tigris
Hamadan
LURISTAN
Cyprus
Famagusta
SYRIA
Tripoli
Beirut
Damascus
Baghdad
Ispahan
Misurata
TRIPOLI
Benghazi
Jaffa
Jerusalem
Gaza
ARABIA
Basra
PERSIAN GULF
Alexandria
EGYPT
Cairo
1517

61. THE NETHERLANDS WAR OF INDEPENDENCE

Boundary of the northern provinces which, after the Union of Utrecht in 1579, formed the republic of the United Provinces

Ghent — Names underlined indicate towns in the Spanish Netherlands which belonged temporarily to the Union of Utrecht

Catholic Union of Arras 1579

Spanish Netherlands

Church lands

62. FRANCE DURING THE HUGUENOT WARS 1562-92

Provinces loyal to the king
Huguenot areas
Provinces supporting the Guises
Spanish territory

0 100 200 300 miles

63. THE RELIGIOUS SITUATION IN EUROPE 1560

64. GERMANY DURING THE THIRTY YEARS' WAR 1618-48

65. ENGLAND, SCOTLAND AND IRELAND IN THE MID-17TH CENTURY
Areas controlled by Charles I in 1642
Charles I's conquests 1643
Area controlled by Parliament in 1642
Conquests by Parliament in 1643
Area controlled by Parliament in 1645
Areas of Ireland where English and Scottish Protestants were settled during the time of Cromwell
Irish areas given to English settlers c. 1650
0 50 100 miles
THE EDINBURGH AREA
Dundee
MURRAY
FIRTH OF TAY
St Andrews
Kinross
LINDSAY
Loch Leven
FIRTH OF FORTH
Leith
Edinburgh
Holyrood
Craigmillar
Bothwell
Carberry Hill
Orkneys
Hebrides
Dunrobin
MORAY FIRTH
Inverness
MORAY
Aberdeen
Balmoral
Dalnaspidal
Killiecrankie
Glencoe
ANGUS
SCOTLAND
Dundee
Perth
Stirling
Dunbar
Glasgow
Edinburgh
Douglas
Ayr
Turnberry
Dumfries
NORTH SEA
ATLANTIC OCEAN
Londonderry
TYRONE
ULSTER
Belfast
CONNAUGHT
Drogheda
IRELAND
Boyne
Dublin
LEINSTER
Limerick
Kilkenny
MUNSTER
Wexford
Cork
Man
IRISH SEA
SOLWAY FIRTH
NORTHUMBERLAND
Newcastle
Carlisle
Durham
WESTMORLAND
YORKSHIRE
Lancaster
York
Preston
Leeds
Bradford
Hull
LANCASHIRE
Manchester
Gainsborough
Lincoln
Conway
Sheffield
CHESHIRE
NOTTINGHAM
Nottingham
Derby
Shrewsbury
LEICESTER
Leicester
Norwich
ENGLAND
NORFOLK
Ely
Naseby
Cambridge
Worcester
Stratford
Bedford
SUFFOLK
Cardigan
Edgehill
Harwich
Buckingham
ESSEX
Pembroke
Gloucester
Berkeley Castle
Oxford
Hatfield
London
Bristol
Reading
Greenwich
Bath
Sedgemoor
Newbury
Canterbury
Bridgwater
SOMERSET
SURREY
KENT
Dover
Taunton
Salisbury
DEVON
DORSET
SUSSEX
Southampton
BEACHY HEAD
Isle of Wight
Tor Bay
CORNWALL
Plymouth
ENGLISH CHANNEL
66 LONDON c. 1600
0 1/2 1 1 1/2 miles
MIDDLESEX
Bethnal Green
Gray's Inn
Bromley
Mile End
WHITECHAPEL
Stepney
Lea
Lincoln's Inn
St Paul's
CITY
MAYFAIR
HYDE PARK
London Bridge
Tower
Poplar
WESTMINSTER
Whitehall
Globe Theatre
Kensington
Buckingham Palace (built 1698)
Westminster Abbey
SOUTHWARK
Parliament
Lambeth
Brompton
Newington
Vauxhall
Walworth
Chelsea
Thames
Nine Elms
SURREY
DEPTFORD
GREENWICH

67. THE HOLY ROMAN EMPIRE AFTER THE PEACE OF WESTPHALIA 164

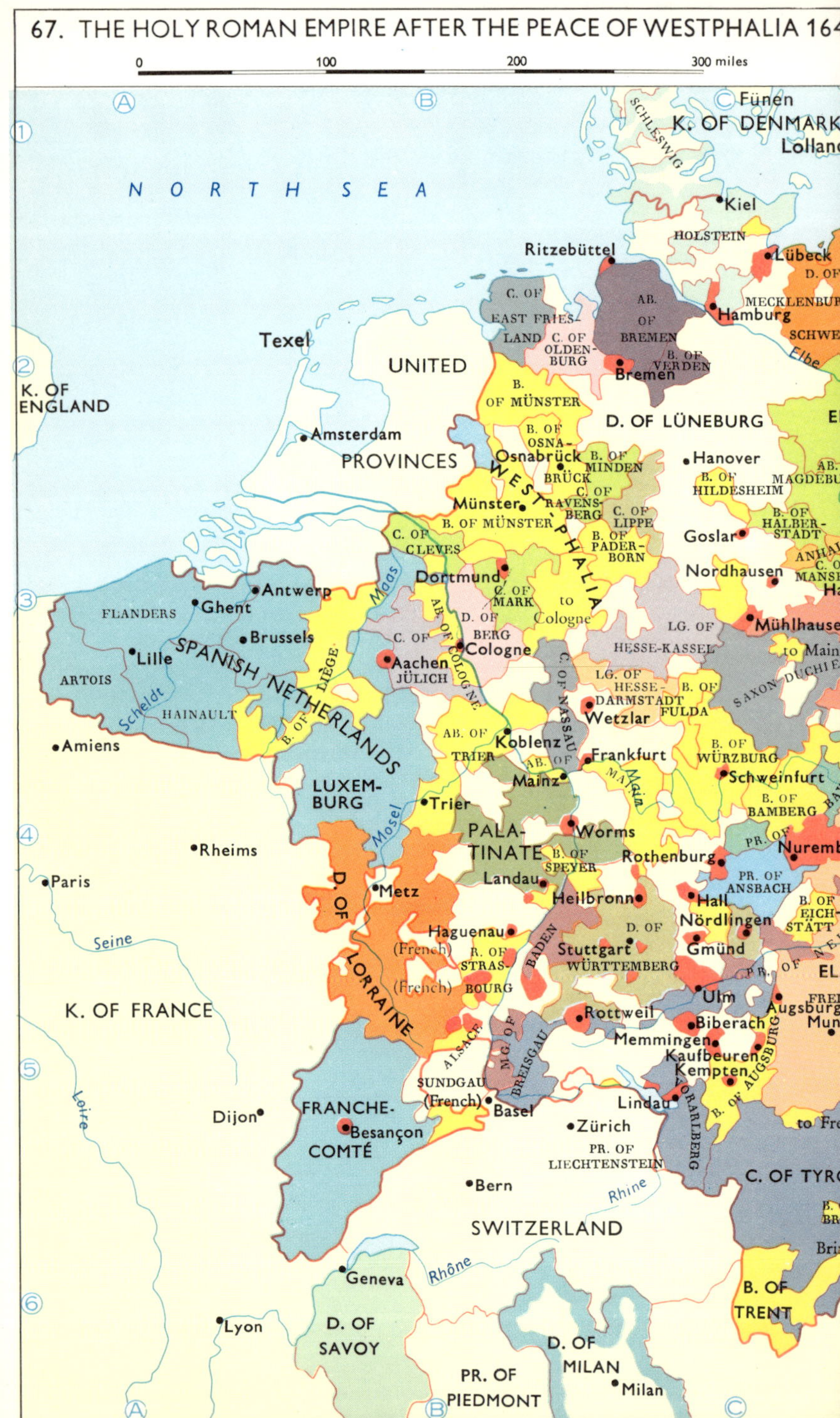

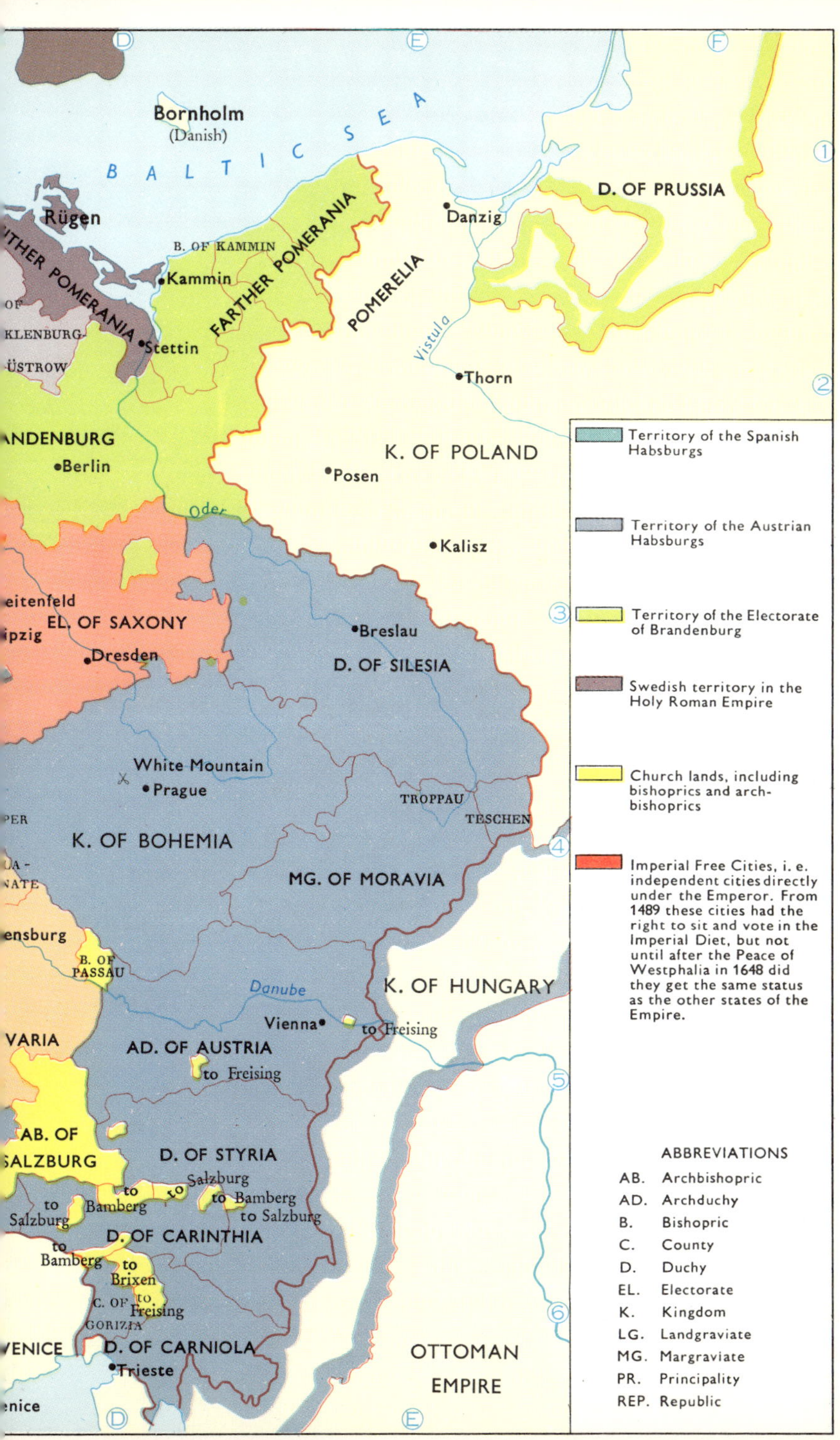

Bornholm
(Danish)
BALTIC SEA
Rügen
B. OF KAMMIN
Kammin
Stettin
FARTHER POMERANIA
POMERELIA
Danzig
D. OF PRUSSIA
Vistula
Thorn
Berlin
Oder
Posen
K. OF POLAND
Kalisz
EL. OF SAXONY
Dresden
Breslau
D. OF SILESIA
White Mountain
Prague
TROPPAU
TESCHEN
K. OF BOHEMIA
MG. OF MORAVIA
B. OF PASSAU
Danube
K. OF HUNGARY
Vienna
to Freising
AD. OF AUSTRIA
to Freising
AB. OF SALZBURG
D. OF STYRIA
to Salzburg
to Bamberg
to Salzburg
to Bamberg
to Bamberg
to Salzburg
D. OF CARINTHIA
to Bamberg
to Brixen
C. OF GORIZIA
to Freising
D. OF CARNIOLA
Trieste
OTTOMAN EMPIRE
Territory of the Spanish Habsburgs
Territory of the Austrian Habsburgs
Territory of the Electorate of Brandenburg
Swedish territory in the Holy Roman Empire
Church lands, including bishoprics and archbishoprics
Imperial Free Cities, i. e. independent cities directly under the Emperor. From 1489 these cities had the right to sit and vote in the Imperial Diet, but not until after the Peace of Westphalia in 1648 did they get the same status as the other states of the Empire.
ABBREVIATIONS
AB. Archbishopric
AD. Archduchy
B. Bishopric
C. County
D. Duchy
EL. Electorate
K. Kingdom
LG. Landgraviate
MG. Margraviate
PR. Principality
REP. Republic

68. THE NETHERLANDS AFTER THE PEACE OF WESTPHALIA 1648
United Provinces
The Generality, i. e. areas seized from the Spanish Netherlands by the United Provinces and administered by the States General
Spanish Netherlands
Church lands
0 25 50 150 miles
West Frisian Is.
Texel
PROV. OF FRIESLAND
PROV. OF GRONINGEN
Groningen
Emden
Stavoren
DRENTHE
ZUIDER ZEE
Alkmaar
PROV. OF HOLLAND
Haarlem
Amsterdam
Kampen
Vecht
Ijssel
PROV. OF OVERIJSSEL
NORTH SEA
Leiden
The Hague
Rijswijk
Delft
Lek
Rotterdam
Briel
Dordrecht
PROV. OF UTRECHT
Utrecht
PROV. OF GELDERLAND
Arnhem
Waal
Nijmegen
Cleves
CLEVES
Lippe
Wesel
Ruhr
Maas
Hertogenbosch
PROV. OF ZEELAND
Middelburg
Breda
THE GENERALITY
UPPER GELDERLAND
Sluys
Ostend
Nieuport
Dunkirk
Calais
Antwerp
D. OF BRABANT
Ghent
Dendermonde
Louvain
Brussels
Roermond
Roer
Rhine
JÜLICH
Cologne
B. OF LIÈGE
Maastricht
Aachen
Neerwinden
Liège
D. OF LIMBURG
C. OF FLANDERS
Ypres
Lys
Scheldt
Steenkerke
Tournai
Fontenoy
C. OF HAINAULT
Mons (Bergen)
Seneffe
Fleurus
Charleroi
C. OF NAMUR
Namur
D. OF LUXEMBURG
C. OF ARTOIS
Arras
Sambre
FRANCE
69. FRENCH CONQUESTS IN THE 17TH CENTURY
to 1648
1648-1697
0 100 200 miles
ENGLISH CHANNEL
Dunkirk
Veurne
Calais
Ypres
FLANDERS
ARTOIS
Arras
Lille
Cambrai
SPANISH NETHERLANDS
Charleroi
Philippeville
Aachen
Rhine
HOLY ROMAN EMPIRE
Frankfurt
Amiens
Rocroi
Bouillon
Mosel
Worms
Heidelberg
Le Havre
Dieppe
PICARDY
Sedan
Trier
PALATINATE
Speyer
Rouen
Beauvais
Luxemburg
Zweibrücken
Saarbrücken
Landau
NORMANDY
Rheims
Marne
Metz
ILE-DE-FRANCE
Paris
Meaux
Verdun
D. OF BAR
Haguenau
Saint-Germain
Versailles
Vitry
LORRAINE
Saverne
Strasbourg
Port Royal
Fontainebleau
Seine
CHAMPAGNE
Maas
Rosheim
Sens
Troyes
ALSACE
Breisach
ORLÉANAIS
Orléans
Freiburg
Vendôme
Sully
Auxerre
SUNDGAU
Blois
Zürich
Tours
K. OF FRANCE
Dijon
FRANCHE-COMTÉ
Besançon
Luzern
Richelieu
Bourges
Nevers
Dôle
Bern
Poitiers
BERRY
BOURBONNAIS
BURGUNDY
Saône
SWITZERLAND
Allier
Loire
MARCHE
Geneva
Angoulême
Clermont
Lyon
LIMOUSIN
ANGOUMOIS
SAVOY
Casale
Turenne
Dordogne
AUVERGNE
Rhône
DAUPHINÉ
Po
Garonne
GUIENNE
Rodez
DIOIS
Genoa
PIEDMONT
Orange (to Nassau 1580-1713)
Lot
Avignon (Church land)
Toulouse
LANGUEDOC
Arles
PROVENCE
Canal du Midi
Montpellier
Narbonne
FOIX
PYRENEES
SPAIN
ROUSSILLON

70. NORTHEASTERN EUROPE IN 1660: EXPANSION OF SWEDEN IN 17TH CENT.

71. EUROPE AT THE OUTBREAK OF THE WAR OF THE SPANISH SUCCESSION 1701
Spanish Habsburgs
Austrian Habsburgs
Marlborough's campaigns
Boundary of the Holy Roman Empire
Prince Eugene's campaigns
Archduke Charles's campaigns
French campaigns
0 200 400 600 miles
ATLANTIC OCEAN
NORTH SEA
BALTIC SEA
MEDITERRANEAN SEA
ADRIATIC SEA
K. OF DENMARK
Copenhagen
UNITED PROVINCES
Emden
Utrecht
London
1704
SPANISH NETHERLANDS
Antwerp
Ramillies
Oudenarde
Lille
Malplaquet
HANOVER
Elbe
BRANDENBURG
SAXONY
Altranstadt
SILESIA
BOHEMIA
Koblenz
Mainz
HOLY ROMAN EMPIRE
Blenheim
Strasbourg
BAVARIA
LORRAINE
Rhine
Danube
Vienna
AUSTRIA
AB. OF SALZBURG
STYRIA
CARINTHIA
TYROL
CARNIOLA
SWITZERLAND
PRUSSIA
Königsberg
Vilna
Niemen
Vistula
K. OF POLAND
(House of Saxony 1697-1763)
Warsaw
Bug
Krakow
Lemberg
GALICIA
Dniester
RUSSIA
Theiss
Pressburg (Bratislava)
K. OF HUNGARY
Buda
Pest
TRANSYLVANIA
Zenta
Drava
Sava
Bender
MOLDAVIA
WALLACHIA
Karlowitz
Belgrade
SERBIA
BOSNIA
Sarajevo
Nish
BULGARIA
Sofia
OTTOMAN EMPIRE
Constantinople
MONTENEGRO
REP. OF RAGUSA
ALBANIA
Salonika
Smyrna
Chios
Athens
MOREA
Zante
Corfu
NORMANDY
BRITTANY
Paris
1708
1709
1704
Nantes
Loire
Orléans
Seine
Maas
K. OF FRANCE
Lyon
Rhône
1706
Bordeaux
Garonne
Toulouse
Avignon
Marseille
Toulon
SAVOY
Turin
Milan
D. OF MILAN
Genoa
Nice
MODENA
Bologna
LUCCA
G. D. OF TUSCANY
PAPAL STATES
Rome
1707
REP. OF VENICE
Venice
Corsica
Sardinia
Naples
K. OF NAPLES
Brindisi
Palermo
K. OF SICILY
Marlborough
Archduke Charles
Oviedo
Vigo
Oporto
Duero
Valladolid
K. OF PORTUGAL
Lisbon
Tagus
Guadiana
Salamanca
CASTILE
Madrid
Toledo
Villaviciosa
Pamplona
Ebro
CATALONIA
Barcelona
K. OF SPAIN
Valencia
Balearic Is.
Minorca
Mallorca
Almanza
Guadalquivir
Seville
Murcia
Granada
Gibraltar

72. THE EXPANSION OF RUSSIA FROM 1300 TO 1825

73. CAMPAIGN OF CHARLES XII 1700-09

Swedish territory at outbreak of Northern War 1700

Charles's campaign. The vertical strokes indicate the beginning of a year

Charles's journey to Stralsund

0 200 400 miles

74. LITHUANIA AND POLAND 13TH-14TH CENTURIES

Lithuania 1263

Expansion 1316-41

Lithuania at the time of union with Poland 1386

Expansion of Lithuania 1392-1430

Poland 1340

Poland at the time of union with Lithuania 1386

0 200 400 miles

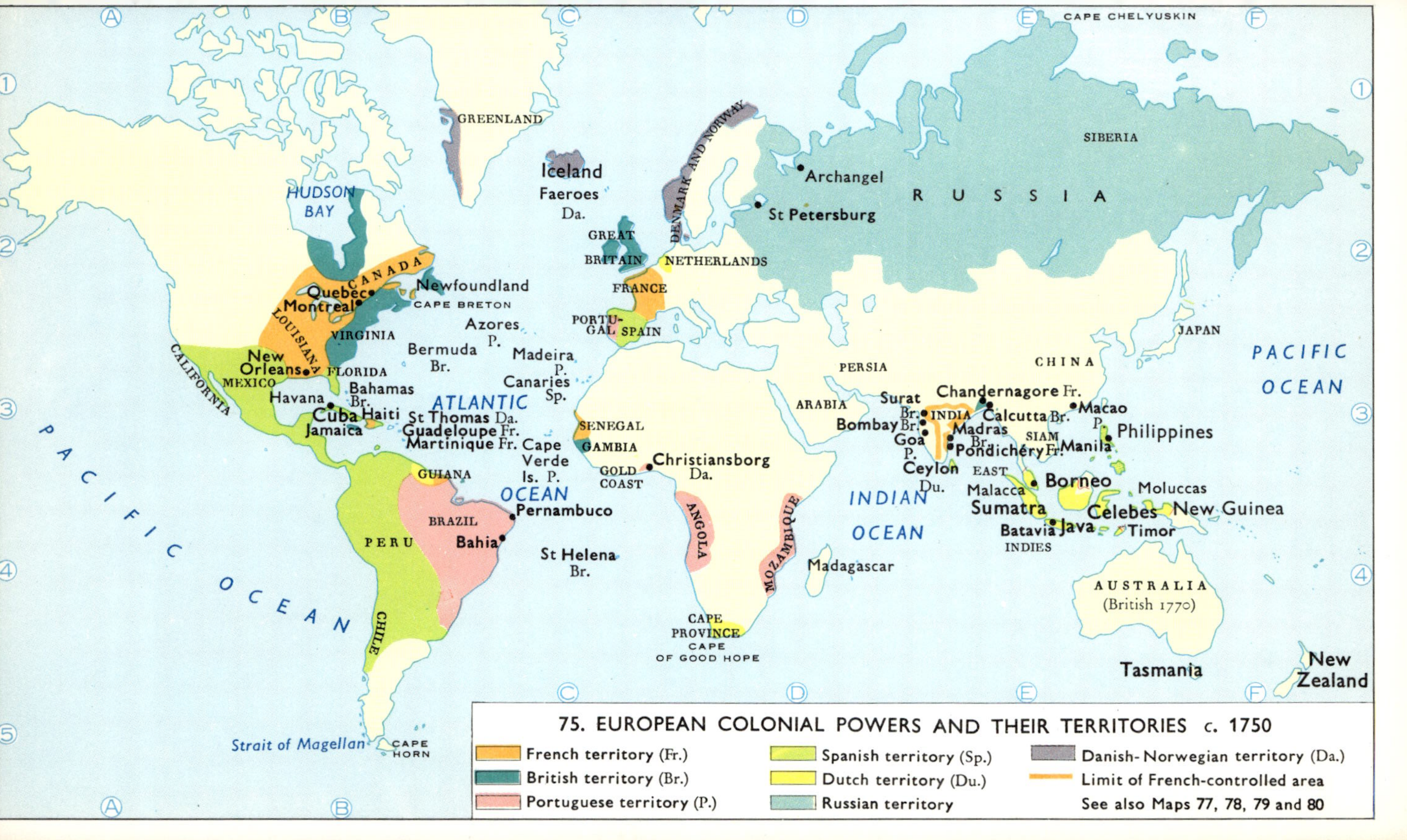

75. EUROPEAN COLONIAL POWERS AND THEIR TERRITORIES *c.* 1750

76. EUROPE IN 1721
Austrian territory
British territory including Hanover, united under the same king 1714-1837
Brandenburg territory
Swedish territory
Boundary of Holy Roman Empire
0
200
400 miles
Shetland Is.
Orkney Is.
Hebrides
Bergen
Stavanger
Culloden
SCOTLAND
Aberdeen
Scone
NORTH SEA
Falkirk
Glasgow
Edinburgh
Berwick
Belfast
Newcastle
K. OF GREAT BRITAIN
Ripon
IRELAND
Dublin
York
Limerick
Newark
Cork
Wexford
Derby
ENGLAND
Southwold
Cambridge
Worcester
Oxford
London
Exeter
Chatham
Dover
Plymouth
Portland
Tor Bay
ATLANTIC OCEAN
UNITED
Amsterdam
The Hague
Utrecht
PROVINCES
Ostend
Dunkirk
AUSTRIAN
Fontenoy
NETHER-
LANDS
Aache
Cambrai
CAP DE LA HOGUE
Rouen
Rheims
Brest
Paris
Versailles
Nancy
Cirey
Fontainebleau
Seine
RAINE
Nantes
Orléans
Loire
Tours
Basel
K. OF FRANCE
Ferney
Rochefort
Geneva
Limoges
Lyon
SAVOY
Bordeaux
Turin
Garonne
Rhône
Oviedo
Bayonne
Toulouse
Avignon
Montpellier
Marseille
Pamplona
Toulon
Burgos
Oporto
Valladolid
Ebro
Duero
Zaragoza
K. OF PORTUGAL
K. OF SPAIN
Barcelona
Tagus
Madrid
Toledo
Lisbon
Guadiana
Balearic Is.
Minorca
(British 1703-83)
Valencia
Mallorca
Almanza
Guadalquivir
Seville
Cartagena
MEDITERRANE
Granada
Cadiz
Gibraltar
(British 1713)
BARBARY STATES

FINLAND
Viborg
Nystad
K. OF SWEDEN
Åbo
Helsingfors
St Petersburg
INGRIA
Narva
Novgorod
Uppsala
Reval
ESTONIA
Christiania
Stockholm
RUSSIA
Fredrikshald
Moscow
LIVONIA
Marstrand
Gotland
BALTIC SEA
Riga
Göteborg
KOURLAND
Dvina
Smolensk
Fladstrand
Kalmar
Karlskrona
Memel
LITHUANIA
penhagen
Lund
Niemen
Vilna
Minsk
Bornholm
Königsberg
PRUSSIA
Grodno
Gottorp
Møen
Dnieper
Rügen
Danzig
Stralsund
Hamburg
BRANDENBURG
Thorn
men
Warsaw
POLAND
(united with Saxony 1697-1763)
NOVER
Elbe
Berlin
Posen
Kiev
Potsdam
Vistula
Lublin
EL. OF SAXONY
Kassel
Altranstadt
Breslau
SILESIA
Oder
Rossbach
Lemberg
Krakow
Bug
Dettingen
Prague
Dniester
Main
BOHEMIA
MORAVIA
AUSTRIA
Prut
nheim
Danube
Passau
MOLDAVIA
BESSARABIA
BAVARIA
Tulln
Vienna
K. OF HUNGARY
Munich
Buda
Pest
Theiss
TRANSYL-VANIA
SALZBURG
Raab
Vasvár
TYROL
Drava
Mohacs
Zenta
BLACK SEA
WALLACHIA
ND
BANAT
Bucharest
LAN
Trieste
Sava
Karlowitz
Milan
Venice
CROATIA
Belgrade
Danube
MANTUA
(Austrian 1718-39)
Parma
RMA
MODENA
BOSNIA
enoa
Bologna
REPUBLIC OF VENICE
SERBIA
Nish
BULGARIA
GENOA
DALMATIA
Sofia
LUCCA
Florence
TUSCANY
PAPAL STATES
Ragusa
MONTE-NEGRO
OTTOMAN EMPIRE
Constantinople
RUMELIA
rsica
Genoa.
nch 1768)
Rome
Salonika
K. OF NAPLES
(Austrian 1714-35)
Brindisi
Naples
Otranto
ALBANIA
rdinia
istrian 1714. To
oy 1720)
(to Venice)
Athens
MOREA
SEA
Palermo
Sicily
(to Savoy 1714.
Austrian 1720-35)
Syracuse
Crete
Malta
(Knights of St John)

77. THE EXPANSION OF NORTH AMERICA 1650-1763

78. THE UNITED STATES OF AMERICA IN 1783

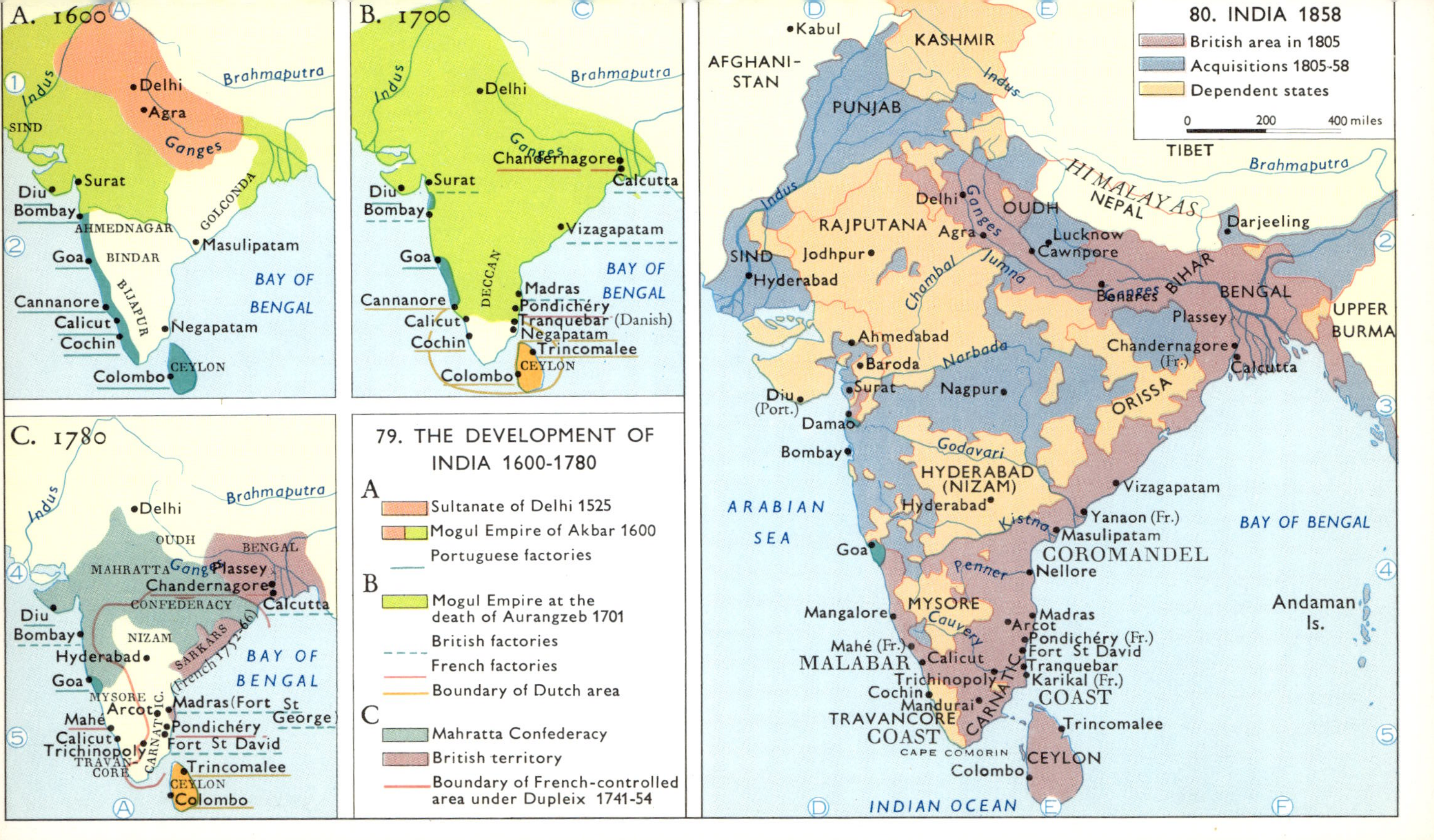

A. 1600
Delhi
Agra
Ganges
Indus
SIND
Brahmaputra
Surat
Diu
Bombay
AHMEDNAGAR
GOLCONDA
Masulipatam
Goa
BINDAR
BIJAPUR
Cannanore
Calicut
Cochin
Negapatam
BAY OF BENGAL
CEYLON
Colombo
B. 1700
Indus
Delhi
Brahmaputra
Ganges
Chandernagore
Calcutta
Surat
Diu
Bombay
Vizagapatam
Goa
DECCAN
Madras
Pondichéry
Tranquebar (Danish)
Negapatam
Trincomalee
Cannanore
Calicut
Cochin
CEYLON
Colombo
BAY OF BENGAL
C. 1780
Indus
Delhi
Brahmaputra
OUDH
BENGAL
MAHRATTA
Ganges
Plassey
Chandernagore
Calcutta
CONFEDERACY
Diu
Bombay
NIZAM
SARKARS (French 1752-66)
Hyderabad
BAY OF BENGAL
Goa
MYSORE
Arcot
Madras (Fort St George)
Mahé
Calicut
Trichinopoly
CARNATIC
Pondichéry
Fort St David
TRAVANCORE
Trincomalee
CEYLON
Colombo
79. THE DEVELOPMENT OF INDIA 1600-1780
A
Sultanate of Delhi 1525
Mogul Empire of Akbar 1600
Portuguese factories
B
Mogul Empire at the death of Aurangzeb 1701
British factories
French factories
Boundary of Dutch area
C
Mahratta Confederacy
British territory
Boundary of French-controlled area under Dupleix 1741-54
80. INDIA 1858
British area in 1805
Acquisitions 1805-58
Dependent states
0 200 400 miles
Kabul
AFGHANISTAN
KASHMIR
Indus
PUNJAB
TIBET
Brahmaputra
HIMALAYAS
NEPAL
Darjeeling
Delhi
OUDH
Ganges
RAJPUTANA
Agra
Lucknow
Cawnpore
SIND
Jodhpur
Hyderabad
Chambal
Jumna
Benares
BIHAR
BENGAL
Plassey
UPPER BURMA
Ahmedabad
Baroda
Narbada
Chandernagore (Fr.)
Calcutta
Surat
Nagpur
ORISSA
Diu (Port.)
Damao
Bombay
Godavari
HYDERABAD (NIZAM)
Hyderabad
Vizagapatam
Yanaon (Fr.)
ARABIAN SEA
Kistna
Masulipatam
BAY OF BENGAL
Goa
COROMANDEL
Penner
Nellore
MYSORE
Mangalore
Madras
Arcot
Cauvery
Andaman Is.
Mahé (Fr.)
Pondichéry (Fr.)
Fort St David
MALABAR
Calicut
Tranquebar
Trichinopoly
Karikal (Fr.)
Cochin
COAST
Mandurai
CARNATIC
TRAVANCORE COAST
Trincomalee
CAPE COMORIN
CEYLON
Colombo
INDIAN OCEAN

81. BRANDENBURG-PRUSSIA
1415-1797
0 50 100 150 miles
NORTH SEA
BALTIC SEA
K. OF DENMARK
K. OF SWEDEN
Bornholm
D. OF SCHLESWIG
D. OF HOLSTEIN
D. OF MECKLEN-BURG
Rügen
Stralsund
SWEDISH POMERANIA
Wollgast
HITHER POMERANIA 1720
Stettin
Kolberg
Rügenwalde
FARTHER POMERANIA 1648
Oliva
Danzig 1793
WEST PRUSSIA 1772
Memel
Königsberg
EAST PRUSSIA
1618
1772
Niemen
1795
Vistula
Warsaw
K. OF POLAND
Posen
Schwiebus
1793
1482
1455
NEUMARK
Küstrin
1472
Rheinsberg 1524
Fehrbellin
BRANDENBURG
ALTMARK
Havel
Canal 1744-46
Berlin
Potsdam
Canal 1743-45
MAGDE-BURG 1680
Wüsterhausen 1680
Canal
HALBER-STADT 1649
1648
1680
1780
1462
1462
Kottbus
Spree
Oder
SILESIA
Liegnitz
Breslau
1742
Mollwitz 1741
Hohenfriedberg 1745
Soor
1795
Rossbach
EL. OF SAXONY
Dresden
Pillnitz
Kesselsdorf
AUSTRIA
Elbe
Prague
BOHEMIA
Chotusitz 1742
Krakow
Hamburg
HANOVER
Elbe
Weser
EAST FRIESLAND 1744
OLDEN-BURG
Ems
NETHERLANDS
1702
LINGEN 1707
MINDEN 1648
RAVENSBERG 1614
Utrecht
MÜNSTER
Cleves
CLEVES 1614
UPPER GELDERLAND 1715
MARK 1614
WEST-PHALIA
JÜLICH
BERG
Cologne
Aachen
Maas
Rhine
NASSAU
Frankfurt
Mainz
Main
Mosel
PALA-TINATE
Metz
D. OF WÜRTTEM-BERG
BAYREUTH 1420-40 1470-86 1791
ANSBACH 1415-40 1470-86 1791
Nurem-berg
Nördlingen
PR. OF NEUCHÂTEL IN SWITZERLAND
FRANCE
NEUCHÂTEL 1707
SWITZERLAND
Electorate of Brandenburg in 1415
Acquisitions 1415-1535
Acquisitions of Johan Sigismund 1608-19
Acquisitions of the Great Elector 1640-88
Acquisitions of Frederick III (I of Prussia) and Frederick William I 1688-1740
Acquisitions of Frederick the Great 1740-86
Acquisitions of Frederick William II 1786-97
Dates show the year of incorporation into Brandenburg-Prussia

82. CENTRAL EUROPE DURING THE SEVEN YEARS' WAR 1756-63
0 50 100 150 miles
Kingdom of Prussia
Habsburg territory
Swedish territory
Church lands
Attack by Frederick the Great on Saxony and Bohemia, 1756
Main outline of counter-attack by Austria, France, Russia and Sweden
Pirna Victory of Frederick the Great and his allies
Kolin Defeat of Frederick the Great and his allies
NORTH SEA
BALTIC SEA
DENMARK
Möen
Falster
Bornholm
Rügen
D. OF HOLSTEIN
Lübeck
Wismar
HITHER POMERANIA
Kolberg
FARTHER POMERANIA
Danzig
WEST PRUSSIA
Königsberg
Grossjägersdorf 1757
EAST PRUSSIA
Marienburg
Marienwerder
Thorn
Netze
Vistula
Warsaw
POLAND
(united with Saxony 1697-1763)
Posen
Warta
Stettin
D. OF MECKLENBURG
Hamburg
EAST FRIESLAND
Weser
Elbe
EL. OF HANOVER
(united with England)
Hanover
Minden 1759
Hastenbeck 1757
Rheinsberg
BRANDENBURG
Oder
Zorndorf 1758
Küstrin
Kunersdorf 1759
Berlin 1760
Charlottenburg
Sans Souci
Potsdam
MAGDEBURG
Magdeburg
HALBER-STADT
Spree
SAXONY
Torgau 1760
Glogau
SILESIA
UNITED PROVINCES
Lingen
Ems
Maas
CLEVES
MARK
B. OF PADERBORN
Göttingen
Wilhelmsthal 1762
Halle
Rossbach 1757
Hubertus-burg
Meissen
Dresden
Liegnitz 1760
Leuthen 1757
Breslau 1757
Bunzelwitz 1761
Schweidnitz
Burkersdorf 1762
Hochkirch 1758
Freiberg 1762
Pirna 1756
Saale
Ostend
Nieuport
AUSTRIAN
Brussels
Fontenoy
Krefeld 1758
Aachen
B. OF LIÈGE
NETHERLANDS
Rhine
Mosel
Frankfurt
Bergen 1759
Dettingen
Main
PALATINATE
P. OF ZWEI-BRÜCKEN
Neckar
Nuremberg
Eger
Eger
Lobositz 1756
Prague 1757
Elbe
Kolin 1757
BOHEMIA
Moldavia
Jägerndorf
Krakow
GALICIA
Olmütz 1758
MORAVIA
EL. OF BAVARIA
Regensburg
Landshut 1760
Danube
Freising
Munich
Isar
Inn
Passau
AUSTRIA
Linz
Vienna
Schönbrunn
Press-burg
Danube
SALZBURG
FRANCE
Strasbourg
Mulhouse
SWITZER-LAND

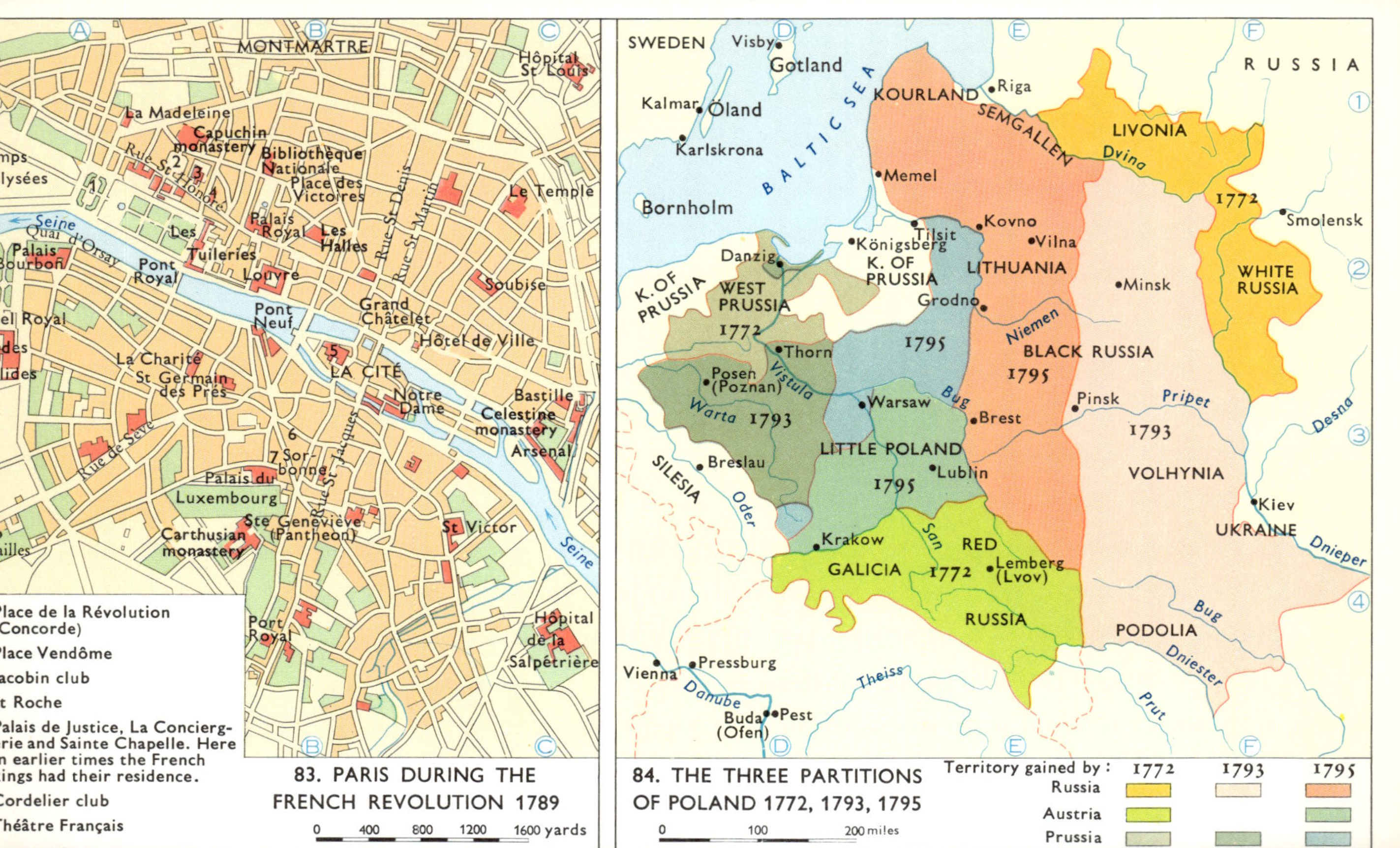

83. PARIS DURING THE FRENCH REVOLUTION 1789

84. THE THREE PARTITIONS OF POLAND 1772, 1793, 1795

85. ITALY c. 1800

86. EUROPE IN NAPOLEON'S TIME 1812

French territory
States ruled by Members of Napoleon's family
Other French-controlled areas
Allies of France
Great Britain and British territory
Neutral states
Napoleon's Eastern campaign 1798
Wellington's Spanish camp. 1808-9
Napoleon's Russian campaign 1812
0 200 400 miles

D
E
F
FINLAND
Viborg
L. LADOGA
Åbo
Helsingfors
St Petersburg
Sveaborg
Åland
Reval
ESTONIA
Novgorod
Stockholm
Volga
LIVONIA
Gotland
Riga
Moscow
Borodino
KOURLAND
Dvina
Öland
Vitebsk
BALTIC SEA
Smolensk
Tilsit
Vilna
RUSSIAN
Königsberg
Friedland
REP. OF DANZIG
Eylau
Niemen
Beresina
OF PRUSSIA
Pripet
G. D. OF
EMPIRE
Vistula
Warsaw
Posen
Trachenberg
Kiev
Bautzen
Oder
WARSAW
Dnieper
Münchengrätz
Krakow
Prague
GALICIA
Troppau
Brünn (Brno)
MORAVIA
Dniester
AUSTRIAN
Wagram
Aspern
Essling
Pressburg
BESSARABIA
MOLDAVIA
Odessa
Buda
Pest
CRIMEA
EMPIRE
TRANSYLVANIA
SLOVENIA
Agram
Laibach
BANAT
WALLACHIA
BLACK SEA
SLAVONIA
Belgrade
Bucharest
BOSNIA
SERBIA
Danube
ILLYRIAN PROVINCES
BULGARIA
Sofia
MONTE-NEGRO
Adrianople
OTTOMAN
RUMELIA
Constantinople
ALBANIA
Salonika
NTECORVO
BENEVENTO
Naples
Salerno
NAPLES
Lemnos
Corfu (French)
EMPIRE
Chios
Athens
Ionian Is.
1797 Fr., 1799 Russ., 1809 Br.
MOREA
Navarino
Rhodes
Cyprus
Malta
Crete
SYRIA
Acre
SEA
Jaffa
Aboukir
Alexandria
EGYPT
Cairo
1
2
3
4
5
6

87. EUROPE AFTER THE CONGRESS OF VIENNA 1815

Boundary of German Confederation

88. SOUTH AMERICA 1810-1914

Boundary of Great Colombia 1819-30

Other boundaries as in 1914

89.-90. UNIFICATION OF ITALY 1859-70
SWITZERLAND
Rhône
Adige
TYROL
AUSTRIA
Adda
Lake Maggiore
Lake Como
Piave
VENETIA
LOMBARDY
1859
K. OF
Novara
Magenta
Milan
Lake Garda
Trieste
ISTRIA
Padua
Venice
Verona
Custozza
Villafranca
Mantua
Solferino
Lodi
Ticino
PIEDMONT
Po
Pavia
Cremona
Adige
Adria
Piacenza
Guastalla (to Parma)
Alessandria
D. OF PARMA
1860
Parma
D. OF MODENA
1860
Ferrara
ROMAGNA
1860
SARDINIA
89. NORTHERN ITALY 1859
Dates show the year of incorporation into the Kingdom of Sardinia
0 25 50 miles
SWITZERLAND
AUSTRIAN EMPIRE
SAVOY (Fr. 1860)
TYROL
LOMBARDY
Milan
Solferino
VENETIA
1866
Venice
Trieste
CROATIA
K. OF
Turin
PIEDMONT
SARDINIA
Genoa
D. OF PARMA
D. OF MODENA
Po
ROMAGNA
FRENCH
EMPIRE
NICE (Fr. 1860)
MONACO
Nice
5 May 1860
PAPAL
STATES
THE MARCHES
UMBRIA
1870
Rome
Florence
G. D. OF TUSCANY
Elba
TURKEY
Zara
DALMATIA
ADRIATIC SEA
Corsica
Caprera
Garibaldi
Sardinia
PONTECORVO
Capua
BENEVENTO
Gaëta
Naples
7 Sept. 1860
Salerno
K. OF THE TWO SICILIES
TYRRHENIAN SEA
Palermo
Messina
20 Aug. 1860
Reggio
Marsala
11 May 1860
Sicily
MEDITERRANEAN SEA
90. THE KINGDOM OF SARDINIA
Sardinia 1859
Austria and Austrian territory 1859
Sardinia, Spring 1860
To Kingdom of Sardinia, Autumn 1860
Garibaldi's exp. against the Two Sicilies
Dates are given for the incorporation of Venetia and the remaining Papal States into the K. of Italy
0 100 200 300 miles

91. THE UNIFICATION OF GERMANY 1865-1871
Prussia 1865
States incorporated into Prussia 1866
Members of the North German Confederation 1866-71
Alsace-Lorraine, ceded to Germany 1871
Boundary of German Empire 1871
0
100
200 miles
NORTH SEA
BALTIC SEA
DENMARK
Fredericia
Fünen
Zealand
SWEDEN
Copenhagen
Bornholm
Dybbøl
SCHLESWIG
Kiel
HOLSTEIN
Heligoland
(Br.)
Rügen
Danzig
Königsberg
EAST PRUSSIA
WEST PRUSSIA
RUSSIAN EMPIRE
Lübeck
MECKLENBURG-SCHWERIN
LAUEN-BURG
Hamburg
POMERANIA
Stettin
Ostrolenka
OLDEN-BURG
Bremen
K. OF HANOVER
K. OF THE NETHERLANDS
Amsterdam
The Hague
Elbe
PRUSSIA
Schönhausen
Hanover
Berlin
Potsdam
BRANDENBURG
POSEN
Vistula
Bug
Warsaw
CONGRESS POLAND
Oder
LIPPE
BRUNSWICK
(to Hanover)
ANHALT
Jüterbog
WESTPHALIA
Rhine
Antwerp
K. OF BELGIUM
Brussels
Düsseldorf
Barmen
Wilhelmshöhe
Göttingen
Kassel
SAXONY
Leipzig
Dresden
Breslau
Aachen
Cologne
K. OF PRUSSIA
RHINE PROVINCE
Bonn
Maas
KURHESSE
Wartburg
Jena
K. OF SAXONY
SILESIA
THURINGIAN STATES
HESSE
Ems
NASSAU
Amiens
Ham
Belgian 1839
LUXEM-BURG
Sedan
Mosel
G.D. OF HESSE
Frankfurt
Main
Münchengrätz
Sadowa
Königgrätz
Elbe
Karlsbad
Prague
Krakow
Auschwitz
GALICIA
FRANCE
Mainz
Trier
Saarbrücken
PALATI-NATE
Hambach
Mannheim
Heidelberg
K. OF BAVARIA
BOHEMIA
Troppau
Gravelotte
Metz
Forbach
K. OF WÜRTTEMBERG
Heilbronn
Nuremberg
AUSTRIAN EMPIRE
Olmütz
MORAVIA
Paris
ALSACE-LORRAINE
Weissenburg
Wörth
Karlsruhe
Toul
Nancy
Strasbourg
Baden
Stuttgart
Tübingen
Danube
Augsburg
Nikolsburg
Vienna
Seine
G.D. OF BADEN
HOHEN-ZOLLERN
Munich
Plombières-les-Bains
SWITZERLAND
Zürich
Innsbruck
TYROL
Gastein
STYRIA
A
B
C
D
E
F
1
2
3
4
5

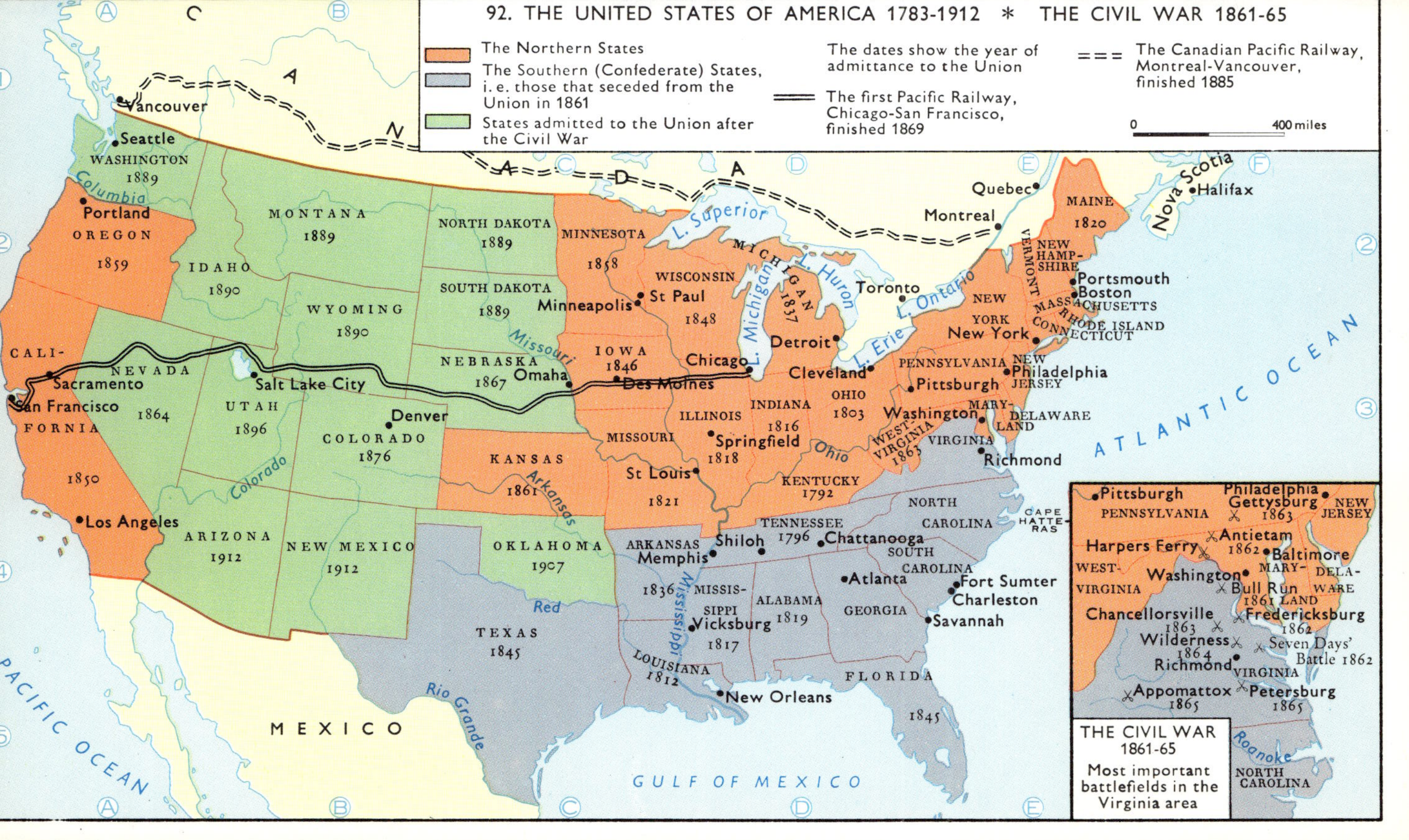

92. THE UNITED STATES OF AMERICA 1783-1912 * THE CIVIL WAR 1861-65
The Northern States
The Southern (Confederate) States, i.e. those that seceded from the Union in 1861
States admitted to the Union after the Civil War
The dates show the year of admittance to the Union
The first Pacific Railway, Chicago-San Francisco, finished 1869
The Canadian Pacific Railway, Montreal-Vancouver, finished 1885
0 400 miles
CANADA
Vancouver
Seattle
WASHINGTON 1889
Columbia
Portland
OREGON 1859
IDAHO 1890
MONTANA 1889
WYOMING 1890
NORTH DAKOTA 1889
SOUTH DAKOTA 1889
NEBRASKA 1867
Missouri
Omaha
MINNESOTA 1858
Minneapolis
St Paul
WISCONSIN 1848
MICHIGAN 1837
L. Superior
L. Michigan
L. Huron
L. Erie
L. Ontario
Toronto
Quebec
Montreal
Nova Scotia
Halifax
MAINE 1820
NEW HAMPSHIRE
VERMONT
Portsmouth
Boston
MASSACHUSETTS
RHODE ISLAND
CONNECTICUT
NEW YORK
New York
NEW JERSEY
Philadelphia
PENNSYLVANIA
Pittsburgh
DELAWARE
MARYLAND
Washington
WEST VIRGINIA 1863
VIRGINIA
Richmond
IOWA 1846
Des Moines
Chicago
Detroit
Cleveland
OHIO 1803
INDIANA 1816
ILLINOIS 1818
Springfield
MISSOURI 1821
St Louis
Ohio
KENTUCKY 1792
CALIFORNIA 1850
Sacramento
San Francisco
Los Angeles
NEVADA 1864
UTAH 1896
Salt Lake City
COLORADO 1876
Denver
Colorado
KANSAS 1861
Arkansas
ARIZONA 1912
NEW MEXICO 1912
OKLAHOMA 1907
Red
TEXAS 1845
Rio Grande
MEXICO
ARKANSAS 1836
Memphis
Shiloh
TENNESSEE 1796
Chattanooga
NORTH CAROLINA
CAPE HATTERAS
SOUTH CAROLINA
Fort Sumter
Charleston
Savannah
Atlanta
GEORGIA
ALABAMA 1819
MISSISSIPPI 1817
Vicksburg
Mississippi
LOUISIANA 1812
New Orleans
FLORIDA 1845
ATLANTIC OCEAN
GULF OF MEXICO
PACIFIC OCEAN
THE CIVIL WAR 1861-65
Most important battlefields in the Virginia area
Pittsburgh
PENNSYLVANIA
Philadelphia
Gettysburg 1863
NEW JERSEY
Antietam 1862
Harpers Ferry
Baltimore
MARYLAND
DELAWARE
WEST-VIRGINIA
Washington
Bull Run 1861
Chancellorsville 1863
Fredericksburg 1862
Wilderness 1864
Seven Days' Battle 1862
Richmond
VIRGINIA
Appomattox 1865
Petersburg 1865
Roanoke
NORTH CAROLINA

93. THE BALKANS AFTER THE CONGRESS OF BERLIN 1878
Turkish territory, occupied and administered by Austria-Hungary
Boundary of the large Bulgaria proposed by Russia in the preliminary treaty of San Stefano
0 100 200 300 miles
RUSSIA
BESSARABIA
Dniester
Jassy
MOLDAVIA
Prut
Romanian 1856-78
CRIMEA
Eupatoria
Sevastopol
Alma
Inkerman
Balaklava
WALLACHIA
Bucharest
ROMANIA
DOBRUJA
Danube
AUSTRIA-HUNGARY
CROATIA
Belgrade
BOSNIA
SERBIA
Sarajevo
HERZEGO-VINA
DALMATIA
MONTE-NEGRO
Plevna
BULGARIA
(under Turkish suzerainty)
Shipka Pass
Sofia
EAST RUMELIA
BLACK SEA
Sinope
Adrianople
Constantinople
San Stefano
Scutari
Ankara
Sea of Marmara
Brussa
Gallipoli
ADRIATIC SEA
ALBANIA
TURKEY
Salonika
DARDANELLES
ITALY
AEGEAN SEA
THESSALY
Lesbos
Ionian Is. (to Greece 1863)
Smyrna
Chios
GREECE
Athens
MOREA
Navarino
Rhodes
Cyprus (Br. 1878)
94. THE BALKANS AFTER THE WARS OF 1912-13
0 100 200 300 miles
RUSSIA
Prut
Dniester
CRIMEA
Sevastopol
AUSTRIA-HUNGARY
TRANSYLVANIA
Drava
Theiss
SLAVONIA
BANAT
Sava
ROMANIA
Bucharest
Belgrade
Danube
DOBRUJA
BLACK SEA
BOSNIA (Annexed 1908)
Sarajevo
HERZEGOVINA (Annexed 1908)
MONTE-NEGRO
SERBIA
BULGARIA
Sofia
Adrianople
Constantinople
Ankara
ADRIATIC SEA
Durazzo
ALBANIA
THRACE
TURKEY
MACEDONIA
Salonika
ITALY
Lemnos
AEGEAN SEA
THESSALY 1881
Lesbos
Corfu
Chios
Athens
GREECE
MOREA
Dodecanese (Ital. from 1912)
Rhodes
Cyprus
Crete (Greek 1908/12)
A B C D E
1 2 3 4 5 6

95. SOUTH AFRICA 1899-1910

96. AFRICA 1914

Simbirsk
Tobolsk
Sverdlovsk (Ekaterinburg)
Samara
Trans-Siberian railway. Finished 1904.
Don
Volga
Constantinople
BLACK SEA
Astrakhan
TURKEY
MEDI-TERRA-NEAN SEA
Cyprus
Kars
ARAL SEA
Baku
CASPIAN SEA
Alexandria
Beirut
Cairo
Suez Canal
Euphrates
Tigris
L. Balkhash
WEST TURKESTAN
Khiva 1847/73
Russian Sphere 1907
Teheran
TURKMENISTAN 1881/86
Bokhara
Tashkent
Samarkand
Merv
BOKHARA
PAMIR 1893
SINKIA
RED SEA
PERSIA
KUWAIT 1901
Kabul
AFGHANISTAN
KASHMIR 1846
ARABIA
PERSIAN GULF
Mecca
Kandahar
PUNJAB 1849
1890
Lahore
Amritsar
British Sphere 1907
1893
BALUCHISTAN 1876
Indus
OMAN (under British protection)
Muscat
Delhi
Meerut
HIMALA
NEPAL
RAJPUTANA
OUDH 1856
SIND
Agra
Lucknow
Cawnpore
Karachi
Ganges
ERITREA
BRITISH
Benares
HADRAMAUT
Aden
FR. SOMALILAND
ARABIAN SEA
Diu (Port.)
Damão (Port.)
Chanderr (Fr.)
INDIA
Bombay
BRITISH SOMALILAND
Socotra
NIZAM
ETHIOPIA
Hyderabad
Goa (Port.)
Yanaor
ITAL. SOMALILAND
MYSORE
Bangalore
Madras
Mahé (Fr.)
Pondichéry (Fr.)
Karikal (Fr.)
CEYLON
INDIAN
Colombo
OCEAN
Russia 1800
Russian acquisitions 1800-78
Russian acquisitions 1878-1914
British territory
French territory
Japanese territory
American territory
Dutch territory
Russian sphere of interest
British sphere of interest
French sphere of interest
Japanese sphere of interest
German sphere of interest
The dates are those of the acquisitions of the various territories. See also Maps 75 and 80
0 200 400 600 800 1000 miles

97. ASIA 1914

SSIA
BERIA
Lake Baikal
Branch line. Finished 1917
Amur
AMUR PROVINCE 1858
1875
SAKHALIN
1905
Kuril Is. (Jap. 1875)
HOKKAIDO
MANCHURIA (Russian 1900-05)
Harbin
Vladivostok
MONGOLIA (Independent 1911)
JAPAN
Mukden
KOREA 1910 (Independent 1895-1910)
Seoul
Pusan
SEA OF JAPAN
Yokohama
Tokyo
Nagoya
Kobe
Osaka
Shimonoseki
Tsushima
Nagasaki
STRAIT OF TSUSHIMA
JEHOL
Peking
Tientsin
Port Arthur (Russ. 1898, Jap. 1905)
Weihaiwei (Br.)
Kiaochow 1898
SHANTUNG
CHINA
Hwang-ho
SHENSI
Yenan
Nanking
Shanghai
Hankow
Yangtse-kiang
Ryukyu Is. 1876
SZECHWAN
Chungking
HUNAN
KIANGSI
FUKIEN
FORMOSA 1895
KWEICHOW
Lhasa
Brahmaputra
BHUTAN
ASSAM
Canton
Hong Kong (Br. 1842)
Macao (Port.)
BURMA 1886
Calcutta
Mandalay
TONKIN 1884
Hanoi
HAINAN
PHILIPPINES (From Spain to the U.S.A. 1898)
Manila
AY OF BENGAL
PEGU 1852
Rangoon
FRENCH
LAOS 1893
ANNAM 1884
SIAM
Mekong
Bangkok
INDO-CHINA
CAMBODIA 1863/1907
Saigon
COCHIN-CHINA 1862/67
Andaman Is. (Br. 1858)
GULF OF SIAM
SOUTH CHINA SEA
Nicobar Is. (Danish to 1848, Br. 1869)
NORTH BORNEO 1883
FEDERATED MALAY STATES 1874/89
Malacca
Singapore 1819
SARAWAK 1888
BORNEO
CELEBES
SUMATRA
INDONESIA
Batavia
JAVA
Timor (Port.)

98. EUROPE DURING THE FIRST WORLD WAR 1914-18
Advance of the Central Powers
Limit of advance of the Central Powers
Advance of the Allies
Limit of Allied advance
0 400 800 miles
Central States
Neutral states which later joined the Central Powers. Dates of joining are shown
The Allies
Neutral states which later joined the Allies Dates of joining are shown
States neutral throughout the war
Areas open to attack by German submarines after 1917
Faeroe Is. (Danish)
Shetland Is.
Orkney Is.
Scapa Flow
Edinburgh
GREAT BRITAIN
Dublin
Manchester
London
Jutland 31 May 1916
Dogger Bank 24 Jan. 1915
NORWAY
Christiania
SWEDEN
Stockholm
SKAGERRAK
Göteborg
DENMARK
Copenhagen
Kiel
BALTIC SEA
FINLAND
Helsinki
Petrograd
Dagö
Ösel
Riga
Moscow
RUSSIA
Eastern Front, Spring 1918
Eastern Front, Oct. 1917
Danzig
1914
Tannenberg
Warsaw
Brest-Litovsk
Kiev
Kharkov
Astrakhan
ATLANTIC OCEAN
NETHER-LANDS
BELG.
Nov. 1914-Mar. 1918
GERMANY
Berlin
Cologne
Dresden
Frankfurt
Prague
GALICIA
1914-15
Paris
FRANCE
Munich
Vienna
AUSTRIA-HUNGARY
Budapest
1916
SWITZ.
TREN-TINO
Caporetto
Isonzo
1917-18
Bordeaux
Lyon
Biarritz
Toulouse
Marseille
MONACO
PORTUGAL 9 Mar. 1916
Lisbon
ANDORRA
Madrid
SPAIN
Seville
Gibraltar (Br.)
Tangier
Balearic Is.
Corsica
Sardinia
ITALY
Rome
23/5 -1915
Naples
BOSNIA
Sarajevo
1914-15
SERBIA
MONTE-NEGRO
ALBANIA
1916-18
ROMANIA 27/8 -1916
BULGARIA
Sofia
14/10-1915
Sevastopol
Salonika
GREECE 1918
Corfu
Gallipoli
1915
TURKEY
Ankara
1/11-1915
Baghdad railway
Oct. 1917
Teheran
PERSIA
MESOPOTAMIA
Baghdad
Dec. 1917
Damascus
ARABIA
Sicily
Tunis
TUNIS
MOROCCO
ALGERIA
Malta (Br.)
MEDITERRANEAN SEA
Crete (Greek)
Rhodes (Ital.)
Cyprus (Br.)
Jerusalem
Gaza
Dec. 1917
SUEZ CANAL
Suez
Cairo
Alexandria
EGYPT
Tripoli
LIBYA
23/5 -1915

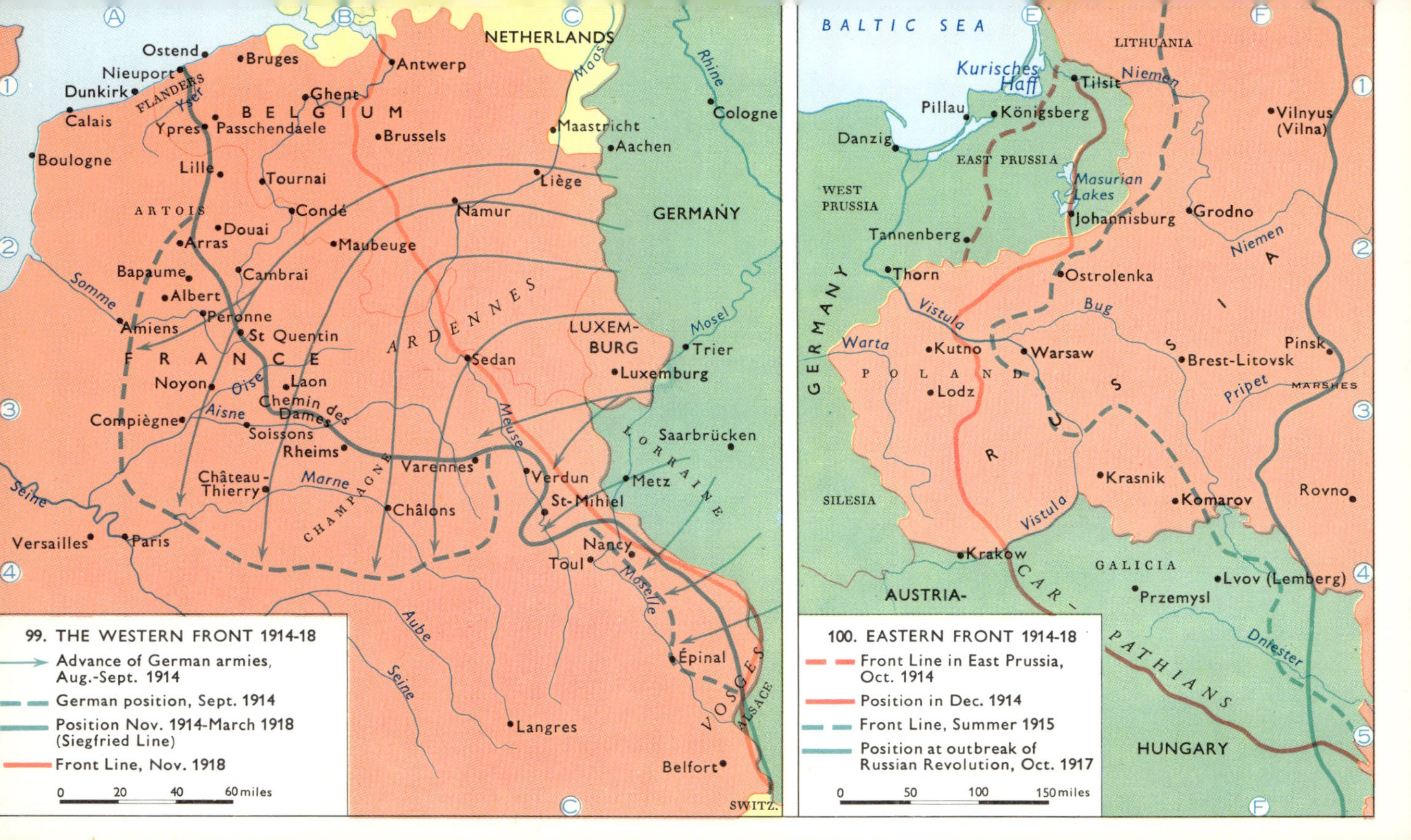
NETHERLANDS
BELGIUM
FRANCE
GERMANY
LUXEMBURG
FLANDERS
ARTOIS
ARDENNES
CHAMPAGNE
LORRAINE
VOSGES
ALSACE
SWITZ.
Ostend
Bruges
Antwerp
Nieuport
Dunkirk
Calais
Ghent
Ypres
Passchendaele
Brussels
Boulogne
Lille
Tournai
Condé
Douai
Arras
Maubeuge
Bapaume
Cambrai
Albert
Peronne
Amiens
St Quentin
Noyon
Laon
Chemin des Dames
Compiègne
Soissons
Rheims
Château-Thierry
Varennes
Châlons
Versailles
Paris
Sedan
Namur
Liège
Maastricht
Aachen
Cologne
Trier
Luxemburg
Saarbrücken
Verdun
Metz
St-Mihiel
Nancy
Toul
Épinal
Langres
Belfort
Yser
Maas
Rhine
Mosel
Meuse
Somme
Oise
Aisne
Marne
Seine
Aube
Moselle
BALTIC SEA
Kurisches Haff
LITHUANIA
EAST PRUSSIA
WEST PRUSSIA
Masurian Lakes
POLAND
RUSSIA
SILESIA
GALICIA
AUSTRIA-HUNGARY
CARPATHIANS
MARSHES
Pillau
Königsberg
Tilsit
Danzig
Tannenberg
Johannisburg
Grodno
Vilnyus (Vilna)
Thorn
Ostrolenka
Kutno
Warsaw
Lodz
Brest-Litovsk
Pinsk
Krasnik
Komarov
Rovno
Krakow
Przemysl
Lvov (Lemberg)
Niemen
Vistula
Bug
Warta
Pripet
Dniester
99. THE WESTERN FRONT 1914-18
Advance of German armies, Aug.-Sept. 1914
German position, Sept. 1914
Position Nov. 1914-March 1918 (Siegfried Line)
Front Line, Nov. 1918
0 20 40 60 miles
100. EASTERN FRONT 1914-18
Front Line in East Prussia, Oct. 1914
Position in Dec. 1914
Front Line, Summer 1915
Position at outbreak of Russian Revolution, Oct. 1917
0 50 100 150 miles

101. EUROPE 1919-35

102. CONQUESTS OF HITLER, MUSSOLINI AND FRANCO

103. EUROPE DURING THE SECOND WORLD WAR, SEPT. 1939-JUNE 1941
Western Powers at outbreak of war 3 Sept. 1939
Germany, Sept. 1939
Italy at war with Western Powers, June 1940, and Bulgaria at war with Great Britain, Mar. 1941
Soviet Union, non-agression pact with Germany from Aug. 1939-June 1941
Neutral countries, Sept. 1939
Axis advances to June 1941
Russian advances to June 1940
Russian boundary, June 1940
Occupied area of France after 26 June 1940
The light red boundaries show the political situation in Sept. 1939. Dates indicate time of German occupation
0 200 400 600 miles
ICELAND
(occupied by Britain 1940)
Faeroe Is.
Petsamo
Murmansk
Narvik
Salla
Suomussalmi
Namsos
FINLAND
Åndalsnes
Steinkjer
Trondhjem
War with Russia Nov. 1939-Mar. 1940
NORWAY 1940
Elverum
Hamar
Bergen
Stavanger
Oslo
SWEDEN
Helsinki
Viborg
Leningrad
Stockholm
Christiansand
ESTONIA
June 1940
LATVIA
June 1940
DENMARK 1940
LITHUANIA
EIRE
Dublin
GREAT BRITAIN
Liverpool
Coventry
London
NETHERLANDS
Danzig
Minsk
Berlin
Sept. 1939
Dunkirk
BELGIUM
GERMANY
Warsaw
POLAND
Rouen
LUXEMBURG
Prague
Kiev
1940
Paris
1939
Sept. 1939
FRANCE
Munich
SLOVAKIA
NORTH BUKOVINA
Vichy
Bern
Vienna
BESSARABIA
SWITZ.
HUNGARY
June 1940
Bordeaux
Toulouse
Milan
ROMANIA
PORTUGAL
Marseille
Belgrade
Bucharest
Lisbon
Madrid
YUGOSLAVIA
SOUTH DOBRUJA
SPAIN
Corsica
Rome
1941
BUL-GARIA
(Bulg. Sept. 1940)
ITALY
Sofia
Sardinia
ALBANIA (It.)
Naples
Gibraltar (Br.)
SP. MOROCCO
Tangier
TURKEY
Ankara
PERSIA
GREECE 1941
Athens
MOROCCO (Fr.)
ALGERIA (Fr.)
TUNISIA (Fr.)
Sicily
SYRIA (Fr. mandate)
IRAQ
Malta
Crete
Cyprus (Br.)
104. EUROPE DURING THE SECOND WORLD WAR, OCT. 1942-MAY 1945
0 400 800 miles
Germany and its allies 1942
Area under German and Ital. control Oct. 1942
Area under Allied control Oct. 1942
Neutral countries 1942
FINLAND armistice 4 Sept. 1944
Viborg June 1944
SWEDEN
Helsinki
Leningrad
Stockholm
GREAT BRITAIN
Edinburgh
Riga
DENMARK
EIRE
Moscow
Copenhagen
Vilnyus
Katyn
SOVIET UNION
Smolensk
Hamburg
Lübeck
Danzig
Minsk
Voronesh
NETHERLANDS
London
Bergen-Belsen
Berlin
Warsaw
Arnhem
Torgau
Brest-Litovsk
Contentin
Caen
BELGIUM
Cologne
(POLAND)
BRITTANY
Remagen
Buchenwald
Stalingrad
Falaise
Paris Aug. 1944
Schweinfurt
Prague
Auschwitz
Kiev
Kharkov
Argentan
Lvov
Pilsen
SLOVAKIA
Nuremberg
Stalino
Dachau
Munich
Vienna
Vichy
SWITZ.
Berchtesgaden
Budapest
Bordeaux
Lyon
HUNGARY
Milan
ROMANIA
Crimea
Yalta
CAUCASUS
PORTUGAL
Belgrade
YUGOSLAVIA
Madrid
SPAIN
Corsica
BULGARIA
Rome
Sofia
ITALY
ALBANIA
Istanbul
Sardinia
Sept. 1943
Naples
TURKEY
Ankara
Amer. and Brit. troops Nov. 1942
Oran
Algiers
Sicily
Tunis May 1943
July 1943
GREECE
MOROCCO
ALGERIA
British troops
Malta
British troops
Cyprus
SYRIA
Crete
IRAQ
Front lines May 1944
Front lines Dec. 1944
Allied advances
Tripoli Jan. 1943
PALESTINE
Tobruk
Benghazi Nov. 1942
JORDAN
El Alamein
Alexandria
LIBYA
EGYPT
ARABIA
Black boundaries show the political situation in September 1939

105. THE FAR EAST DEC. 1941-AUG. 1942

106. THE FAR EAST AUG. 1942-AUG. 1945

107. EUROPE TODAY

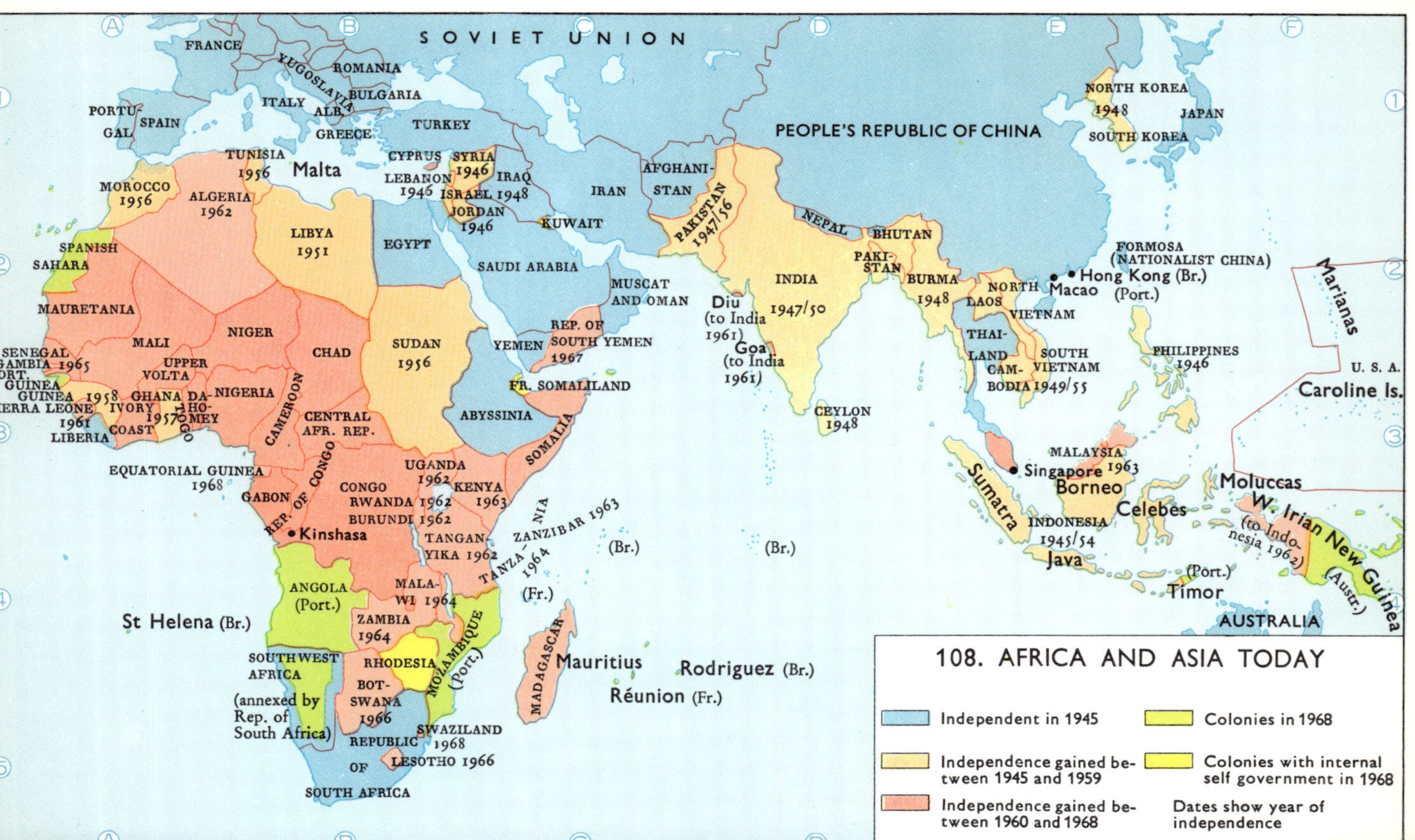
108. AFRICA AND ASIA TODAY
Independent in 1945
Independence gained between 1945 and 1959
Independence gained between 1960 and 1968
Colonies in 1968
Colonies with internal self government in 1968
Dates show year of independence
SOVIET UNION
FRANCE
ROMANIA
YUGOSLAVIA
BULGARIA
PORTUGAL
SPAIN
ITALY
ALB.
GREECE
TURKEY
PEOPLE'S REPUBLIC OF CHINA
NORTH KOREA 1948
SOUTH KOREA
JAPAN
TUNISIA 1956
Malta
CYPRUS
SYRIA 1946
LEBANON 1946
IRAQ
ISRAEL 1948
JORDAN 1946
KUWAIT
IRAN
AFGHANISTAN
PAKISTAN 1947/56
NEPAL
BHUTAN
PAKISTAN
INDIA 1947/50
BURMA 1948
MOROCCO 1956
ALGERIA 1962
LIBYA 1951
EGYPT
SAUDI ARABIA
MUSCAT AND OMAN
SPANISH SAHARA
MAURETANIA
MALI
NIGER
CHAD
SUDAN 1956
YEMEN
REP. OF SOUTH YEMEN 1967
FR. SOMALILAND
ABYSSINIA
SOMALIA
SENEGAL
GAMBIA 1965
PORT. GUINEA
GUINEA 1958
SIERRA LEONE 1961
LIBERIA
IVORY COAST
UPPER VOLTA
GHANA 1957
TOGO
DAHOMEY
NIGERIA
CAMEROON
CENTRAL AFR. REP.
EQUATORIAL GUINEA 1968
GABON
REP. OF CONGO
Kinshasa
CONGO
RWANDA 1962
BURUNDI 1962
UGANDA 1962
KENYA 1963
TANGANYIKA 1962
ZANZIBAR 1963
TANZANIA 1964
MALAWI 1964
ZAMBIA 1964
ANGOLA (Port.)
MOZAMBIQUE (Port.)
RHODESIA
BOTSWANA 1966
SOUTH WEST AFRICA (annexed by Rep. of South Africa)
REPUBLIC OF SOUTH AFRICA
SWAZILAND 1968
LESOTHO 1966
St Helena (Br.)
MADAGASCAR
Mauritius
Réunion (Fr.)
Rodriguez (Br.)
(Br.)
(Br.)
(Fr.)
Diu (to India 1961)
Goa (to India 1961)
CEYLON 1948
NORTH VIETNAM
LAOS
THAILAND
CAMBODIA
SOUTH VIETNAM 1949/55
Hong Kong (Br.)
Macao (Port.)
FORMOSA (NATIONALIST CHINA)
PHILIPPINES 1946
Marianas
U. S. A.
Caroline Is.
MALAYSIA 1963
Singapore
Borneo
Sumatra
INDONESIA 1945/54
Java
Celebes
Moluccas
W. Irian (to Indonesia 1962)
New Guinea (Austr.)
Timor (Port.)
AUSTRALIA

INDEX

The index contains all the place names on the maps, and also names of peoples (e.g. Goths), historical events (e.g. Civil War in England), military expeditions (e.g. Marlborough), voyages of discovery (e.g. Columbus), etc.

Towns and cities which appear on more than one map are generally given a reference to only one map—the one on which they are most important historically, or, for very common names, the one on which they can be most easily found, i.e. generally the map drawn to the largest scale.

More than one reference is given to places important at different times for different reasons. Poitiers, for example, has a reference to Map 33—the battle between Charles Martel and the Moslems in 732—and to Map 43, where it is shown as important in the civilization of medieval Europe.

Countries, provinces, regions, etc.—the boundaries of which may alter with time—are given several references in chronological order, so that their development may be traced. Bulgaria, for example, has sixteen references for the period 900 to 1968; and if one is interested in the political situation in Italy at the beginning of the eighteenth century there are references to two maps, showing the situation in 1701 and 1721.

For references to wide historical periods or concepts which cannot be immediately found in the index, the list of contents at the beginning of the book should be consulted.

The italic number is the number of the map; the letter and number which follow show the area on the map in which the name will be found. (It is to be supposed that each map is divided into squares by lines drawn down the page midway between the letters and across the page midway between the numbers.)

Names in parentheses are alternative names or spellings; those preceded by *mod.* are the modern or present-day names of the localities. Classical names of towns and cities are given in their Latin form.

Aachen (Aix-la-Chapelle)
*36*C4, *43*C2, *61*D4, *67*B3
Aalborg *44*C2, *70*A4
Aargau *48*C5
Aarhus *70*A4
Abadan *107*F5
Abdera (*mod.* Adra), Spain *11*A3
Abdera, Thrace *14*D1
Aberdeen *65*D2
Åbo *72*A3
Aboukir *86*F6
Abruzzi *45*E4
Abu Simbel *2*A4
Abusir *2*A1
Abydos, Egypt *1*B3, *2*A3
Abydus, on the Hellespont *14*E1
Abyla *11*A3
Abyssinia (Ethiopia)
1914 *96*E4, 1968 *108*C3
Acadia *77*A1
Acarnania *14*A2
Acco (Acre) *41*B5
Achaea, ancient *14*B3
during Persian Wars *20*B3
Roman province *28*D4, *29*C4
1230 *40*D4 1265 *52*A2
1355 *53*A5
Achaeans *12*
Achelous (river) *14*B2
Acqui *49*D5
Acrae *16*C3
Acragas (Agrigentum, *mod.* Agrigento) *16*B3
Acre *40*F5, *41*B5, *86*F6
Acropolis, Athens *13*, *17*
Actium *14*A2, *28*D3
Adab *8*C4
Adalia *60*C4
Adana *41*B1
Adda (river) *89*B1
Addis Ababa *96*E4
Aden, 1914 *97*A4
Adige (river) *89*C1–2
Adria *89*D2
Adrianople (*mod.* Edirne)
*32*E4, *40*E3, *52*B1
Aduatuca *27*F1
Aduwa *96*E4
Aegates Is. *23*C3
Aegean Sea *20*C–D1–5
Aegina (island, *mod.* Aigina) *15*C6
Aegina (town, *mod.* Aigina) *15*C6
Aegira *15*A6
Aegitium *15*A5
Aegium *15*A5
Aegospotami *21*F2
Aegyptus
44 B.C. *28*E5 A.D. 117 *29*D5
See also Egypt
Aemilius Paulus, trophy of, Delphi *19*C4
Aenus (*mod.* Enez) *11*E2
Aeolians *14*
Aequi *23*C2
Aetolia *14*B2

Afghanistan, 814 *33*F2
1914 *97*B–C3 1968 *108*C2
Africa (Roman province)
146 B.C. *25*E5 44 B.C. *28*C4
A.D. 117 *29*B4
Africa (continent)
c. 1600 *58*C–D3–5
1750 *75*C–D3–4
1914 *96* 1968 *108*
Agadir *96*A3
Agedincum (*mod.* Sens) *27*E2
Agen *49*B5
Agincourt *51*C3
Agra *80*E2
Agram *86*D4
Agrigentum
(Acragas, *mod.* Agrigento) *16*B3
Ahmedabad *80*D3
Ahmednagar *79*A2
Aigues-Mortes *40*A2
Aire *49*B5
Aisne (river) *99*B3
Aix(-en-Provence) *43*C4, *49*C5
Aix-la-Chapelle (Aachen) *86*C3
See also Aachen
Ajaccio *85*A3
Akbar *see* Mogul Empire
Akershus (county), 1660 *70*A–B3
Akershus *70*B3
Akhetaton
(*mod.* Tell-el-Amarna) *2*A2
Akkad *8*B–C4
Alabama (river) *78*D4
Alabama (state), 1861–65 *92*D4
Alaça Hüyük *6*B1
Alais *49*C5
Alalakh (*mod.* Tell Atchana) *6*C2
Alamannia *36*C5
Alamans, 526 *32*C3
Åland Is.
1370 *44*D1 1660 *70*C3
1812 *86*D1 1825 *72*A3
Alaric, route of *32*E4
Alba, central Italy *21*A1
Alba, north Italy *49*C5
Albania
1265 *52*A2 1556 *57*D4
1701 *71*E4–5 1721 *76*E5
1812 *86*D4–5 1878 *93*B2
1912–13 *94*B5–6
1914–18 *98*D4 1919–35 *101*C2
1939 *102*E5 1939–41 *103*C3
1945 *104*C5–6 1968 *107*C4–5
Albano *39*D5
Albany *78*E2
Albenga *49*D5
Albert *99*A2
Albi *43*B4, *51*C6
Albret *50*A6
Alcibiades' journey to Sicily, 415 B.C. *21*
Alençon *61*C3
Aleppo *41*D2
Aleria *25*E2
Alesia *27*E2

Alessandria *89*A2
Alet *49*B5
Alexander the Great
Empire of *22*
route of, 334–323 B.C. *22*
Alexandria (*mod.* Iskenderun)
Asia Minor *22*B2
Alexandria, Babylonia *22*D4
Alexandria, Bactria *22*F2
Alexandria, Carmania *22*E4
Alexandria, Egypt *22*B3
Alexandria, Gedrosia *22*F4
Alexandria (*mod.* Ghazni) *22*F3
Alexandria (*mod.* Herat) *22*E3
Alexandria, India Inferior *22*F4
Alexandria (*mod.* Kandahar) *22*F3
Alexandria Eschata *22*F1
Alexandria Margiane (*mod.* Merv) *22*E2
Alexandria Sogdiana *22*F3
Alexandropolis *22*E2
Algarve *55*A6
Algeciras *96*B3
Algeria, 1812 *86*B5
1914 *96*B3
1914–18 *98*B5
1919–35 *101*A2
1939–41 *103*A3
1942–45 *104*A-B6
1968 *107*B5, *108*A1–2
Algiers, 1556 *57*B6
Algiers (town) *107*B5
Algonkin *59*D3
Alicante *39*B6
Alkmaar *61*C2
Allegheny Mts. *78*E3
Allen, route of, 1885 *59*B1
Allier (river) *69*E3–4
Allies, during First World War *98*
Alma *93*E1
Almaden *46*A6
Almagro *see* Pizarro
Almanza *76*B6
Almendralejo *32*A4
Almeria *55*C6
Al Mina (Posidium) *11*F3
Almissa *49*E5
Almoravides, Dominions of the 1100 *39*B6
Alpes Montes (the Alps) *27*F3–4
Alpheus (river) *14*B3
Alsace
936 *38*B2–3
c. 1630 *64*B6
1914–18 *99*D5
1919–35 *101*B2
Alsace-Lorraine, 1871 *91*B4–5
Alstahaug *70*B1
Altamaha (river) *78*D-E4
Altamira *1*A2
Altdorf *48*C5
Althing *37*A1
Altmark (town) *70*C5
Altmark, Brandenburg, 1415 *81*C3
Altranstadt *73*B2
Amalfi *39*D5
Amanus, Mt. *6*C2
Amasia *26*C1

Amazon (river) *88*E-F2
Ambarri *27*F3
Amboise *62*C3
Ambracia *20*B2
Ameland *61*D1
Amenophis II
Mortuary temple of *5*
Amenophis II
Temple of *4*
Amenophis III
Mortuary temple of *5*
American Indians *59*
Amiens *43*C2, *51*C3
Amisus (*mod.* Samsun) *26*C1
Amiternum
(*mod.* San Vittorino) *25*E2
Amman *41*C6
Ammon, 800 B.C. *9*F4
Amon, Oracle of *10*A4
Amon, Temple of, Karnak *4*
Amorgos *14*E3
Amphipolis *14*C1
Amq *6*C2
Amritsar *97*C3
Amsterdam *61*D2
Amur (river) *42*E1
Amur Province, 1914 *97*E-F1
Anapus (river) *16*C3
Anas (*mod.* Guadiana, river) *25*A3–4
Anatolia *53*D5
Ancona *35*E2, *45*E3
Ancyra (*mod.* Ankara) *22*B2, *26*C2
Åndalsnes *103*B1
Andalusia *55*B6
Andaman Is.
1858 *80*F4
1914 *97*D5
Andorra
1812 *86*B4
1815 *87*B4
1914–18 *98*B3
1968 *107*B4
Andros *14*D3, *15*E6
Andrussov *72*B4
Ångermanland *70*C2
Angers *43*B3
Anghiari *45*D3
Angles *32*C1
Anglicans in Europe, 1560 *63*
Anglo-Egyptian Sudan, 1914 *96*D4
Anglo-Saxon kingdoms *32*B1–2
Angola
1750 *75*D4
1914 *96*C5
1968 *108*B4
Angora (*mod.* Ankara) *42*A2, *52*D2
Angoulême (province) *50*B6
Angoulême (town) *36*B5, *43*B3
Angoumois *69*D4
Angus *65*D2
Anhalt
1648 *67*C3
1871 *91*C3
Anibe *2*A4
Anjou
1100 *39*B3
1180–1453 *50*
1429 *51*B4
1562–92 *62*B3
Ankara *93*E2
Anna, Empress of Russia
expansion under, 1730–40 *72*
Annam, 1914 *97*E4

Ansbach
1415–40, 1470–86, 1791 *81*C5
1648 *67*C4
Antietam *92*F4
Anti-Lebanon *9*F1
Antilles, Greater *56*C-E1
Antioch, Syria *see* Antiochia
Antioch, Principality of
1140 *41*C2–3 1265 *52*E2
Antiochia, Persia *20*F3
Antiochia (Antioch, *mod.* Antakya) Syria *29*D4, *41*C2
Antoninus and Faustina, Temple of Rome *31*C6(5)
Antwerp *43*C2, *44*A5, *61*C3
Anyang *1*E2
Aosta *49*C4
Apaches *59*B3
Apamea *26*B3
Apennines *25*E2
Aphroditopolis *2*A2
Apollo, Sanctuary of, Delphi *19*
Apollo Sitalkas, Delphi *19*B4
Apollonia *11*E2
Appenzell *48*D5
Appomattox *92*E5
Aptara *12*B
Apulia, 264 B.C. *23*D2
10th century *38*D5
1100 *39*D5
Aqua Appia, Rome *30*D-E3
Aquae Sextiae
(*mod.* Aix-en-Provence) *27*F4
Aquileia (*mod.* Aglar) *32*C3
Aquincum (*mod.* Budapest) *29*C2
Aquino *45*E4
Aquitaine, 1100 *39*B-C4
1180–1453 *50* 1429 *51*B5
Aquitania, *c.* 50 B.C. *27*D-E4
A.D. 117 *29*A-B2
843 *36*B5
See also Aquitaine
Arabia (Roman province) *29*D5
Arabia
632–814 *33* 1914 *97*A2–4
1914–18 *98*E-F5
Arabian Sea *97*B4
Arachosia *7*E6
Aragon, 1037 *54*E1
c. 1100 *54*B2, *39*B5
1180 *54*E2 1230 *40*A3
1476 *55*D-E4–5
Aral Sea *10*E1
Aranjuez *55*C5
Ararat, Mt. *6*D1
Aras (river) *72*D-E6
Arausio (*mod.* Orange) *27*F4
Araxes (river) *10*C2
Arbe *49*E5
Arbela (*mod.* Erbil) *22*C3
Arcadia *14*B3, *15*A6
Arcadians *14*
Archangel *72*C2
Arcole *85*B1
Arcot *79*A5, *80*E4
Arctic Ocean *58*F1

Ardakhan *72*D6
Ardennes *99*B-C2
Arelate (*mod.* Arles) *27*F4
Arendal *70*A3
Arezzo *45*D3
Argentan *104*B5
Argentina, 1914 *88*E3–5
Argentoratum
(*mod.* Strasbourg) *29*B2
Argolis *14*C3, *15*B6
Argos (state) *20*B4
Argos (town) *21*D3
Aria *22*E3
Ariminum (*mod.* Rimini) *23*C1
Arizona, 1912 *92*A-B4
Arkansas (river) *59*B3-C4, *92*C4
Arkansas (state), 1861–65 *92*C-D4
Arles *39*C4
Armagh *43*A1
Armagnac, 1429 *51*B-C6
Armenia, 600 B.C. *7*B-C5
44 B.C. *28*F2–3
A.D. 117 *29*E3
814 *33*D2 1230 *40*F4
1520–1680 *60*E3
Arnhem *44*B4, *61*D3, *104*B4
Arno (river) *45*C-D3
Arques *62*C2
Arras *49*B2, *51*D3, *99*A2
Arretium (*mod.* Arezzo) *23*B1
Artaxata *29*E3
Artemis of Brauron, Temple of
Acropolis, Athens *17*B4
Artemisium, Greece *20*C3
Artemisium, Spain *11*B3
Artois, 1429 *51*D3
1579 *61*A4 1914–18 *99*A2
Arx, Rome *31*A5
Ascalon
1400 B.C. *6*B3 860 B.C. *9*D4
A.D. 1140 *41*A6
Asclepius, Temple of
Acropolis, Athens *17*C-D5
Ascoli *45*E3
Asculum *23*C2
Ashur *8*B2
Asia (Roman province) *28*E3, *29*D3
Asia (continent)
c. 1300 *42*, 1914 *97*, 1968 *108*
Asia Minor, 189 B.C. *26*
Asine *15*B6
Asisium (*mod.* Assisi) *29*B3
Asklepios (Asclepius), Temple of
Acropolis, Athens *17*C-D5
Askra *15*B5
Aspern *86*D3
Assam, 1914 *97*D4
Assassins *41*C3
Assen *61*E1
Assiniboine (river) *59*C3
Assisi *43*D4, *45*D3
Assiut *2*A2
Assyria
1400 B.C. *6*D2
greatest expansion of Empire
c. 700 B.C. *7*A-C5–6

500 B.C. *10*C3 400 B.C. *24*D5
under Alexander the Great *22*C3
Roman province *29*E3
Asti *45*A2
Astrakhan *42*B2, *72*E5
Astrakhan, Khanate of *72*D5
Asturias, 814 *33*A3
c. 900 *37*A4, *54*A1
Aswan 2B3, *96*D3
Atacama *56*D3
Atchana, Tell *6*C2
Athabasca (river) *59*B2
Athabasca, Lake *59*B-C2
Athena, Altar of
Acropolis, Athens *17*D4
Athena, Statue of
Acropolis, Athens *17*B4
Athena, Temple of
Acropolis, Athens *17*C4
Athenopolis *11*C2
Athens *14*C3, *28*D3, *43*E5
Athens, Acropolis of, from
Mycenaean times to 470 B.C. *13*
in classical times *17*
Athens, Duchy of
1265 *52*A-B2
1355 *53*A-B5
Athos, Mt. *20*C2
Athos (monastery) *43*E4
Atlanta *92*D4
Atlantic Ocean *58*B-C2–4
Atlas Mons (Atlas Mts.) *29*A3–4
Atri *45*E3
Attalia *26*B3, *40*F4
Attica *14*C3, *15*D6
Attila, kingdom of, *c.* A.D. 450 *32*
residence of, 434–53 *32*D3
Aube (river) *99*B-C4–5
Auch *49*B5
Auerstädt *86*C3
Augsburg *38*C3, *46*C5, *64*D6, *67*C5
Augsburg, Bishopric of
1648 *67*C5
Augusta Emerita
(*mod.* Merida) *29*A3
Augusta Taurinorum
(*mod.* Turin) *23*A1
Augusta Treverorum
(*mod.* Trier) *29*B2
Augustus, Triumphal arch of
Rome *31*C6(10)
Aulis *15*C5
Aurangzeb *see* Mogul Empire
Aurignac *1*A2
Auschwitz *91*E4, *104*C5

Austbygda *58*C2
Austerlitz *86*D3
Australia *58*F5
Austrasia, 814 *33*B2
843 *36*C4
Austria
1556 *57*D3 1648 *67*D-E5
1701 *71*D-E3 1721 *76*D-E3-4
during Seven Years' War, 1756–63
*82*D-E5
c. 1800 (southwestern area)
*85*B-E1
1812 *86*D-E3-4 1815 *87*C3
1859-66 *89*, *90*B-E3
1919–35 *101*B-C2
1938 *102*D4
1968 *107*B-C4
See also Austria-Hungary
Austria-Hungary, 1878 *93*A-C1–2
1912–13 *94*A-B4–5
1914–18 *98*C-D3
Austrian territories, 1721 *76*
Autun *49*C4
Auvergne
1180–1453 *50* 1429 *51*C5
1562–92 *62*C-D4
Auxerre *51*D4
Ava *42*D4
Avallon *57*B3
Avaricum (*mod.* Bourges) *27*E3
Avars *33*C3
Avars, Kingdom of the, 843 *36*E5
Aventine, Rome *30*C3
Avezzo *35*E3
Avignon *39*C4, *43*C4, *51*D6, *57*C3
Avignon, adherents of the Popes at
during the Great Schism
1378–1417 *47*
Avila *43*A4, *55*B5
Avranches *49*B3
Axis Powers
during Second World War *103*
Axius (river) *14*B1
Ay, tomb of *5*
Ayacucho *88*E2
Ayr *65*C2
Azerbaijan *60*E3
Azores
c. 1600 *58*C3
1914 *96*A3
Azov *60*D1, *72*C5
Azov, Sea of *72*C5
Aztec civilization *56*A1
Aztec Kingdom
1486 *56* 1519 *56*

B

Baalbek *41*C4
Babylon *8*C4
Babylonia, 1400 B.C. *6*E3
600 B.C. 7C6 500 B.C. *10*C4

under Alexander the Great *22*C3
Back, route of, 1833 *59*C2
Back (river) *59*C2
Bactra (*mod.* Balkh) *22*F2

Bactria *22*F2
Baden, *c.* 1630 *64*C6
1648 *67*B4–5 1812 *86*C3
1815 *87*B3 1871 *91*B4–5
Baden, Switzerland *48*C5
Baecula *25*B4
Baetis (*mod.* Guadalquivir, river) *25*A4
Baghdad *8*C3, *42*A3, *98*F5
Baghdad Railway *98*D-F4
Bahamas, *c.* 1600 *58*B3
1750 *75*B3 1650–1763 *77*
Bahia *58*B4, *88*F2
Baiae *29*C3
Baikal, Lake *97*D1
Bailen *86*A5
Baku *72*E6
Balaklava *93*E1
Baleares (Balearic Is.) *28*B3
Balearic Is., 264 B.C. *25*C3
526 *32*B4 814 *33*A-B4
c. 900 *37*B5 1100 *39*B5
1230 *40*A3 1476 *55*E5
1556 *57*B4 1701 *71*C5
1721 *76*C5–6 1812 *86*B5
1815 *87*B4 1914–18 *98*B4
Balkans, 1878
(after Congress of Berlin) *93*
1912–13 (after Balkan Wars) *94*
Balkh *42*C3
Balkhash, Lake *97*C2
Balmoral *65*C2
Baltic Sea *44*D-E1–3, *70*B-D2–4
Baltimore *78*E3, *92*F4
Balts *32*D1
Baluchistan *22*E4, *97*B3
Bamberg *39*D3, *43*D2
Bamberg, Bishopric of, 1648 *67*C4
Banat, 1721 *76*E4
1812 *86*D4 1912–13 *94*B4
Bangalore *97*C5
Bangkok *105*A2
Bangor *49*A1
Bapaume *99*A2
Bar *69*E2
Barbarian invasions *32*
Barbarian migrations, 526 *32*
Barbary states *76*C6
Barcelona (county), 1037 *54*E1
c. 1100 *39*B5, *54*B2
Barcelona (town) *39*B5, *43*B4
Barents, William
route of, 1596 *58*C2
Barents Sea *58*D1
Bari *85*E3
Barmen *91*B3
Baroda *80*D3
Bärwalde *64*E4
Basel *43*C3, *48*B5
Basilica Aemilia
Rome *31*C6
Basilica Julia
Rome *31*B6
Basilica of Constantine
Rome *31*D6
Basilica Ulpia
Rome *31*B4

Basques *32*A3
Basra *60*F5
Bastille, Paris *83*C3
Basutoland, 1868–1910 *95*C1–2
1968 (Lesotho) *108*B5
Batavia (*mod.* Jakarta) *97*E6
Bath *51*B2
Batum *72*D6
Bautzen *86*D3
Bavaria
936 *38*C-D3 *c.* 1630 *64*D6
1648 *67*C-D4–5
1721 *76*D3–4
1756–63 *82*C-D4–5
1812 *86*C3 1815 *87*C3
1871 *91*C4–5
Bavarian Palatinate *87*B3
Bayeux *39*B3
Bayonne *76*B5
Bayreuth
1420–40, 1470–86, 1791 *81*C4
1648 *67*C4
Bazas *49*B5
Beachy Head *65*E5
Béarn
1429 *51*B6 1562–92 *62*B5
Bear Pass *59*B3
Beaulieu *62*C4
Beauvais *43*B2, *69*E1
Bec *43*B2
Bechuanaland, 1885–1910 *95*B1
1914 *96*D6
1968 (Botswana) *108*B5
Bedford (county) *51*C2
Bedford (town) *65*E4
Behistun *10*D3
Beira *96*D6
Beirut *41*B4
Belfast *65*C3
Belfort *57*C3, *99*D5
Belgae *27*D-E1
Belgian Congo, 1914 *96*C-D4–5
Belgica (Roman province) *28*B1
Belgium, 1871 *91*A3–4
1914–18 *98*C2, *99*A-C1–3
1919–35 *101*B1
1939–41 *103*B2
1968 *107*B3
See also Netherlands, Spanish
Netherlands, Austrian
Belgrade *39*E4, *93*B2
Belle I., Strait of *59*E3
Belluno *49*D4
Benares *80*E2
Bender *73*D3
Benevento *85*D3
Benevento, Duchy of
c. 1000–1150 *38*D5
1812 *86*D5 1860 *90*D4
Bengal, 1780 *79*A4
1858 *80*F2 1914 *97*C-D4
Bengal, Bay of *97*C-D4
Benghazi *60*B5, *104*C5
Berber *96*D4
Berbers *33*B5
Berceto *45*B2

Berchtesgaden *104*C5
Berezina (river) *86*E2
Berg, Duchy of, 1648 *67*B3
Bergamo *45*B1
Bergen (Mons)
Spanish Netherlands *61*C4
Bergen, Hesse *82*B4
Bergen, Norway *44*B1, *70*A3, *103*B1
Bergen-Belsen *104*C4
Bergenhus (county), 1660 *70*A3
Bergerac *62*C4
Bergslagen *70*B3
Berkeley *51*B2
Berkeley Castle *65*D4
Berlin *44*C4, *82*D2, *107*C3
Bermuda, 1750 *75*B3
Bern (canton) *48*B5
Bern (town) *48*B5
Berry *51*C4
Berwick *76*B2
Besançon *49*C4, *51*E4, *67*B5
Bessarabia
1721 *76*F4
1812 *86*E3
1878 *93*C-D1
1919–35 *101*C2
Bethel *9*E4
Bethlehem *9*E4, *41*B6
Bethnal Green, London *66*D5
Béziers *49*B5
Bhutan, 1914 *97*D3–4
1968 *108*D2
Biarritz *98*B3
Biberach *67*C5
Bibliothèque Nationale, Paris *83*B1
Bibracte (*mod.* Mont Beuvray) *27*E3
Bicocca *45*B1
Bidassoa (river) *55*C4
Bihar *80*F2
Bijapur *79*A2
Bilbao *102*B5
Billungs, March of the *38*C1
Bindar *79*A2
Bingen *38*B2
Birka *37*C1
Birmingham, England *86*B2
Birmingham, U.S.A. *59*C4
Biscay, Bay of *51*A5
Bismarck Archipelago
1941–42 *105*C3
1942–45 *106*C6
Bithynia
under Alexander the Great *22*B2
189 B.C. *26*B1
Roman province *28*E3, *29*D3
Bizerta *85*B5
Björneborg *70*C3
Blackfoot Indians *59*B2
Black Russia, 1793–95 *84*E-F2–3
Black Sea *11*E-F1–2
Blankenberghe *51*D3
Blaye *51*D3
Blekinge, 1660 *70*B4
Blenheim *71*D2
Bloemfontein *95*C1
Blois *51*C4, *62*C3
Bobbio *49*D5

Bocchus, Kingdom of *25*
Bodensee *48*D5
Boeotia *14*C2, *15*B-C5
Boer Republics *95*C-D1
Boer War *95*
Bogaz-Köy *6*C1
Bogota *88*E1
Bohemia, 814 *33*B2
c. 900 *37*C3
1556 *57*D2
c. 1630 *64*E5
1648 *67*D4
1721 *76*D3
1756–63 *82*D4
1871 *91*C-D4
1939 *102*D4
Bohemond of Taranto *40*D3
Bohus (county)
1370 *44*C2
1660 *70*B3
Bohus (town) *70*B3
Bokhara (state), 1914 *97*C2
Bokhara (town) *33*E1, *42*B3, *97*B2
Bolivia, 1914 *88*E2–3
Bologna *35*D1, *43*C4, *45*C2
Bolsena *35*D2
Bombay *79*A2, C2, A4, *80*D3
Bône (*mod.* Annaba) *85*A5
Bonin Is. *106*C5
Bonn *43*C2, *91*B3
Bononia (*mod.* Bologna) *23*B1
Bordeaux *36*A5, *43*B3
Borg *37*A1
Borgundarholm (Bornholm) *37*C2
Borneo
c. 1600 *58*F4
1750 *75*E3
1914 *97*E-F5–6
1941–42 *105*A-B3
1942–45 *106*A-B6
1968 *108*E3
Bornholm
526 *32*C1
c. 900 *37*C2
1100 *39*D2
1370 *44*D3
1660 *70*B4
1700 *73*B1
Borodino *86*E1
Borough, Steven
route of, 1556 *58*D1
Borysthenes
(*mod.* Dnieper, river) *28*E1
Bosnia
1556 *57*D4
1701 *71*E4
1721 *76*E4
c. 1800 *85*E2
1812 *86*D4
1878 *93*A2
1912–13 *94*A5
1914–18 *98*C3
Bosporus *39*F5
Boston, England *44*A4
Boston, Massachusetts *78*F2
Bosworth *51*C2
Bothnia, Gulf of *70*C2
Bothwell *65*E1
Botswana
(formerly Bechuanaland) *108*B5
Bouillon *61*D5
Boulogne *62*C2
Bourbon
1429 *51*D5
1562–92 *62*D3
Bourbonnais *69*E3
Bourges *36*B5, *43*B3
Bouvines *39*C3
Boyne (river) *65*B3

Brabant
1429 *51*E3
1579 *61*C-D3–4
Bradford *65*D3
Braga *55*A5
Brahestad *70*D2
Brạhmaputra (river) *80*F2
Brandenburg (town) *44*C4
Brandenburg-Prussia
1415–1797 *81* c. 1630 *64*D4
1648 *67*C-D2 1700 *73*B2
1701 *71*D1–2 1721 *76*D3
Bratislava (Pressburg) *71*E3
Brazil
c. 1600 *58*B4 1750 *75*B-C4
1815–1914 *88*E-F1–4
Breda *61*C3
Breida Fjord *37*A1
Breisach *69*F2
Breisgau, 1648 *67*B5
Breitenfeld *64*D5
Bremen *38*B1, *43*C1, *44*B4, *67*C2
Bremen, Archbishopric of
c. 1630 *64*C4
1648 *67*C2
Brenner Pass *38*C3
Brescia *45*C1
Breslau *44*D5, *82*E3
Brest-Litovsk *100*F3
Brétigny *51*C4
Bretland (Wales) *37*B2
Briel *61*C3
Brienne *86*C3
Brihuega *102*B5
Brindisi *38*E5
Bristol *65*D4
Britannia *28*B1
Britannia Inferior, A.D. 117 *29*B1
Britannia Minor (Brittany) *32*B2
Britannia Superior, A.D. 117 *29*A1
British colonies, 1750 *75*
British East Africa, 1914 *96*E4–5
British Guiana (*mod.* Guyana)
1914 *88*E1
British India, 1914 *97*B-D3–5
See also India
British (Celtic) kingdoms
526 *32*A-B1–2
British Somaliland
1914 *96*E4, *97*A4
Brittany (Britannia Minor) *32*B2
814 *33*A3 843 *36*A4
c. 900 *37*B3 1100 *39*B3
1180–1453 *50* 1429 *51*A4
Brixen *49*D4
Brixen, Bishopric of, 1648 *67*C6
Brno (Brünn) *86*D3
Bromley, London *66*E6
Brompton, London *66*A6
Brömsebro *70*B4
Bruges *44*A5, *61*B3
Brule, route of *59*C3
Brundisium (*mod.* Brindisi) *23*E2
Brunete *102*A5
Brünn (Brno) *86*D3
Brunswick *44*C4
Brunswick, Duchy of, 1871 *91*C3
Brussa *60*C3
Brussels *43*C2, *61*C4
Bruttium *23*D3
Bucephala *22*F3
Bucharest *60*C2, *76*F4, *93*C1
Buchenwald *104*C5
Buckingham *65*D4
Buckingham Palace, London *66*B6
Buda *39*E4, *43*D3, *60*B1
Budapest *98*C4, *104*C5, *107*C4
Buenaventura *56*D2
Buenos Aires (province) *88*E4
Buenos Aires (town) *88*E4
Bug (river running into Black Sea)
*74*C-D6
Bug (tributary of the Vistula)
*74*B5
Bulawayo *96*D6
Bulgar *42*B1
Bulgaria, *c.* 900 *37*D4
1230 *40*D-E2–3
1265 *52*B1 1355 *53*B4
1453 *60*C2 1556 *57*E3
1701 *71*F4 1721 *76*F4
1812 *86*E4 1878 *93*B-C2
1912–13 *94*C5 1914–18 *98*D4
1919–35 *101*C2
1939–41 *103*C3
1942–45 *104*D5
1968 *107*D4
Bulgars
526 *32*D-E4 814 *33*C3
Bull Run *92*F4
Bunzelwitz *82*E3
Burdigala (*mod.* Bordeaux) *27*D4
Burgos *39*B4, *43*B4, *49*A5
Burgundian kingdom, 526 *32*B3
Burgundian migrations *32*
Burgundy, Domains of, 1429 *51*
Burgundy, Duchy of, 1100 *39*C3–4
1180–1453 *50* 1429 *51*D5
16th century *62*D3
Burgundy, Kingdom of, 1100 *39*C4
Burgundy, Lower, *c.* 900 *37*B4
Burgundy, Upper, *c.* 900 *37*C4
Burkersdorf *82*E3
Burma
1914 *97*D4
1941–42 *105*A2
1942–45 *106*A5
1968 *108*D-E2
Burma Road *106*A5
Burundi *108*B4
Bury St Edmunds *43*B1
Byblos
1400 B.C. *6*C2 860 B.C. *9*E1
Byzantine Empire
526 *32*D-F4–5 814 *33*B-D3–4
c. 900 *37*C-E5 1100 *39*E-F5–6
1256 *52* 1355 *53*
Byzantine territories, 1100 *40*
Byzantium (*mod.* Istanbul)
*21*F1, *28*E3

Cabinda *96*C5
Cabot, John, route of, 1497 *58*B2
Cabot, John and Sebastian, route of 1498 *58*B3
Cabral, Pedro, route of 1500 *58*C5 and D-E4
Cadiz *55*B6
Caelius, Rome *30*D3
Caen *43*B2, *51*B3
Caere *23*C2
Caesarea (Mazaca, *mod.* Kayseri) Cappadocia *26*C2
Caesarea (*mod.* Cherchel) North Africa *25*C5
Caesarea (*mod.* Kaisariyeh) Palestine *29*D4, *41*B5
Cagliari *40*B4, *85*A4
Cahors *43*B3, *51*C5
Cairo *33*D4, *60*C5, *86*F6
Cajamarca *56*D3
Calabria *23*E3
Calais, 1180–1453 *50*
1429 *51*D3
Calauria *14*C3
Calcutta *79*C2, B4, *80*F3
Calicut (*mod.* Kozhikode) *58*E4, *79*A2, C2, A5, *80*D5
California
1750 *75*A3
1861–65 *92*A2–4
California Trail *59*A-C3
Caliphate of Cordoba (dominions of the Almoravides)
1100 *39*B6, *54*A-B3
1180 *54*D-E3
Calvinists in Europe, 1560 *63*
Camarina *16*C3
Cambodia
1914 *97*E5
1968 *108*E3
Cambrai *61*B5, *69*E1
Cambridge *43*B2, *51*C2
Camerinum (*mod.* Camerino) *23*C2
Cameroon (Kamerun)
1914 *96*C4
1968 *108*B3
Campania *23*C3
Campo Formio *85*C1
Campus Martius (Field of Mars) *30*B-C1–2
Canaan *9*E3
Canada, 1750 *75*B2, 1783 *78*E1
Canal du Midi *69*D-E5
Canary Is. *58*C3, *75*C3, *96*A3
Candia (Iraklion) *40*E5
Cannae *25*F3
Cannanore *79*A2, C2
Cannes *86*C4
Canossa *38*C4
Cantabria *29*A2
Canterbury *43*B2, *51*C3
Canton *42*E4, *97*E4
Canute, Kingdom of *39*
Cap de la Hogue *76*B-C3
Cape Bojador *58*C3

Cape Breton I. *75*B2
Cape Chelyuskin *75*E1
Cape Colony, *c.* 1900 *95*A-C2
1914 *96*C-D6
Cape Comorin *80*E5
Cape Finisterre *86*A4
Cape Hatteras *92*E4
Cape Horn *75*B5
Cape of Good Hope *75*D4
Cape Province, 1750 *75*D4
Cape St Vincent *55*A6
Cape Sunium (*mod.* Sounion) *14*C3, *15*D6
Cape Town *95*A2
Cape Trafalgar *86*A5
Cape Verde *58*C3
Cape Verde Is. *58*C3, *75*C3
Capitol, Rome *30*C2, *31*A6
Caporetto *98*C3
Cappadocia, 500 B.C. *10*B-C2
under Alexander the Great *22*B2
189 B.C. *26*C2–3
44 B.C. *28*E-F3 A.D. 117 *29*D3
Caprera *90*B4
Caprese *45*D3
Capua *38*D5
Capua, Duchy of *38*D5
Capuchin monastery, Paris *83*A-B1
Caracas *88*E1
Carales (*mod.* Cagliari) *23*A3
Carberry Hill *65*E1
Carcassonne *39*B5
Carchemish *6*C2
Cardiff *39*B2
Cardigan *65*C4
Careggi *57*C3
Caria, 189 B.C. *26*A3
Caribbean Sea *56*D1
Carinthia
936 *38*D3 1648 *67*D6
1701 *71*D3 *c.* 1800 *85*C1
Carlat *62*C4
Carlisle *51*B1
Carmania *22*E4
Carnatic *79*A5, *80*E4–5
Carniola
1556 *57*D3 1648 *67*D6
1701 *71*D3 *c.* 1800 *85*D1
Carolina, 1700 *77*B2
See also North Carolina and South Carolina
Caroline Is.
c. 1600 *58*F4 1968 *108*F3
Carpathian Mts. *100*E-F4–5
Carpi (Carpathian Mts.) *29*C2
Carrhae *28*F3
Carrion *55*B4
Cartagena *32*B5
Carthage *25*E4, *28*C4, *29*B3
Carthago Nova (*mod.* Cartagena) *25*B4
Carthusian Monastery, Paris *83*B4
Cartier, Jacques, route of
1534 *58*B-C3 1536 *59*D-E3
Carystus *14*D3, *15*E6

Casale *45*A2
Cashel *49*A1
Caspian Sea *10*D1–2
Cassano *85*B1
Cassotis, well of, Delphi *19*A4
Castanea *20*B2
Castel del Monte *38*E5
Castelfranco *45*D1
Castellon *1*A2
Castile, 1037 *54*D1
c. 1100 *39*A-B4–5, *54*A-B2
1180 *54*D2
1476 *55*A-C4–6
1701 *71*A-B4
Castor and Pollux, Temple of
Rome *31*B6(11)
Castres *51*C6
Catalaunian Plain *32*B2
Catalonia
526 *32*B4
1100 *39*B5
1562–92 *62*C5
1701 *71*B-C4
Catana (*mod.* Catania)
*16*C3, *23*D4
Catania *43*D5, *85*D5
Cataract, First *2*A4
Cataract, Second *2*A4
Cataract, Third *2*A5
Cataract, Fourth *2*B5
Cataract, Fifth *2*B5
Cateau-Cambrésis *61*B5
Catherine the Great
conquests of, 1762–96 *72*
Catholic Union of Arras, 1579 *61*
Caucasus Mts. *22*C2
Caulonia *16*E2
Cauvery (river) *80*E4
Cawnpore *80*E2
Cayenne *88*F1
Cebu *58*F4
Cefalu *38*D6, *43*D5
Celebes, *c.* 1600 *58*F4
1750 *75*E4
1914 *97*F6
1941–2 *105*B3
1968 *108*E4
Celestine Monastery, Paris *83*C3
Celts *11*B-C1, *25*E1
Cenabum (*mod.* Orléans) *27*E2
Central African Republic *108*B3
Central Powers
during First World War *98*
advance of, during First World War *98*
Ceos *14*D3, *15*D6
Cephallenia (Cephalonia) *14*A3, *20*A3
Cephallenia, County of *52*A2
Cerasus (*mod.* Kiresum) *24*C4
Cerilli· *16*D1
Ceuta *39*A6, *57*A5, *102*A6
Ceylon, *c. 1600* *58*E4, *79*A2
1700 *79*C2
1780 *79*A5
1858 *80*E5
1914 *97*C5
1968 *108*D3
Chablais *48*A6
Chad *108*B2–3
Chaeronea *15*B5
Chaise-Dieu, La *43*B3
Chalcedon (*mod.* Kadiköy) *26*B1

Chalcidice *14*C1
Chalcis *14*C2, *15*C5
Chaldaea *8*C5
Chalon *49*C4
Châlons *49*C3, *51*D4, *99*B4
Chambal (river) *80*D-E2
Chambord *62*C3
Champagne, 1100 *39*C3
1180–1453 *50*
1429 *51*D4
Champlain, route of *59*D3
Champlain, Lake *77*B3
Champs Elysées, Paris *83*A1
Chancellor, Richard, route of
1556 *58*D2
Chancellorsville *92*F4
Chandernagore *79*C1, A4, *80*F3
Charlemagne, Empire of, 814 *33*
Charleroi *68*B5
Charles, Archduke, expedition of *71*
Charles V
hereditary dominions of, 1556 *57*
Charles XII
expedition of, 1700–09 *73*
Charles XII
journey to Stralsund, 1714 *73*
Charles the Bald
Kingdom of, 843 *36*
Charleston *59*D4, *92*E4
Charlottenburg *82*D2
Chartres *39*B3, *43*B3
Château-Gaillard *39*C3
Château-Thierry *99*B3
Chatellerault *62*C3
Châtillon *86*B3
Chattanooga *92*D4
Chaumont *86*C3
Chazars *37*E3
Chelles *1*A2
Chelsea, London *66*A6
Chemin des Dames *99*B3
Chensu, Temple of *4*
Cheops, Pyramid of *3*
Chephren, Pyramid of *3*
Cherokee Indians *59*C4
Cherson *52*D1
Chersonesus *14*E1
Cheshire *65*D4
Chester *43*B1, *49*B1
Cheyenne Indians *59*C3
Chibcha civilization *56*D2
Chicago *92*D3
Chichen Itza *56*B1
Chichester *49*B2
Chiemsee *49*D3
Chienti (river) *35*E2
Chigirin *73*E2
Chile, 1533 *56*D5
1750 *75*B4
1914 *88*E3–5
China, between 1000 B.C. and
A.D. 200 *1*E-F3
c. 1300 *42*D-E4
1914 *97*C-E2–4
1941–42 *105*A-B1–2
1942–5 *106*A-B4–5

1968 *108*D-E1–2
Chinon *51*C4
Chinook Indians *59*B2
Chios *14*E2
during Persian wars *20*D3
1878 *93*C3 1912–13 *94*C6
Chipas *56*B1
Chiusi *45*D3
Cholula *56*A1
Chorasan *22*E3
Chotusitz *81*D5
Chou-Kow-Tien *1*E2
Christiania (*mod.* Oslo) *70*B3, *98*C1
Christiansand *70*A3
Christiansborg *75*C3
Chungking *97*E3, *106*A5
Chur *48*D5
Church in west and central Europe *c.* 1500 *49*
Cibyra *26*B3
Cilicia
under Alexander the Great *22*B2
189 B.C. *26*C3
Roman province *28*E-F3
Cimbrians *29*B-C1
Cintra *86*A4
Circus Flaminius, Rome *30*C2
Circus Maximus, Rome *30*D3
Cirta (*mod.* Constantine) *25*D5
Cisalpine Republic 1797–1802 *85*A-C1–2
Cîteaux *43*C3
Citium (*mod.* Larnaca) *11*F3
City, London *66*C6
Cividale *34*B1
Civilization
expansion to A.D. 200 *1*
Civil War in England in 1640's *65*
Civitavecchia *35*D3
Clairvaux *39*C3, *43*C3
Clepsydra, Acropolis, Athens *13, 17*A4
Clermont *39*C4, *43*B3
Cleveland *92*D3
Cleves *61*E3, *81*A3
Cleves, Duchy of, 1614 *81*A-B3
1648 *67*B3
1756–63 *82*B3
Clitor *14*B3, *15*A6
Clivus Argentarius, Rome *31*A-B4–5
Clivus Oppius, Rome *31*D5
Cloaca Maxima, Rome *31*B6
Cluny *39*C4, *43*C3
Cnidians, Assembly hall of the Delphi *19*A4
Cnidus *26*A3
Cnossus *12*C
Coca *55*B5
Cochin *58*E4, *79*A3, B3, *80*D5
Cochin-China, 1914 *97*E5
Cognac *62*B4
Coimbra *43*A4, *55*A5
Colchis *10*C2, *28*F2
Colenso *95*C1
Collina, Rome *30*D2(3)
Colmar *36*C5

Cologne *43*C2, *44*B5, *67*B3
Cologne, Archbishopric of 1648 *67*B3
Colombia, 1914 *88*E1
Colombia, Great 1819–30 *88*E1-2
Colombo *79*A2, C2, A5, *80*E5
Colonia Agrippinensis (*mod.* Cologne) *29*B1
Colonial Powers
and their possessions, *c.* 1750 *75*
Colophon *20*D3
Colorado (river, N. America) *59*A-B3, *92*AB3-4
Colorado (river, S. America) *56*E6
Colorado (state), 1876 *92*B3
Colossae *20*E4
Columbia (river) *59*A-B3, *92*A-B2
Columbus, travels of, *58*B-C3
Columnae Herculis (Pillars of Hercules) *29*A3
Comacchio *49*D5
Como *45*B1
Como, Lake *89*B1
Comoro Is., 1914 *96*E5
Compiègne *51*D3, *61*A5
Concord, Temple of, Rome *31*B5
Condé *62*D2
Condom *49*B5
Confederate States of America 1861–65 *92*
Congo (river) *96*C-D4–5
Congo, Republic of *108*B3
Congo (Congolese Republic) *108*B3–4
Congress Poland *91*E2–3
Connaught *65*A3
Connecticut
1783 *78*E-F2
1861–65 *92*E2
Conrad III (2nd Crusade) *40*C1
Consentia (*mod.* Cosenza) *16*D1
Constance *48*D5
Constantinople (*mod.* Istanbul) *32*E4, *43*F4
Conway *65*C3
Copais, Lake *15*B5
Copenhagen *43*D1, *44*C3
Coral Sea *105*C3
Corcyra (Corfu) *20*A2
Cordelier Club, Paris *83*B3(6)
Cordoba *37*A5, *54, 55*B6
Corduba (*mod.* Cordoba) *28*A3
Corfinium (*mod.* Pentima) *23*C2
Corfu
1265 *52*A2 1701 *71*E5
1812 *86*D5 1912–13 *94*B6
Corinth *14*B3, *15*B6, *28*D4
Corinth, Gulf of *14*B2–3, *15*A-B5–6
Cork *65*A4
Corneto *45*D4
Cornwall *65*C5
Coromandel Coast *80*E4–5
Coronado, route of *59*A-B3–4
Coronea *15*B5
Correggio *45*C2

Corregidor *106*B5
Corsica, 264 B.C. *23*A2
526 *32*C4 — *c.* 775 *34*A2
814 *33*B3 — 843 *36*C6
c. 900 *37*C4 — 1100 *39*C5
1230 *40*B3 — 1454 *45*B4
1556 *57*C4 — 1701 *71*D4
c. 1800 *85*A-B3 — 1815 *87*B4
1860 *90*B4 — 1914–18 *98*C4
1919–35 *101*B2
1968 *107*B4
Cortez, march of
1519 *58*A3, *59*C-B4–5
Cortona *35*D2
Corunna (La Coruña) *57*A3
Corvey *38*B1, *43*C2
Cos *26*A3
Cosenza *32*D5
Costa Rica *56*C2
Cotentin *104*B5
Cotrone *38*E6
Coutances *49*B3
Coutras *62*B4
Coventry *49*B1, *103*B2
Craigmillar *65*E1
Crato *55*A5
Crécy *51*D3
Cree Indians *59*C2
Creek Indians *59*C-D4
Crema *45*B2
Cremona *23*B1, *89*B2
Crete *11*E3, *12*
44 B.C. *28*D4 — 526 *32*E5
814 *33*C4 — 1100 *39*F6
1230 *40*E5 — 1265 *52*B3
1355 *53*B6 — 1556 *57*E5
1680 *60*B4 — 1721 *76*F6
1812 *86*E6 — 1914–18 *98*D5
1919–35 *101*C3 — 1968 *107*D5
Crete, Sea of *14*C-D4
Crimea *11*E1
526 *32*E3 — 814 *33*C2
1520 *60*D2 — 1796 *72*B-C5
1878 *93*E1
Crimea, Khanate of
1556 *57*F2 — 1762–96 *72*C5
Croatia, *c.* 900 *37*C4, *38*E4
c. 1100 *39*D4 — 1680 *60*B1
1721 *76*D4 — *c.* 1800 *85*D1
1859 *90*D3
Croats, 526 *32*D3
Crocodilopolis *2*A2

Cro-Magnon *1*A2
Croton (*mod.* Crotone) *21*B3, *23*E3
Crusades, 1096–1270 *40*
Csanad *49*F4
Ctesiphon *8*C4, *10*C3
Cuba *56*C-D1
c. 1600 *58*B3 — 1650–1763 *77*
1750 *75*B3
Cuicul (*mod.* Djemila) *29*B3
Culloden *76*B1
Cumae (*mod.* Cuma) *21*A1
Cumans *39*F3–4
Cumberland (county) *51*B1
Cumberland (river) *78*D3
Cumberland (town) *59*D4
Cumberland Road *59*C-D3
Cunaxa *24*E6
Curia, Rome *31*B5(4)
Curzola *49*E5
Custozza *89*C2
Cuzco *56*D4, *88*E2
Cyclades *14*D3
Cyme *26*A2
Cyprus, *c.* 1400 B.C. *6*B2
c. 700 B.C. 7A5
at the time of Alexander the Great *22*B3
189 B.C. *26*B-C4
44 B.C. *28*E4 — A.D. 526 *32*F5
814 *33*D3 — *c.* 900 *37*E5
1140 *41*A3 — 1230 *40*F4
1265 *52*D2 — 1355 *53*D6
1556 *57*F5 — 1680 *60*D4
1812 *86*F5 — 1878 *93*E3
1914 *96*D3 — 1914–18 *98*E5
1919–35 *101*D2
1939–41 *103*D3
1942–45 *104*E6
1968 *107*D-E5
Cyrenaica at the time of Alexander the Great *22*A3
Roman province, 44 B.C. *28*D5
A.D. 117 *29*C5
Cyrene (*mod.* Cirene) *22*A3, *28*D5
Cyrus (river) *10*C2
Cythera *14*C4
Cythnos *14*D3
Cyzicus *20*E1
Czechoslovakia, 1919–35 *101*B-C1–2
1938–39 *102*D-E4
1968 *107*C3
Czestochowa *74*A5

D

Dachau *104*B5
Dacia (Roman province) *29*C2
Dagö, 1100 *39*E1
1370 *44*E1 — 1660 *70*D3
1725 *72*A3 — 1914–18 *98*D1
Dahomey *108*A3
Dahshur *2*A2

Dakar *96*A4
Dalarna, 1660 *70*B3
Dalmatia
A.D. 117 (Roman province) *29*C3
1721 *76*D-E5 — 1800 *85*D-E2
1859 *90*D3 — 1878 *93*A2
Dalnaspidal *65*C2

Damão *80*D3, *97*C4
Damascus *28*F4 1400 B.C. *6*C2
600 B.C. *7*B6 860 B.C. *9*F2
500 B.C. *10*B3 1140 *41*C4
Damascus, Emirate of *41*D4
Damietta *40*F5
Danelaw *37*B2
Danish-Norwegian colonies
1750 *75*
Danube (river) *32*C-E3, *39*C-F3–4
Danubius (*mod.* Danube, river)
*28*C-D1–2
Danzig
1370 *44*D4 1660 *70*C5
1721 *76*E2 1793 *84*D2
1812 *86*D2 1935–39 *102*E4
Dardanelles *93*C2
Dar-es-Salaam *96*E5
Darjeeling *80*F2
Datis, naval attack of
490 B.C. *20*
Dauphiné
1429 *51*E5 1562–92 *62*E4
Davis, John, route of, 1585 *58*C2
Davis Strait *58*B2
Dawson *59*B1
Dax *49*A5
Dead Sea *9*E4
Dead Sea Scrolls, location *9*E4
Deccan *79*C2
Decelea *15*C6
Deir-el-Bahri *5*
Delaware (river) *78*E2
Delaware (state) 1783 *78*E3
1861–65 *92*F4, *92*E3
Delaware Indians *59*D3
Delft *61*C3
Delhi *42*C4, *80*E2
Delhi, Sultanate of, 1525 *79*A
Delian Confederacy *21*
Delos *14*D3
Delphi *14*B2, *15*A5
Demarcation lines
of 1494 and 1529 *58*
Dendera *2*B3
Dendermonde *68*B4
Dendra (Midea) *15*B6
Denmark
c. 900 *37*C2 *c.* 1100 *39*D2
1370 *44*C3 1556 *57*C1
1660 *70*A-C1–4 1700 *73*A1
1721 *76*C-D1–2
1756–63 *82*C1 1812 *86*C1–2
1815 *87*B-C2 1871 *91*B-C1
1914–18 *98*C2 1919–35 *101*B1
1939–41 *103*B-C2
1942–45 *104*B-C4
1968 *107*B2
Denver *92*B3
Deptford, London *66*E6
Derby *65*D4
Des Moines *92*C3
Desna (river) *84*F3
de Soto, route of *59*C4
Detroit *78*D2
Dettingen *76*D3

Deva (*mod.* Chester) *29*B1
de Vaca, route of *59*C4
Deventer *44*B4, *61*E2
Devon *51*B3, *65*C5
Diaz, Bartolomeu
route of, 1486 *58*C4–5
Die *49*C5
Dieppe *69*D1
Digne *49*C5
Dijon *51*D4, *62*D3
Dinant *44*B5
Diois *69*E4
Dionysus, Sanctuary of
Delphi *19*B5
Dionysus, Theatre of
Acropolis, Athens *17*D-E5
Dioscurias *11*F1, *29*D3
Diu *79*A2, *80*D3, *97*C4, *108*D2
Diyala (river) *8*C2–3
Djakowo *49*F4
Dnieper (river) *74*D-E5–6
Dniester (river) *73*D3
Dobruja, 526 *32*E3
1912–13 *94*C-D5
Dodecanese Is., 1912 *94*D6
1919–35 *101*C2
1968 *107*D5
Dodge City *59*C3
Dodona *20*A2
Dogger Bank
battle of 24 Jan., 1915 *98*C2
Dol *49*A3
Dôle *69*E3
Domrémy *51*E4
Domus Caligulae, Rome *31*B6
Domus Tiberiana, Rome *31*C6
Don (river) *72*C-D4–5
Dor *9*E3
Dordogne (river) *51*C5
Dordrecht *44*B4, *61*C3
Dorians *14*
Dorpat *44*E1, *70*D3
Dorset *51*B3
Dortmund *44*B5, *67*B3
Dorylaeum *40*E3
Douai *61*B4, *99*A2
Dover *65*E4
Drake, Francis
voyage round the world, 1577–80
*58*A3, B5 and D-E4–5
Drammen *70*A3
Drangiana *22*E3
Drava (river) *76*D-E4
Drenthe *61*E2
Drepanum *16*A2
Dresden *82*D3
Dreux *62*C2
Drogheda *65*B3
Dublin *37*B2, *39*B2
Duero (river) *55*A-C5
Duisburg *44*B5
Dulduli (Hit) *8*B3
Dumfries *65*C2
Dunbar *65*D2
Dundee *65*E1
Dunkirk *61*A4, *99*A1

Dunrobin *65*C1
Dupleix, French territory in India under, 1741–54 *79*C
Dura-Europus *22*C3, *29*E4
Duranius (*mod.* Dordogne, river) *27*E4
Durazzo *40*D3, *52*A1, *94*A-B5
Durban *95*D2
Durham *39*B2, *65*D3
Durili *8*C4
Durius (*mod.* Duero, river) *25*A3

Dürnstein *39*D3
Durocortorum (*mod.* Rheims) *27*E2
Dutch colonies, 1750 *75*
Dutch East Indies
1941–42 *105*A-B3
Dutch Guiana (Surinam)
1914 *88*E-F1
Dvina (river) *44*E-F2, *84*E-F1
Dybbøl *91*C1

E

East, The, *c.* 600 B.C. *7*
East Anglia *36*B4
Eastern Front, 1914–18 *100*
October 1917 *98*D1–3
Spring 1918 *98*D-F1–3
Eastern Roman Empire
see Byzantine Empire
East Frankish Kingdom
c. 900 *37*C3
East Friesland, 1648 *67*B2
1744 *81*B2 1756–63 *82*B2
East Indies
c. 1600 *58*E4 1750 *75*E3–4
1941–42 *105*A-B3
East Prussia
14th and 15th centuries *74*B4
1618 *81*E-F1–2 1756–63 *82*F1
1865 *91*E1 1914–18 *100*E1
1919–35 *101*C1
1935–39 *102*E4
East Rumelia, 1878 *93*C2
East Slavs *37*D3
Ebro (river) *55*B-D4–5
Eburacum (*mod.* York) *29*B1
Ecbatana (*mod.* Hamadan)
*22*D3, *29*E4, *33*E3
Ecuador, 1533 *56*D3
1811, 1821–31, 1914 *88*E2
Edessa *41*E1
Edessa, County of, 1140 *41*D-E1
Edfu *2*B3
Edgehill *65*D4
Edinburgh *39*B1, *65*E1
Edom *9*E5
Eger, Bohemia *82*C4
Eger (river) *82*C4
Eger (Erlau), Hungary *49*F3
Egmont *61*C2
Egypt, ancient *2*
Egypt
Old Kingdom,
southern boundary *2*A-B4
Middle Kingdom,
southern boundary *2*A4
New Kingdom,
southern boundary *2*A-B5
1400 B.C. *6*A-C2–4
700 B.C. *7*A6
500 B.C. *10*A-B4–5

under Alexander the Great *22*A-B4
44 B.C. *28*E-F5
A.D. 117 *29*D5
656–814 *33*D4–5
1453–1680 *60*C5
1812 *86*F6 1914 *96*D3
1914–18 *98*D-E5
1919–35 *101*D2
1942–45 *104*D-E6
1968 *108*B2
Egypt, Lower *2*A1
Egypt, Upper *2*B3
Ehrensdorf *1*A1
Eichstätt *49*D3
Eichstätt, Bishopric of, 1648 *67*C4
Einsiedeln *48*D5
Eire (Republic of Ireland)
1939–41 *103*A2
1942–45 *104*A4
See also Ireland, Irish Free State
Eisenach *39*D3
Ekaterinburg (*mod.* Sverdlovsk) *97*C1
Ekron *9*D4
El Alamein *104*D6
Elam *6*E2–3
Elba, 1454 *45*C3
c. 1800 *85*B2 1859–60 *90*B4
Elbe (river) *81*C-D2–4
Elbing *44*E4, *70*C5
Elea *21*B2
Elephantine I. *2*B3
El Escorial *55*C5
Eleusis *15*C6
El-Fustat (Cairo) *33*D4
Elis (town) *14*A3
Elis (region) *14*A-B3
Elizabeth, Empress of Russia
conquests of, 1741–62 *72*
Ellice Is. *105*D3, *106*E6
El Paso *59*B4
Elverum *103*C1
Ely *43*B1, *51*C2
Embrun *49*C5
Emden *71*C1
Emesa *29*D4
Ems (river) *81*B2–3
Ems (town) *91*B4
Enghien *61*C4
England, 526 *32*B1–2

900 *37*B2 1100 *39*B2
1429 *51* 1556 *57*A-B1
c. 1650 *65*
1721 *76*B-C2–3
See also Britannia and Great Britain
English Channel *51*A-C3
Eniwetok I. *106*D5
Ephesus *22*A2
Epidamnus *11*D2, *21*C1
Epidaurum *11*D2
Epidaurus *14*C3, *15*B6
Epinal *99*C5
Epirus (Roman province) *28*D3, *29*C3
Epirus, Despotate of
1230 *40*D3–4
1265 *52*A2
Erech (Warka) *8*C5
Erechtheum, Acropolis, Athens *17*C4
Eretria *14*C2, *15*D5
Erfurt *43*D2, *44*C5, *86*C3
Erie, Lake *59*D3, *78*E2
Eridu *8*C5
Eritrea, 1914 *96*E4
Erivan (Yerevan) *101*E2
Erlau (Eger) *49*F3
Eryces (river) *16*C3
Eskilstuna *70*C3
Eskimo *59*C-D2
Esna *2*B3, *22*B4
Esquilina, Rome *30*D2(2)
Esquiline, Rome *30*E2
Essex *51*C2
Essling *86*D3
Este *45*D2
Estonia, 1100 *39*E1

1660 *70*D3 1700 *73*C1
1721 *76*E3 1725 *72*B3
1812 *86*D-E1
1919–35 *101*C1
1939–41 *103*C2
1968 *107*C2
Estonians *37*D2
Esztergom (Gran) *49*F3
Ethiopia *see* Abyssinia
Etna, Mt. *16*C2
Etruria, 264 B.C. *23*B2
kingdom, 1801–08 *85*B-C2
Ettenheim *86*C3
Eu *62*C2, *86*B3
Euboea *14*C2, *15*D5
Eugene, Prince, expedition of *71*
Eumenes, Stoa of
Acropolis, Athens *17*B-C5
Eumenia *20*F3
Eupatoria *93*E1
Euphrates (river) *6*C-E1–3, *28*F3
Europe, 526 *32*
814 *33* 900 *37*
1100 *39* 1230 *40*
1370 *44* 1556 *57*
1701 *71* 1721 *76*
1812 *86* 1815 *87*
1914–18 *98* 1919–35 *101*
Sept. 1939–June 1941 *103*
Oct. 1942–May 1945 *104*
1968 *107*
Europus (river) *14*B1
Evesham *43*B1
Evreux *49*B3
Exarchate, The *35*D1
Exeter *39*B2, *43*B2
Eylau (*mod.* Bagrationovsk) *86*D2

F

Faenza *45*D2
Faeroe Is.
800 *37*B1 1914–18 *98*B1
1939–41 *103*B1 1968 *107*A1
Falaise *104*B5
Falkirk *76*B2
Falkland Is. *88*E5
Fallen Timber *59*C3
Falster *82*C1
Falsterbo *44*C3
Falun *70*B3
Famagusta *40*F4
Far East, The
1941–42 *105* 1942–45 *106*
Farfa *43*D4
Fargo *59*C3
Fashoda *96*D4
Fayum, Oasis of *2*A2
Fehmarn *70*A4
Fehrbellin *81*C3
Fellujah (Palukut) *8*B3
Feltre *45*D1, *57*C3

Feodosiya (Kaffa) *72*C5
Fermo *45*E3
Ferney *76*C4
Ferns *49*A1
Ferrara *43*D3, *45*D2
Ferrara, Duchy of, 1454 *45*D2
Fez 1556 *57*A5
Fez (town) *33*A4, *96*B3
Fezzan *33*B-C5
Fidenae (*mod.* Castel Giubileo) *23*C2
Fiesole *45*C3
Fiji *105*D3, *106*E6
Finland
1660 *70*D2 1721 *76*E1
1812 *86*D1 1815 *87*C1
1825 *72*B2 1914–18 *98*D1
1919–35 *101*C1
1939–41 *103*C1
1942–45 *104*C4
1968 *107*C1
Finland, Gulf of *70*D3
First World War, 1914–18

Europe *98*
Firth of Forth *65*E1
Firth of Tay *65*E1
Five Boroughs, The *37*B2
Fladstrand *76*D2
Flanders, *1100* *39*C3
1370 *44*A5 1429 *51*D3
1579 *61*A-B3–4
1914–18 *99*A1
Fleurus *68*B5
Fleury *43*B3
Florence *43*D4, *45*C3
Florence, Republic of, 1454 *45*C3
Florentia (*mod.* Florence) *23*B1
Florida
1650 *77*A2 1700 *77*B2
1713 *77*A4 1750 *75*B3
1763 *77*B4 1783 *78*D-E5
1861–65 *92*D-E5
Flushing *61*B3
Foix *62*C5
Foix, County of *50*B6
Foligno *49*E5
Fontainebleau *76*C4
Fontenoy, Austrian Netherlands *76*C3
Fontenoy, Yonne *36*B5
Forbach *91*B4
Forez *62*D4
Forli *49*D5
Formosa, 1914 *97*F3
1941–45 *105*B2, *106*B5
1968 *108*E2
Fort Chipewyan *59*B2
Fort Duquesne (Pittsburgh)
*77*B4, *78*E2
Fort Frontenac *78*E2
Fort Hall *59*B3
Fort Laramie *59*B3
Fort le Boeuf *78*E2
Fort Mims *59*C4
Fort Necessity *78*E2
Fort Niagara *78*E2
Fort Oswego *78*E2
Fort Reliance *59*C2
Fort St David *79*A5, *80*E4
Fort St George (Madras) *79*A5
Fort St Louis *78*D2
Fort Sault Ste Marie *78*D1
Fort Sumter, 1861–65 *92*E4
Fort William Henry *78*E2
Forum Augusti, Rome *31*C5
Forum Boarium, Rome *30*C3
Forum Julium, Rome *31*B5
Forum Pacis, Rome *31*C5
Forum Romanum *30*D2, *31*B6
Fossanova *45*E4
Fotheringhay *62*C1
France, at time of Caesar *27*
44 B.C. *28*B2 A.D. 117 *29*B2
526 *32*B2–3 814 *33*A-B2–3
843 *36* 900 *37*B3–4
1100 *39*B-C3–4
1180–1453 *50* 1230 *40*A1–2
1429 *51* 1556 *57*B2–3
1562–92 (Huguenot wars) *62*
1701 *71*B-C2–4
1721 *76*B-C3–5
1812 *86*B-C2–4
1815 *87*B3–4
1914–18 *98*B-C3
1919–35 *101*A-B1–2
1939–41 *103*A-B2–3
1968 *107*A-B3–4
Franche-Comté, 1429 *51*E5
1562–92 *62*E3 1648 *67*B5
end of 17th century *69*E-F3–4
Franco, conquests of, 1936–39 *102*
Franconia
936 *38*B-C2 *c.* 1630 *64*C6
Frankenhausen *57*C2
Franks, homeland *32*B-C2
Franks, kingdom, 526 *32*B-C2–3
814 *33*
Franks, migrations *32*
Frascati *35*E3
Fraser (river) *59*B2
Frauenburg *57*D1
Fraustadt *73*B2
Fredericia *70*A4
Frederick II *40*D4
Frederick Barbarossa *40*C1
Fredericksburg *92*F4
Frederick the Great *82*
Fredrikshald *70*B3
Fredrikshamn *70*E3
Freiberg *82*D3
Freiburg, Germany *43*C3
Freiburg, Switzerland *48*B6
Freising *38*C3, *82*C5
Freising, Bishopric of,
1648 *67*C5
Fréjus *49*C5
Frémont, routes of *59*A-B3
French colonies, 1750 *75*
French conquests,
in 17th century *69*
French Equatorial Africa
1914 *96*C4–5
French Guiana, 1914 *88*F1
French Guinea, 1914 *96*A4
French Indo-China, 1914 *97*E4–5
1941–42 *105*A2
1942–45 *106*A5
French North Africa, 1914 *96*B3
French Somaliland, 1914 *96*E4
French West Africa, 1914 *96*A-B4
Fretum Gallicum (English Channel)
*27*E1
Friedland, Bohemia *64*E5
Friedland, East Prussia *86*D2
Friesland
936 *38*A1 1579 *61*D1
Fritzlar *38*B2
Fuentes de Onoro *86*A4
Fugger operations in western and
central Europe, *c.* 1500 *46*
Fukien *97*E3
Fulda *43*C2, *44*C5
Fulda, Bishopric of, 1648 *67*C3
Fünen *44*C3
Fünfkirchen (Pécs) *49*F4
Furness *37*B2

Gabon *108*B3–4
Gades (*mod.* Cadiz) *25*A4
Gaeta *90*C4
Gaetulia *25*C5
Gainsborough *65*E3
Galapagos Is. *56*B3
Galatia, 189 B.C. *26*B-C2
44 B.C. *28*E3 A.D. 117 *29*D3
Galicia, Spain *55*A4
Galicia, Poland
1701 *71*E-F2 1756–63 *82*F4
1772 *84*D4 1812 *86*D-E3
1914–18 *98*D3, *100*E-F4
Galilee *41*B5
Galilee, Sea of *9*E2–3
Gallia Belgica *27*E-F1
Gallia Celtica *27*D-F2–4
Gallia Cisalpina *25*D-E1
Gallia Cispadana *23*B1
Gallia Narbonensis *27*E-F4
Gallia Transalpina *25*C-D2
Gallia Transpadana *23*A1
Gallipoli *60*C3, *98*D4
Galveston *59*B4
Gama, Vasco da, route of
1498 *58*C4–5, and D-E4
Gambia, 1750 *75*C3
1914 *96*A4 1968 *108*A3
Ganges (river) *80*E-F2
Gangra *26*C1
Gap *49*C5
Garda, Lake *45*C1
Garibaldi, expedition against
the Kingdom of the
Two Sicilies, 1860 *90*
Garigliano (river) *45*E4
Garonne (river) *51*C6
Garumna (*mod.* Garonne, river)
*27*D-E4
Gascony, 1100 *39*B4
1429 *51*B6 1562–92 *62*B4
Gastein *91*C5
Gath *9*D4
Gaugamela *22*C2
Gaul *27*
Gävle *70*C3
Gaza *22*B3
Gedrosia (Baluchistan) *22*E4
Gela *16*B3
Gelas (river) *16*C3
Gelderland, 1579 *61*D-E2
Gelderland, Upper
1579 *61*D-E3 1715 *81*A3
Gelnhausen *39*C3
Gembloux *61*C4
Genava (*mod.* Geneva) *27*F3
Generality, The, 1648 *68*B-C3–4
Geneva *48*A6
Geneva, Lake of *48*A6
Genghis Khan, Empire of, 1227 *42*
most important campaigns *42*
Genoa *45*B2
Genoa, Republic of, 1454 *45*A2
1556 *57*C3–4
1721 *76*C-D4–5

Genoese settlements in Aegean Sea
and on Black Sea coast, 1355 *53*
Genseric *32*C5
Genua (*mod.* Genoa) *23*A1
Georgetown *88*E1
Georgia, Asia *60*E3
Georgia, U.S.A., 1763 *77*B4
1783 *78*D4 1861–65 *92*D4
Gepides, Kingdom of the, 526 *32*D3
Gergovia *27*E3
Gerizim, Mt. *9*E3, *41*B5
German Confederation, 1815 *87*
German Democratic Republic
1968 *107*B-C3
German East Africa (Tanganyika)
1914 *96*D-E5
German Empire, 1701 *71*C-E1–3
1721 *76* 1871 *91*
See also Germany
Germania, A.D. 117 *29*B-C1–2
Germania Inferior, A.D. 117 *29*B1
Germania Magna *28*C-D1
Germania Superior, A.D. 117 *29*B2
German South-West Africa
c. 1900 *95*A1 1914 *96*C6
Germany
526 *32*C-D2–3 843 *36*C-E4–5
c. 900 *37*C3 936 *38*A-D1–3
1100 *39*C-D2–4
1230 *40*B-C1–2
1370 (North Germany) *44*B-D4–5
1378–1417 *47*C-E2
1556 *57*C-D1–3
during Thirty Year's War
1618–48 *64*
1648 *67*
1701 *71*C-D1–3
1721 *76*C-D3–4
during Seven Year's War,
1756–63 *82*
1812 *86*C-D2–3
1815 *87*B-C2–3
1865–71
(unification of Germany) *91*
1914–18 *98*C2–3
1919–35 *101*B-C1–2
1936–39 *102*
1939–41 *103*B-C2
1942–45 *104*B-C4–5
1968 *107*B3
Germany, Federal Republic of
*107*B3
Gettysburg *92*F4
Ghana, 1968 *108*A3
See also Gold Coast
Ghent *61*B4, *99*B1
Gibraltar (Jebel Tarik)
*33*A4, *55*B6, *76*B6, *98*B4, *107*A5
Gien *62*C3
Gilbert Is. *105*D3, *106*D6
Gilboa, Mt. *9*E3, *41*B5
Giza *2*A1, *3*
Glandève *49*C5
Glarus *48*D5
Glasgow *43*B1, *65*C2

Glastonbury *43*B2
Globe Theatre, London *66*C6
Glogau *82*E3
Glomma (river) *70*B2–3
Gloucester (county) *51*B2
Gloucester (town) *43*B2, *65*D4
Gmünd *67*C4
Goa *58*E4, *79*A2, *80*D4, *97*C4, *108*D3
Gobi Desert *42*E2
Godavari (river) *80*E3
Godfrey of Bouillon *40*B1
Gokstad *37*C1
Golconda *79*A2
Gold Coast
1750 *75*C3 1914 *96*B4
See also Ghana
Golden Horde, The, *c.* 1300 *42*A-C1–2
Goldingen *44*E2
Goletta (La Goulette) *57*C5
Gomorrah *9*E5
Gonzaga *45*C2
Gordium *22*B2, *26*B2
Gorizia, County of, 1648 *67*D6
Gorki *101*D1
Goshen *7*A6
Goslar *38*C1, *44*C5, *67*C3
Göteborg (Gothenburg) *70*B4
Gothalunia *32*B2
Goths *32*
Gotland
526 *32*D1 1100 *39*D1
1370 *44*D2 1660 *70*C4
Göttingen *44*C5, *82*C3
Gottorp *70*A4, *76*D2
Gran (Esztergom) *49*F3
Granada *55*C6
Granada, Kingdom of, 1476 *55*B-C6
Grand Châtelet, Paris *83*B2
Granicus (river) *22*B2
Grasse *49*C5
Graubünden (Grisons) *48*D-E6
Gravelotte *91*A4
Gray's Inn, London *66*C6
Graz *57*D3
Great Britain
1721 *76*B-C1–3
1812 *86*A-B1 2
1815 *87*A-B1–2
1914–18 *98*B1–2
1919–35 *101*A-B1
1939–41 *103*A-B2
1942–45 *104*B4
1968 *107*A-B2–3
See also England and Scotland
Great Fish (river) *95*C2
Great Khan, Empire of the *42*
Great Slave Lake *59*B-C2
Great Trek, 1835 *95*

Great Wall of China *42*E3
Greece
in ancient times *14*
during Persian Wars *20*
during Peloponnesian War *21*
under Alexander the Great *22*A2
A.D. 117 *29*C3 1100 *39*E5–6
1878 *93*B-C3
1912–13 *94*B-C5·6
1914–18 *98*D4
1919–35 *101*C2
1939–41 *104*C3
1942–45 *104*C-D6
1968 *107*C-D5
Greek Orthodox Church in Europe
1560 *63*
Greek settlements
around the Mediterranean *11*
Greenland
c. 1600 *58*C1 1750 *75*B-C1
Greensboro *59*D4
Greenwich *65*E4, *66*E6
Greifswald *43*D1
Grenoble *36*C5, *43*C3
Grimaldi *1*A2
Grimsby *44*A3
Grimstad *70*A3
Grodno *73*C2
Groningen (province) *61*E1
Groningen (town) *44*B4, *61*E1
Grosseto *45*C3
Gross-Görschen *86*C3
Grossjägersdorf *82*F1
Grosswardein (Oradea Mare) *49*F3
Guadalajara *102*B5
Guadalcanal, Pacific Ocean *106*D6
Guadalcanal, Spain *46*A6
Guadalquivir (river) *55*B6
Guadeloupe, 1750 *75*B3
Guadiana (river) *39*A5
Guam *105*C2, *106*C5
Guastalla *89*C2
Guatemala *56*B1
Guayaquil *88*E2
Guernica *102*B5
Guiana
1750 *75*B3 1914 *88*E2
Guienne
1429 *51*B5 1562–92 *62*B4
Guinea *108*A3
Guinea, Gulf of *58*C4
Guise *62*D2
Guises, domains of, during
Huguenot wars, 1562–92 *62*
Gurk *49*E4
Gustavus Adolphus
campaign of, 1630–32 *64*
Györ (Raab) *49*E3

H

Haarlem *61*C2
Habsburg *48*C5
Habsburg dominions

1556 *57* 1648 *67*
1701 *71* 1756–63 *82*
Hadramaut *33*E-F5

Hadria *11*C1
Hadrianopolis *29*D3
Hadrumetum (*mod.* Sousse) *25*E5
Hague, The *61*C2, *107*B3
Haguenau *67*B4, *69*F2
Haifa *107*E5
Hainan, 1914 *97*E4
1941–42 *105*A2
1942–45 *106*A5
Hainault, 1579 *61*B-C4
Haiti *56*D-E1
1650–1763 *77* 1750 *75*B3
Halberstadt *49*D2
Halberstadt, Bishopric of
1648 *67*C3, *81*C3
1756–63 *82*C3
Haleb (Aleppo) *6*C2, *107*E5
Haliacmon (river) *14*B1
Halicarnassus *20*D4
Halifax, Nova Scotia *59*E3, *78*F1
Halland, 1660 *70*B4
Halle *44*C5, *67*C4, *82*C3
Halles, Les, Paris *83*B2
Halupe *8*A1
Halycus (river) *16*B3
Halys (river) *10*B2
Ham *91*A4
Hama *41*C3
Hamadan *33*E3, *42*B3
Hamar *103*C1
Hambach *86*C3
Hamburg *44*C4
Hameln *44*B5
Hampshire *51*B-C3
Hangchow *42*F3
Hangö (Gangud) *70*D3
Hankow *97*E3, *105*B2
Hannibal
expedition of, 220–203 B.C. *25*
Hanoi *97*E4
Hanover (town) *44*C4, *82*C2
Hanover
1701 *71*D1–2 1721 *76*D3
1756–63 *82*B-C2
1815 *87*B-O2
1866 *91*B-C2–3
Hanse towns *44*
Hanseatic League *44*
Hanseatic trading depots and settlements *44*
Harbin *97*E1
Harfleur *51*C3
Härje Valley, 1660 *70*B2
Härnösand *70*C2
Harpers Ferry *92*F4
Harwich *65*E4
Harzburg *38*C1
Hasdrubal
expedition of, 208–207 B.C. *25*
Hastenbeck *82*C2
Hastings *39*B3
Hatfield *65*E4
Hatshepsut, tomb of *5*
Hattushash (*mod.* Bogaz-Köy) *6*B1
Havana *56*C1, *58*A3, *59*C4
Havel (river) *81*C-D2–3

Havelberg *49*D1
Hawaiian Is. *105*E2
Hazor *9*E2
Hebron *41*B6
Hecatompylus *22*D2
Hedemora *70*B3
Heidaby *37*C2
Heidelberg *43*C2, *91*B4
Heilbronn *67*C4
Hejaz *33*D4
Helena *59*B3
Helicon, Mt. *15*B5
Heligoland *36*C4, *91*B1
Heliopolis *2*A1
Helios, chariot of, Delphi *19*C4
Hellespont *14*E1
Helluland *58*B2
Helsingfors (*mod.* Helsinki) *86*D1
Helsingland *70*B-C2
Helsinki (Helsingfors) *98*D1
Helvetian Republic
1800 *85*A-B1 1812 *86*C3
Helwan *2*A2
Hera, Temple of, Olympia *18*B1
Heraclea *41*A1
Heraclea (*mod.* Eregli)
Bithynia *26*B1
Heraclea (*mod.* Sevastopol)
Crimea *11*E1
Heraclea, Lucania *21*B2, *23*D3
Heraclea Minoa, Sicily *16*A3
Heracleopolis *2*A2
Heracleum
(*mod.* Candia, Iraklion) *12*C
Herat *22*E3, *42*B3
Herculaneum *23*C2
Hercules, Pillars of *25*A5
Hereford (county) *51*B2
Hereford (town) *49*B1
Hermannstadt *60*C2
Hermonthis *2*B3
Hermopolis *2*A2
Hermus (river) *20*D-E3
Herodes, Odeum of, Acropolis
Athens *17*B5
Hersfeld *43*C2
Hertford *51*C2
Hertogenbosch *68*C3
Herzegovina, 1556 *57*D4
1878 *93*A2 1912–13 *94*A5
Hesse
936 *38*B2 *c.* 1630 *64*C5
Hesse, Grand Duchy of, 1871 *91*B4
Hesse-Darmstadt, Landgraviate of
1648 *67*C3
Hesse-Kassel, Landgraviate of
1648 *67*C3
Hibernia *29*A1
Hieraconpolis *2*B3
Hierosolyma (Jerusalem) *28*F4
Hildesheim *38*C1
Hildesheim, Bishopric of
1648 *67*C3
Himalayas *80*E-F1–2
Himera (river) *16*B3
Himera (town) *16*B2

Hindu Kush *22*F2
Hipponium *16*D2
Hippo Regius (*mod.* Annaba)
*25*D4, *32*C5
Hiroshima *106*C5
Hirsau *43*C2
Hispania *25*A-B2–4
Hispania Citerior
Roman province *28*A-B3
Hispania Ulterior
Roman province *28*A3
Hispaniola (Haiti) *56*D-E1
Hit (Dulduli) *8*B3
Hitler, conquests of, 1936–39 *102*
Hittite Empire
c. 1400 B.C. *6*A-C1–2
Hjaltland (Shetland Is.) *c.* 900 *37*B1
Hjardarholt *37*A1
Hochkirch *82*D3
Hohenfriedberg *81*D4
Hohenlinden *86*C3
Hohenstaufen *39*D3
Hohenzollern, 1865 *91*B5
Hokkaido *97*F1
Holar *37*A1
Holland, County of, 1579 *61*C2
Holland, Kingdom of, 1812 *86*C2
See also Netherlands
Holmgard (Novgorod) *37*D1
Holovzin *73*D1
Holstein, 1100 *39*D2
c. 1630 *64*C4 1648 *67*C1
1660 *70*A4 1756–63 *82*C1
1815 *87*C2 1866 *91*B-C2
Holstein-Gottorp, 1660 *70*
Holy Roman Empire, 962 *38*
c. 1100 *39* 1230 *40*
1556 *57* 1648 *67*
Holyrood *65*E1
Homs *41*C3
Honduras *56*C1
Hong Kong
*97*E4, *105*B2, *106*B5, *108*E2

Hoorn *61*D2
Hôpital de la Salpétrière
Paris *83*C4
Hôpital St Louis, Paris *83*C1
Horemheb, tomb of *5*
Horseshoe Bend *59*C4
Hôtel Royal des Invalides
Paris *83*A2–3
Hôtel de Ville, Paris *83*C2
Hubertusburg *82*C3
Hudiksvall *70*C3
Hudson, Henry, routes of
1609, 1610–11 *58*B2, *59*D3
Hudson (river) *59*D3
Hudson Bay *58*B2, *59*C-D2
Hudson's Bay Co. *77*A3, *77*B3
Huesca *43*B4
Huguenot wars, 1562–92 *62*
Hull *44*A3, *65*E3
Hunaflo (river) *37*A1
Hunan *97*E3
Hungary, 1100 *39*D-E4
1230 *40*C-D1–2
1556 *57*D3 1701 *71*E3
1721 *76*E4 *c.* 1800 *85*E1
1919–35 *101*C2
1939–41 *103*C2
1942–45 *104*C5
1968 *107*C4
Huns (migrations) *32*
Huron, Lake *59*D3, *78*D-E1–2
Hwang-ho (river) *42*D3, *97*D-E2–3
Hydaspes (river) *22*F3
Hyde Park, London *66*A6
Hyderabad, Hyderabad *80*E4
Hyderabad (Nizam's Dominions)
*80*E3–4
Hyderabad, Sind *80*D2
Hydra *14*C3
Hymettus, Mt. *15*D6
Hypsos (river) *16*A2
Hyrcania *29*E-F3
Hythe *102*B4

I

Iberian Peninsula
900–1180 *54* 1476 *55*
See also Spain and Portugal
Iberians *11*A2
Iberus (*mod.* Ebro, river)
*25*B-C2–3
Ibiza *55*E5
Icaria *14*E3
Iceland
at time of the Sagas *37*A1
1750 *75*C1–2
1939–41 *103*A1
1968 *107*A1
Iconium (*mod.* Konya) *24*B5, *26*B3
Ida, Mt. *12*B
Idaho, 1890 *92*A-B2

Idre, 1660 *70*B2
Ifni *108*A2
Ile-de-France *51*C-D4
Ilium (Troy) *14*E1
Ilkhan Empire, *c.* 1300 *42*A-C2–4
Illinois (river) *78*D2
Illinois (state), 1861–65 *92*D3
Illyria, *c.* 200 B.C. *25*F1–2
526 *32*D4
Illyrian Provinces, 1812 *86*D4
Illyrians *11*D2
Illyricum
(Roman province) *28*C-D2–3
Ilmen, Lake *70*E3
Ilva (*mod.* Elba) *23*B2
Imbros *14*E1

Imperial fora, Rome *31*
Imperial free cities
in Holy Roman Empire, 1648 *67*
Inca civilization *56*D-E4
Inca Empire, 11th century *56*
1533 *56*
Independence *59*B3
India, between 1000 B.C. and A.D. 200 *1*D3
c. 1600 *58*E3–4
1600–1780 *79*
1750 *75*E3
1858 *80*
1914 *97*B-D3–5
1968 *108*D2–3
India Inferior *22*F4
India Superior *22*F3
Indian Ocean *58*E4
Indiana, 1861–65 *92*D3
Indonesia
1914 *97*E6
1968 *108*E3–4
Indus (river) *80*D-E1
Ingelheim *38*B2
Ingolstadt *64*D6
Ingria, 1660 *70*E3
1721 *76*E1
1725 *72*B3
Inkerman *93*E1
Inn (river) *38*C3
Innsbruck *85*C1
Ionia *20*D3
Ionian Is., 1797–1809 *86*D5
1815 *87*C5
1863–78 *93*B3
Ionians *14*
Ionian Sea *21*C3
Ios *14*D4
Iowa, 1861–65 *92*C3
Ipsus *26*B2
Ipswich *44*A4
Iquique *56*E5
Iran (Persia) *107*F4, *108*C2
Iraq
1919–35 *101*E2
1939–41 *103*E3
1942–45 *104*E6
1968 *107*E-F5
Ireland, A.D. 117 *29*A1
526 *32*A1
c. 900 *37*B2
1100 *39*B2
1556 *57*A-B1
c. 1650 *65*A-B3–4
1721 *76*B2
1812 *86*B2
See also Ireland, Republic of and Irish Free State

Ireland, Republic of *107*A2–3
Irish Free State
1919–35 *101*A1
1936–39 *102*A3
Irish Sea *65*C3
Iroquois Indians *59*C-D3
Isar (river) *82*C5
Isin *8*C5
Islamic Empire, 814 *33*
Isonzo *98*C3
Ispahan (Isfahan) *33*E3
Israel, 860 B.C. *9*E3–4
1968 *107*E5, *108*B2
Issus *22*B2
Istanbul *107*D4
Ister (*mod.* Danube, river) *28*D2
Istria *85*C-D1
Istrus *11*E1
Italian Republic, 1802–5 *85*A-C1–2
Italian Somaliland, 1914 *96*E4
Italica *25*A4
Italy
*11*C2
264 B.C. *23*
during Punic Wars, 264–146 B.C. *25*D-F1–4
44 B.C. *28*C2–3
A.D. 117 *29*B-C3
526 *32*C-D3–5
774 *34*
814 *33*B3–4
843 *36*C-E5–6
c. 900 *37*C4
962 *38*B-E3–6
1100 *39*D5
1230 *40*B-C2–4
1454 *45*
1556 *57*C-D3–5
1701 *71*D-E3–5
1721 *76*C-E4–6
c. 1800 *85*
1812 *86*C4
1815 *87*B-C3–4
1859–70 (unification) *89*, *90*
1914–18 *98*C3–4
1919–35 *101*B2
1935–39 *102*
1939–41 *103*B-C3
1942–45 *104*B-C5–6
1968 *108*B-C4–5
Itanus *12*D
Ithaca *14*A2
Ivory Coast
1914 *96*A-B4
1968 *108*A3
Ivrea *49*C4
Ivry *62*C2
Iwo Jima *106*C5

J

Jacobin Club, Paris *83*A1(3)
Jaffa (Joppa) *9*D4, *41*A6, *86*F6
Jagatai, Empire of *42*C-D1–3
Jägerndorf *82*E4
Jakarta *105*A3
Jamaica
1650–1763 *77*
1750 *75*B3

Jämtland
c. 900 *37*C1
1660 *70*B2
Janina *60*B3
Jan Mayen I. *58*C2
Japan, 1914 *97*F1–2
and Japanese-controlled areas, 1941 *105*, 1942–45 *106*

Japan, Sea of *97*F2
Jarnac *62*B4
Jarrow *43*B1
Jassy *93*C1
Java *1*F5
c. 1600 *58*E-F4 1750 *75*E4
1914 *97*E6 1968 *108*E4
Jaxartes (river) *22*E1
Jebel Tarik (Gibraltar) *33*A4
Jehol, 1914 *97*E2
Jellinge *37*C2
Jena *86*C3
Jerez de la Frontera *33*A4
Jericho *9*E4
Jerusalem, 1400 B.C. *6*B3
860 B.C. *9*E4 1140 *41*B6
Jerusalem, Kingdom of
*41*B4–6
Jervaulx *43*B1
Joan of Arc, campaign of *51*
Jodhpur *80*D2
Johannesburg *95*C1

Johannisburg *100*E2
Jomsborg *38*D1
Jönköping *70*B4
Joppa (Jaffa) *9*D4
Jordan (river) *9*E3–4
Jordan (state)
1942–45 *104*E6
1968 *108*B-C2
Judah, 860 B.C. *9*D-E5
Jugurtha, Kingdom of *25*
Jülich *61*E4
Jülich, County of, 1648 *67*B3
Julius Caesar, Temple of
Rome *31*C6(7)
Jumna (river) *80*E2
Juno Moneta, Temple of
Rome *31*A5
Jupiter, Temple of, Rome *31*A6
Jüterbog *91*C3
Jutland *44*C3
Jutland, Battle of
31 May 1916 *98*C2

K

Kabelvåg *70*C1
Kabul *22*F2, *42*C3
Kadesh *6*C2
Kadesia *33*D3
Kaffa (*mod.* Feodosiya)
*42*A1, *52*D1, *72*C5
Kaffraria, *c.* 1900 *95*C2
Kaine *11*A3
Kairouan *57*C5
Kaiserswerth *38*B2
Kajana *70*E2
Kalach (Nimrud) *8*B1
Kalahari Desert *95*B1
Kalisz *67*E3
Kalka *42*B1
Kalmar *44*D2, *70*B4
Kalocsa *49*F4
Kama (river) *72*E3
Kamchatka *105*C-D1
Kamerun (Cameroon) *96*C4
Kammin (town) *44*D4, *70*B5
Kammin, Bishopric of, 1648 *67*D1
Kampen *61*D2
Kandahar *22*F3, *42*B4
Kanesh *6*B1
Kano *96*C4
Kansas, 1861–65 *92*C3
Kappel *48*C5
Karachi *97*B3
Karakorum *42*D2
Karbala *8*B4, *33*D3
Kardis *70*D3
Karelia
1660 *70*E3 1725 *72*B3
Karikal *80*E5, *97*C5
Karlowitz (Karlovci)
*71*E3, *76*E4

Karlsbad (Karlovy Vary)
*86*C3, *91*C4
Karlshamn *73*B1
Karlskrona *70*B4, *76*D2
Karlsruhe *91*B4
Karlstad *70*B3
Karnak *2*B3
Kars *97*B2
Kashgar *42*C3
Kashmir
1858 *80*D-E1
1914 *97*C3
Kassel *73*A2, *91*B3
Kassites *6*E2
Katyn *104*D4
Kaufbeuren *67*C5
Kazan *72*D3
Kazan, Khanate of *72*D-E3–4
Keksgolm (county), 1660 *70*E2–3
Keksgolm (town) *70*E3
Kempten *67*C5
Kenilworth *51*C2
Kenninghall *62*C1
Kensington, London *66*A6
Kent *51*C3, *65*E4
Kentucky, 1861–65 *92*D3–4
Kenya, 1968 *108*B-C3
Kerbela *see* Karbala
Kerch *11*F1
Kerma *2*A5
Kesselsdorf *81*C4
Kharkov *72*C4
Khartoum *96*D4
Khiva *97*B2
Khorsabad *8*B1
Kiangsi *97*E3
Kiaochow *97*E2

Kiel *44*C4, *91*C1
Kiev *42*A1, *72*B4, *74*D5
Kilkenny *65*B4
Killiecrankie *65*C2
Kimberley *95*B1
Kings, Valley of the *2*A3, *5*
King's road, between
Susa and Sardes *10*A-D2–4
Kinross *65*E1
Kinsai (*mod.* Hangchow) *42*F3
Kinshasa (Leopoldville)
*108*B4
Kipr (Cyprus) *37*E5
Kirkholm *70*D4
Kirkuk *8*C2
Kish *8*C4
Kistna (*mod.* Krishna, river) *80*E4
Klara (river) *70*B3
Kobe *97*F2
Koblenz *38*B2
Koburg *63*D5
Kokenhusen *44*F2
Kolberg *44*D4, *82*D1
Kolin *82*D4
Komarov *100*F4
Königsberg *44*E3, *76*E2
Konya *60*D4
Korea, *c.* 1300 *42*F2
1914 *97*F2
1941–42 *105*B1
1942–45 *106*B4
1968 *108*E1
Kottbus *81*D3
Kotyora *24*C4
Kourland

1370 *44*E3 1660 *70*D4
1721 *76*E2 1795 *84*E1
1796 *72*A3 1812 *86*D1
Kovno *73*C1
Kragerø *70*A3
Krak *41*C3
Krakow *39*E3, *43*D2, *44*E5
Krakow, Republic of,
1815 *87*C3
Krasnik *100*E3
Krefeld *82*B3
Kremsmünster *36*E5
Kringen *70*A2
Kronborg *70*A4
Kronstadt *72*B3
Kuban (province) *60*D2
Kuban (river) *72*C5
Kufa *33*E3
Kunersdorf *82*D2
Kura (river) *72*D-E6
Kurdistan *24*D5
Kurhesse *91*B-C3
Kuril Is. *97*F1, *105*C1
Kurisches Haff *100*E1
Kurna *2*B3
Kush (Nubia) *2*A-B5
Küstrin *81*D3
Kut *8*C4
Kutno *100*E3
Kuwait, 1914 *96*E3, *97*A3
1919–35 *101*E2 1968 *107*F5
Kvikne *70*A2
Kwajalein *106*D6
Kweichow *97*E3
Kyffhäuser *39*D3

L

Labrador *58*B2
La Chapelle *1*A2
La Charité, Paris *83*A3
Lachish *9*D4
La Cité, Paris *83*B3
La Conciergerie, Paris *83*B2(5)
Laconia *14*B3
Lade *37*C1
Ladoga, Lake *70*E3
Ladrone (Mariana) Is. *58*F4
Ladysmith *95*C1
Laerdal *70*A2
Lagash *8*C5
Lagos *96*B4
La Grosse *59*C3
Lahore *97*C3
Laibach (*mod.* Ljubljana) *86*D4
Lake of the Woods *59*C3
La Madeleine, Paris *83*A1
La Mancha *55*C5
La Marche *62*C4
Lambaesis (*mod.* Lambèse) *29*B4
Lambeth, London *66*C6
Lamia *14*B2

Lampsacus (*mod.* Lapseki) *11*E2
Lancashire *65*D3
Lancaster (county) *51*B1
Lancaster (town) *51*B1
Landau *67*B4
Landsberg *64*E4
Landshut *82*D5
Langanes *37*A1
Langres *50*E1, *99*C5
Languedoc, 1429 *51*C-D6
1562–92 *62*C-D4–5
Lanuvium (*mod.* Lanuvio) *25*E2
Laon *43*C2, *51*D3
La Orilla *59*B5
Laos
1914 *97*E4 1968 *108*E2
La Paz *56*E4, *88*E3
Lapland *70*D1
La Rabida *55*A6
Larach *8*C4
Laredo *59*B4
Larisa *14*B2
La Rochelle *62*B3
Larsa *8*C5

La Salle, route of *59*C3–4
Las Vegas *59*B3
Latin Empire, 1100 *40*
greatest extent (1204) *52*
Latin States
1265 *52* 1355 *53*
Latium *23*C2
Latvia, *1919–35* *101*C1
1939–41 *103*C2 1968 *107*C2
Lauenburg, 1865 *91*C2
Laus *16*D1 . .
Lausanne *48*A6
Lausitz, 1630 *64*E5
Lavant *49*E4
La Vérendrye, route of *59*B-C3
Lavinium *21*A1
Lea (river) *66*E6
Lebanon Mts. *9*E1
Lebanon *107*E5
Lechfeld *38*C3
Leeds *65*D3
Leghorn *85*B2
Legnano, Milan *39*C4
Legnano, Verona *85*C1
Le Havre *62*B2
Leicester (town) *65*E4
Leicester (county) *65*D-E4
Leiden *61*C2
Leighlin *49*A1
Leinster *65*B4
Leipzig *43*D2, *64*D5
Leith *65*E1
Lek (river) *68*B3
Le Mans *43*B3, *49*B3
Lemberg (Lvov) *84*E4, *100*F4
Lemnos *20*C2
Leningrad (St Petersburg, Petrograd)
*101*C1, *104*D4
Leon (town) *43*A4, *55*B4
Leon (kingdom), 1037 *54*D1
c. 1100 *39*A4, *54*A2
1180 *54*D2
Leonidaeum, Olympia *18*A2
Leontini (*mod.* Lentini) *16*C3
Leopoldville *see* Kinshasa
Lepanto *57*D5
Leptis magna (*mod.* Lebda)
*11*C4, *28*C5
Leptis minor (*mod.* Lamta) *11*C3
Le Puy *43*C3, *51*D5
Lerida *39*B5, *43*B4
Lesbos, ancient *14*E2
1878 *93*C3 1912–13 *94*C6
Lescar *49*B5
Lesna *73*D2
Lesotho (formerly Basutoland) *108*B5
Lesser Armenia, 1140 *40*B-C1
1265 *52*D2 1355 *53*D5
Le Temple, Paris *83*C2
Leucas *14*A2, *20*A3
Leuctra *14*C2, *15*B5
Leuthen *82*E3
Leven, Loch *65*E1
Lewis and Clark, route of *59*A-C3
Lexington *78*F2
Leyte *106*B5

Lhasa *97*D3
Libau *73*C1
Liberia
1914 *96*A4 1968 *108*A3
Libreville *96*C5
Libya, 500 B.C. *10*A3
814 *33*C4
1914–18 *98*C-D5
1919–35 *101*B-C2
1942–45 *104*B-C6
1968 *108*B2
Libyan Desert *10*A4
Lichfield *43*B1, *49*B1
Liechtenstein, Principality of
*67*C5
Liège *61*D4
Liège, Bishopric of, 1579 *61*D4
1648 *67*B3 1756–63 *82*A3
Liegnitz *82*D3
Lierre *61*C3
Liger (*mod.* Loire, river) *27*D-E3
Ligny *86*C3
Liguria *23*A1
Ligurian Republic, 1797–1805
*85*A-B2
Ligurians *11*B-C1–2
Lille *61*B4
Lilybaeum (*mod.* Marsala)
*16*A2, *23*C4
Lima *56*D4
Limassol *40*F4
Limburg
1429 *51*E3 1579 *61*D4
Limerick *65*A4
Limoges *43*B3, *51*C5
Limonum (*mod.* Poitiers) *27*E3
Limousin *69*D4
Lincoln (county) *51*C2
Lincoln (town) *43*B1, *49*B1
Lincoln's Inn, London *66*B6
Lindau *67*C5
Lindisfarne *37*B2
Lingen (county), 1702–07 *81*B3
Lingen (town) *82*B2
Linz *82*D5
Lipara (*mod.* Lipari) *16*C2
Liparaeae Is. *16*C2
Lippe (river) *68*C3
Lippe, County of
1648 *67*C3 1871 *91*B3
Lippespring *36*D4
Lisbon *37*A4, *43*A5
Lisieux *49*B3
Lithuania
1100 *39*E1 1263–1386 *74*
1370 *44*F3 1556 *57*D-E1
1660 *70*D-E4–5
1721 *76*E2 1795 *84*E2
1796 *72*A-B4
1919–35 *101*C1
1939–41 *103*C2
1968 *107*C2
Little Bighorn *59*B3
Little Falls *59*D3
Little Poland, 1795 *84*D-E3
Little Rock *59*C3

Little Russia *72*B4
Liverpool *86*B2
Livingstone, route of, 1849–56 *96*
Livonia
1660 *70*D4 1700 *73*C-D1
1721 *76*E1 1725 *72*B3
1772 *84*E-F1 1812 *86*D-E1
Llandaff *49*A2
Lobositz *82*D4
Locri *16*E2
Locris, on Gulf of Corinth *14*B2
Locris, on Strait of Euboea *14*B-C2
Lodi *45*B2, *89*B2
Lodi, Peace of, 1454 *45*
Lodz *100*E3
Lofoten Is. *70*B1
Loire (river) *51*D4
Lolland *44*C3
Lombards *32*D3
Lombardy
774 *34* 962 *38*B3–4
1800 *85*B1 1815 *87*B-C3
1859 *89*B1 1860 *90*B3
Londinium (*mod.* London) *29*B1
London *39*B2, *43*B2, *44*A4
c. 1600 (detail) *66*
London Bridge *66*C6
Londonderry *65*B3
Long Island *78*F2
Lorch *43*C2
Lorraine, 1100 *39*C3
c. 1630 *64*B6 1648 *67*B4–5
1914–18 *99*C3–4
1919–35 *101*B2
Lorraine, Lower, Duchy of
936 *38*A2
Lorraine, Upper, Duchy of
*38*A-B2
Los Angeles *59*A3, *92*A4
Lot (river) *69*D-E4
Lothair, Kingdom of, 843 *36*
Louis VII (Crusade) *40*B1
Louis IX (Crusade) *40*B3
Louis the German, Kingdom of,
843 *36*
Louisburg *77*B3
Louisiana, 1700 *77*B2
1713 *77*A4 1763 *77*B4
1861–65 *92*C-D4–5
Louvain *43*C2, *61*C4
Louvre, Paris *83*B2

Luanda *96*C5
Lübeck *44*C4, *67*C2
Lublin *74*B5
Lucania *23*D3
Lucca (town) *43*C4, *45*C3
Lucca, 1454 *45*C3
1701 *71*D4 1721 *76*D5
1799–1805 *85*B2
1812 *86*C4 1815 *87*C4
Lucera *38*D5
Lucknow *80*E2
Luçon *49*B4, *62*B3
Lugano *102*D5
Lugdunensis (Roman province)
*28*B1, *29*B2
Lugdunum (*mod.* Lyon) *27*F3
Luleå *70*D2
Luna *37*C4
Lund *39*D2, *43*D1
Lüneburg (town) *44*C4
Lüneburg, Duchy of
c. 1630 *64*C4
1648 *67*C2
Lunéville *86*C3
Luristan *60*E-F4
Lusatia, March of *38*D1
Lusitania, during Punic Wars *25*A3
A.D. 117 *29*A3
Lutetia (*mod.* Paris) *27*E2
Lutherans in Europe, 1560 *63*
Lützen *64*D5
Luxemburg *61*E5
Luxemburg, Grand Duchy of
1579 *61*D-E5 1815 *87*B3
1871 *91*A-B4
1914–18 *99*C2–3
1968 *107*B3
Luxor *2*B3
Luzern (canton) *48*C5
Luzern (town) *48*C5
Luzon *106*B5
Lvov (Lemberg) *84*E4, *100*F4
Lycaonia, 44 B.C. *28*E3
A.D. 117 *29*D4
Lycia, 189 B.C. *26*B3
44 B.C. *28*E4 A.D. 117 *29*D4
Lyctus *12*C
Lycopolis (*mod.* Assiut) *2*A2
Lydia *10*A-B2, *11*E3
Lynn *44*A4
Lys (river) *61*A-B4

M

Maas (Meuse, river)
*61*D4–5, *99*C1–4
Maastricht *61*D4
Macao *75*E3, *97*E4
Macaria *49*E5
Macedonia *14*A-B1
during Peloponnesian War *21*D1
under Alexander the Great *22*A1

44 B.C. *28*D3 A.D. 117 *29*C3
1453 *60*B3
1912–13 *94*B-C5
Macchu Picchu *56*E4
Mackenzie, routes of *59*B1–2
Mackenzie (river) *59*B1–2
Mâcon *49*C4
Mactan *58*F4

Madagascar, *c.* 1600 *58*D4
1914 *96*E5–6 1968 *108*C4–5
Madeira (river) *88*E2
Madeira (island), *c.* 1600 *58*C3
c. 1750 *75*C3 1914 *96*A3
Madras *79*C2, A5, *80*E4
Madrid *55*C5, *86*B4
Maeander (*mod.* Menderes, river) *20*E3
Maeotis Palus (*mod.* Sea of Azov) *28*E2
Maere *37*C1
Mafeking *95*C1
Magdeburg *43*D2, *44*C5
Magdeburg, Archbishopric of
1648 *67*C2 1680 *81*C3
1756–63 *82*C2
Magellan, route of, 1519–22 *58*
Magellan, Strait of *58*B5
Magenta *89*A2
Magersfontein *95*B1
Maggiore, Lake *89*A1
Magna Graecia *16*
Magyars, *c.* 900 *37*D3–4
raids in 10th century *38*
Mahé *79*A5, *80*D4, *97*C5
Mahratta confederacy, 1780 *79C*
Maillezais *49*B4
Main (river) *67*C4
Maine, France
1100 *39*B3 1180–1453 *50*
1429 *51*B4
1562–92 *62*B3
Maine, U.S.A., 1861–65 *92*E2
Mainz *37*C3, *43*C2, *44*B5
Mainz, Archbishopric of
1648 *67*B-C4
Majuba Hill *95*C1
Malabar Coast *80*D5
Malaca (*mod.* Malaga) *11*A3
Malacca (town) *97*E5
Malacca (state), *c.* 1600 *58*E4
1941–42 *105*A3
1942–45 *106*A6
Malaga *55*B6
Malatya *6*C1
Malawi (formerly Nyasaland) *108*B4
Malaya, 1914
(Federated Malay States) *97*E5
Malaysia, Federation of *108*E3
Mallorca
1476 *55*E5 1701 *71*C5
1721 *76*C6
1812 *86*B5
See also Balearic Is.
Malmaison *86*B3
Malmö *44*C3
Malplaquet *71*C2
Malta
1230 *40*C5 1556 *57*D5
1721 *76*D6
1798–1800 *85*D5
1812 *86*D6 1815 *87*C5
1914 *96*C3
1914–18 *98*C5
1919–35 *101*B2
1968 *107*C5
Maltaya *8*B1
Mameluke Empire *42*A3, *52*E2
Man, I. of
c. 900 *37*B2
1100 *39*B2 1429 *51*B1
c. 1650 *65*C3
Manchester *65*D3
Manchukuo (Manchuria), 1941–2 *105*B1
Manchuria
1914 *97*E1 1941–2 *105*B1
Mandalay *97*D4
Mandurai *80*D5
Mangalore *80*D4
Manila *97*F4, *105*B2
Mannheim *91*B4
Mansfeld, County of, 1648 *67*C3
Mantinea *15*A6
Mantua *23*B1, *45*C2
Mantua, Duchy of
1454 *45*C2 1721 *76*D4
Manzanares el Real *55*C5
Maras *6*C2, *41*C1
Marathon *14*C3, *15*D6
Marburg *38*B2, *44*B5
Marche *69*D3
Marches, The *90*C3–4
Marcianople *32*E4
Marcomanni *29*C2
Mardonius, naval attack of 492 B.C. *20*
Mare Adriaticum (Adriatic Sea) *28*C-D2–3
Mare Cantabricum (Bay of Biscay) *28*A2
Mare Caspium (Caspian Sea) *29*E3
Mare Ibericum *28*A4
Mare Internum (Mediterranean Sea) *28* A-E3–4
Marengo *85*A2
Mare Tyrrhenum (Tyrrhenian Sea) *28*C3
Mari *8*A3
Mariana (Ladrone) Is.
1941–45 *105*C2, *106*C5
1968 *108*F2
Marienbad *102*D4
Marienburg, Livonia *70*E4
Marienburg, East Prussia *44*E4, *70*C5
Marienwerder *82*E1
Marignano *57*C3
Maritsa (river) *39*F5
Mark, 1614 *81*B3–4
1648 *67*B3 1756–63 *82*B3
Markland *58*B2
Marlborough, expedition of *71*
Marmara, Sea of *20*D-E1
Marne (river) *51*D4, *99*A-C4
Marrakesh *33*A5
Mars, Field of
(Campus Martius) *30*B-C1–2
Marsala *90*C6
Marseille *36*C6, *76*C5

Marshall Is. *105*D2, *106*D5
Marstrand *76*D1
Martinique, 1750 *75*B3
Maryland
1700 *77*B1 1783 *78*E3
1861–65 *92*E3, F4
Masovia *74*B5
Massachusetts
1783 *78*F2 1861–65 *92*E2
Massagetae *22*D-E2
Massawa *96*E4
Massilia (*mod.* Marseille)
*25*D2, *27*F4
Massinissa, Empire of *25*
Masulipatam (*mod.* Bandar) *79*A2
Masurian Lakes *100*E2
Matrona (*mod.* Marne, river) *27*E-F2
Maubeuge *99*B2
Mauretania, 104–46 B.C. *25*B5
44 B.C. *28*A4 A.D. 117 *29*A3
1914 *96*A4 1968 *108*A2
Mauritius *108*C5
Maya civilization *56*C1
Mayan Kingdom
7th century *56* 1520 *56*
Mayapan *56*B1
Mayfair, London *66*B6
Mazaca (Caesarea, *mod.* Kayseri)
*26*C2
Mazara *16*A3
Meaux *49*B3, *62*D2
Mecca *33*E5
Mechelen *61*C4
Mecklenburg
1100 *39*D2 *c.* 1630 *64*D4
1812 *86*C2 1815 *87*C2
Mecklenburg-Güstrow, Duchy of
1648 *67*D2
Mecklenburg-Schwerin, Duchy of
1648 *67*C2 1871 *91*C2
Media *10*D3
Median Kingdom, 600 B.C. *7*
Medici, activities in west and
central Europe *c.* 1500 *46*
Medina *33*E4
Medinaceli *55*C5
Medina Sidonia *55*B6
Mediolanum (*mod.* Milan) *23*B1
Mediterranean Sea *11*
Meerut *97*C3
Megara, Greece *14*C3, *15*C6
Megara, Sicily *16*C3
Megiddo *9*E3
Meidum *2*A2
Meissen *49*D2, *82*D3
Meissen, March of *38*D2
Mekong (river) *42*E5
Melinde *58*D4
Melita (Malta) *11*C3
Melos *14*D4
Memel (river) *39*E2
Memel (town) *44*E3, *70*D4, *76*E2,
*102*E3
Memelland, 1939 *102*E3
Memmingen *64*C6, *67*C5
Memnon, Colossi of *5*

Memphis, Egypt *2*A1, *29*D5
Memphis, Tennessee *59*C4, D4
Mende *49*B5
Mentuhotep, Mortuary temple of *5*
Merano *39*D4
Mercia *36*B4
Merenptah, Mortuary temple of *5*
Merida *39*A5
Merseburg *44*C5
Merv *42*B3, *97*B2
Mesopotamia
at the time of Hammurabi *8*
under Alexander the Great *22*C3
Roman province *29*E4
814 *33*D3
1680 *60*E4
Mespila (Nineveh) *24*D5
Messana (*mod.* Messina) *16*D2
Messenia *14*B3
Messina *43*D5
c. 1800 *85*D4 1860 *90*D5
Messina, Strait of *16*D2
Metauro (river) *35*E2
Metaurum *16*D2
Methone *53*A6
Metz *37*C3, *64*B6, *99*C3
Meuse (Maas, river)
*61*D5, *99*B-C2–4
Mexico
c. 1600 *58*A3 *c.* 1750 *75*B3
Mexico, Gulf of *77*
Mexico City *56*A1, *58*A3, *59*B5
Mézières *62*D2
Michigan *92*D2
Michigan, Lake *59*C3, *78*D1–2
Middelburg *68*B4
Middlesex *66*C6
Midea (Dendra) *15*B6
Midway I. *105*D2
Miklagard (*mod.* Istanbul) *37*E4
Milan *43*C3, *45*B1
Milan, Duchy of, 1454 *45*B1–2
1701 *71*D3–4 1721 *76*D4
Mile End, London *66*D6
Miletus *20*D4
Minden (town) *49*D1, *82*C2
Minden, Bishopric of
1648 *67*C2, *81*B3
Minerva, Temple of, Rome *31*C5
Minneapolis *92*C2
Minnesota *92*C2
Minoan-Mycenaean territory
*6*A-B2
Minoans *12*
Minorca
*55*E5 1701 *71*C5
1721 *76*C5 1812 *86*B5
See also Balearic Is.
Minsk *73*D2
Mirandola *45*C2
Mississippi (river) *59*C3–4, *78*D1–3
Mississippi (state) *92*D4
Missouri (river) *59*B-C3, *92*C2–3
Missouri (state) *92*C-D3–4
Misurata *60*A4
Mitanni, *c.* 1400 B.C. *6*C-D2

Moab *9*E5
Modena *45*C2
Modena, Duchy of
1454 *45*C2 1701 *71*D4
1721 *76*D4 1815 *87*C4
1859–60 *89*C2, *90*B3
Modoc Indians *59*A3
Modrusch *49*E4
Møen *82*C1
Moeris, Lake *2*A2
Moesia, A.D. 117 *29*C3
Mogilev *73*D2, *101*D1
Mogul Empire *79A, B*
Moguntiacum (*mod.* Mainz) *29*B2
Mohacs *60*B1, *76*E4
Moldavia (river) *82*D4
Moldavia
1556 *57*E3 1680 *60*C2
1701 *71*F3 1721 *76*F3–4
1812 *86*E3 1878 *93*C1
Molde *70*A2
Mollwitz *81*E4
Moluccas *58*F4, *108*F3
Mombasa *58*D4, *96*E5
Monaco (town) *85*A2
Monaco, Principality of, 1860 *90*A3
1914–18 *98*C3 1968 *107*B4
Mondovi *49*C5, *85*A2
Mongolia, *c.* 1300 *42*D-E2
1914 *97*D-E2
1941–42 *105*A1
Monreale *38*D6, *43*D5
Monrovia *96*A4
Mons (Bergen) *68*B5
Montana *92*B2
Mont Cenis *25*D1
Monte Alban *56*A1
Monte Cassino *34*B2, *43*D4
Montenegro, 1520 *60*B2
1701 *71*E4 1721 *76*E5
1812 *86*D4 1878 *93*A-B2
1912–13 *94*A-B5
1914–18 *98*D4
1919–35 *101*C2
Montereau *51*D4
Montevideo *88*E4
Montferrat, 1454 *45*A2
Montmartre, Paris *83*B1
Montone (river) *35*D1
Montpellier *43*C4
Montreal *59*D3, *92*E2
Mont St Michel *43*B2
Montu, Temple of *4*
Monza *38*B3
Moravia, 814 *33*B2
843 *36*E4 *c.* 900 *37*C3
962 *38*E2 1100 *39*D3
1556 *57*D2 1648 *67*E4
1721 *76*D3 1756–63 *82*E4
1871 *91*D4 1939 *102*D4
Moray *65*C2
Moray Firth *65*D1
Morea, 1556 *57*E5
1701 *71*F5 1721 *76*E6
1812 *86*E5 1878 *93*B3
1912–13 *94*B-C6

Morgarten *48*C5
Morges *48*A6
Morocco
814 *33*A4–5 *c.* 1600 *58*C3
1812 *86*A5–6
1914 *96*B3
1914–18 *98*A-B4
1919–35 *101*A2
1939–45 *104*A6
1968 *108*A2
Morotai *106*B6
Mosa (*mod.* Maas or Meuse, river)
*27*F1–2
Moscow *42*B1, *72*C3
Moscow, Principality of
c. 1300 *72*C3
Grand Duchy of, 1462 *72*C-D3–4
Mosel or **Moselle** (river)
*67*B4, *99*C2–4
Mosella (*mod.* Mosel or Moselle, river)
*27*F2
Moslems in Europe, 1560 *63*
Moss *70*B3
Mossel Bay *95*B2
Mosul *33*D3, *60*E4
Moulins *62*D3
Moutiers *49*C4
Mozambique (state),
1750 *75*D4
1915 *96*D-E5–6
1968 *108*B-C4–5
Mozambique (town) *58*D4, *96*E5
Mühlberg *57*D2
Mühlhausen *57*C2, *64*C5, *67*C3
Mukden (*mod.* Shenyang)
*97*E2, *105*B1
Mülhausen (Mulhouse)
*48*B5, *64*B6, *82*B5
Mulhouse *82*B5
Münchengrätz *91*D4
Munda *28*A3
Munich *76*D4
Munster *65*A4
Münster *44*B5, *67*B3
Münster, Bishopric of
1648 *67*B3
Murat *62*C4
Murcia *55*D6
Murmansk *103*D1
Murray *65*E1
Muscat *97*B3
Muscat and Oman *108*C2
Mussolini, conquests of
1935–39 *102*
Mut, Temple of *4*
Mutina (*mod.* Modena) *23*B1
Mycale, Mt. *20*D4
Mycenae *14*B3, *15*B6
Mycerinus, pyramid of *3*
Myconos *14*D3
Mylae *16*C2, *25*F4
Myriandrus *11*F3, *24*C5
Mysia *26*A2
Mysore *79*A5, *80*D-E4
Mytilene *14*E2, *21*F2
Mytistratum *16*C2

Nagasaki *97*F2, *106*B5
Nagoya *97*F2
Nagpur *80*E3
Nahr-el-Kelb *9*E1
Nairobi *96*E5
Naissus (Nish) *32*D4
Nakwitchevan *60*E3
Namur *61*C4
Namur, County of
1579 *61*C4 1648 *68*B5
Nancy *64*B6
Nanking *97*E3, *105*B2
Nantes *43*B3, *62*B3
Naples *43*D4, *90*D4
Naples, Kingdom of
1454 *45*E4 1556 *57*D4–5
1701 *71*D-E4–5
1721 *76*D-E5–6
c. 1800 *85*C-E3–4
See also Two Sicilies, Kingdom of the
Narbada (*mod.* Narmada, river) *80*E3
Narbo Martius (*mod.* Narbonne) *27*E4
Narbonensis, 44 B.C. *28*B2–3
A.D. 117 *29*B2–3
Narbonne *32*B4, *51*D6
Narni *35*E2
Narva *44*F1, *70*E3
Narvik *103*C1
Naseby *65*D4
Nassau
1648 *67*B3–4 1866 *91*B4
Natal, *c.* 1900 *95*C-D1
NATO countries, 1968 *107*
Naucratis *2*A1
Naulochus *28*C4
Naumburg *49*D2
Naupactus *14*B2
Navaho Indians *59*A3
Navarino *86*E5
Navarre
c. 900 *54*B1 1037 *54*D1
c. 1100 *54*B2 1180 *54*D2
1230 *40*A2 1476 *55*C4
1556 *57*B3
Naxos (island) *14*E3
Naxos, Duchy of *52*B2
Naxus (*mod.* Capo di Schiso) Sicily *16*D2
Nazareth *41*B5
Neanderthal *1*A1
Neapolis (*mod.* Naples), Italy *23*C2
Neapolis, Sardinia *23*A3
Nearchus, voyage of, 325 B.C. *22*
Near East, *c.* 1400 B.C. *6*
Nebraska *92*C3
Neckar (river) *82*B4
Necropolis, Thebes *5*
Neerwinden *68*C5
Negapatam *79*A2, C2
Negeb *9*D5
Negro (river) *56*E3
Nellore *80*E4
Nelson (river) *59*C2

Nemausus (*mod.* Nîmes) *27*F4
Nemea *15*B6
Neo-Babylonian Empire
600 B.C. *7*A-C5–6
Nepal, 1858 *80*E2
1914 *97*C3 1968 *108*D2
Nera (river) *35*E2
Nero, Palace of, Olympia *18*D2
Nerva, Forum of, Rome *31*C5
Netherlands, 1556 *57*C1–2
war of independence *61*
after Peace of Westphalia, 1648 *68*
Netherlands, Kingdom of the
1815 *87*B2–3 1871 *91*A-B2–3
1914–18 *98*C2 1919–35 *101*B1
1939–41 *103*B2 1942–45 *104*B4
1968 *107*B3
See also United Provinces and Holland
Netherlands, Austrian
1721 *76*C3
1756–63 *82*A3–4
See also Netherlands, Spanish and Belgium
Netherlands, Spanish, 1579 *61*
1648 *67*A-B3–4
1701 *71*C2
See also Netherlands, Austrian and Belgium
Netherlands, United
see United Provinces
Netze (river) *82*E2
Neuburg, Principality of
1648 *67*C4–5
Neuchâtel, 1536 *48*A-B5
1707 *81*F4 1800 *85*A1
Neumark, 1455 *81*D3
Neuss *64*B5
Neustria
814 *33*A3 843 *36*B5
Neutra *49*E3
Neva (river) *37*D1
Nevada *92*A3
Nevers (province) *51*D4
Nevers (town) *51*D4
New Amsterdam (*mod.* New York) *77*A1
Newark *76*C2
New Brunswick, 1783 *78*F1
Newbury *65*D4
New Caledonia
1941–42 *105*D3
1942–45 *106*D6
Newcastle *65*D3
New England *77*A1
Newfoundland, 1650–1763 *77*
c. 1750 *75*B2
New Granada, 1831–63 *88*E1
New Guinea
c. 1600 *58*F4 1750 *75*F4
1941–42 *105*C3 1942–45 *106*C6
1968 *108*F4
New Hampshire
1783 *78*F2 1861–65 *92*E2

New Hebrides *105*D3, *106*D6
New Holland (Australia) *58*F5
Newington, London *66*C6
New Jersey
1783 *78*E2–3 1861–65 *92*E3
New Karleby *70*D2
New Mexico, 1912 *92*B4
New Orleans *59*C4, *78*D4, *92*D5
New Sweden *77*A1
New York (state)
1783 *78*E2 1861–65 *92*E2
New York (town) *77*B1, *78*E2, *92*E3
New Zealand *75*F5
Nez Perce Indians *59*A-B3
Niaux *1*A2
Nicaea, Asia Minor
*29*D3, *39*F5, *43*F4
Nicaea (*mod.* Nice) *11*C2, *23*A1
Nicaea, Empire of *40*E3
Nicaragua *56*C2
Nice *36*C5, *90*A3
Nice, County of, 1859–60 *90*A3
Nicephorium *22*C2
Nicobar Is., 1849–1914 *97*D5
Nicolet, route of *59*C3
Nicomedia *20*E1
Nicopolis *53*B4
Nicosia *107*D5
Niemen (river) *70*D4
Nieuport *68*A4, *99*A1
Niger (river) *96*A-B4
Niger (state) *108*A-B2–3
Nigeria
1914 *96*B-C4 1968 *108*A-B3
Nijmegen *68*C3
Nike, sanctuary of
Acropolis, Athens *13*
Nike, Paeonius's statue of
Olympia *18*C2
Nike, statue of, Delphi *19*D4
Nike, Temple of
Acropolis, Athens *17*B4
Nikolsburg *91*D5
Nile (river) *2*, *96*D3–4
Nilus (*mod.* Nile, river) *28*D5
Nîmes *36*B5
Nimrud *8*B1
Nine Elms, London *66*B6
Nineveh *6*D2, *8*B1, *24*D5
Nipigon, Lake *59*C3
Nippur *8*C4
Nish *32*D4, *76*E5
Nizam, dominions of the
1858 *80*E3–4
1914 *97*C4
Nizhni-Novgorod (*mod.* Gorki) *72*D3
Noli *49*C5
Nordhausen *67*C3
Nördlingen *64*C6, *67*C4, *81*C5
Nordmark *38*C-D1
Noreia (*mod.* Neumark) *28*C2
Norfolk *65*E4
Noricum (Roman province) *29*B-C2
Normandy
c. 900 *37*B3 1100 *39*B3
1180–1453 *50* 1429 *51*B-C3

Normans, Kingdom of the, 1154 *38*
Norrköping *70*C3
North America
c. 1600 *58* 1650–1763 *77*
1750 *75* 1783 *78*
1783–1912 *92*
1861–65 (Civil War) *92*
North Borneo, 1914 *97*E-F5
North Bukovina *103*C2
North Cape *72*B1
North Carolina
1783 *78*E3
1861–65 *92*E4
North Dakota, 1889 *92*C2
Northeastern Europe, 1660 *70*
Northern Rhodesia *see* Zambia
Northern States, 1861–65 *92*
North German Confederation
1886–71 *91*
North Korea *108*E1
North Schleswig *101*B1
North Sea *76*C2
Northumberland *51*C1
North Vietnam *108*E2
North Wales *36*A4
Northwest Greeks
(North Dorians) *14*
Norton Sound *59*B1
Norvasund (Strait of Gibraltar) *37*A5
Norway, *c.* 900 *37*C1
1370 *44*B-C1–2
1815 *87*B-C1
1914–18 *98*C1 1919–35 *101*B1
1939–41 *103*B-C1
1942–45 *104*C4
1968 *107*B1–2
See also Denmark for the
period 1397–1814
Norwich *65*E4
Nöteborg *70*E3, *72*C3
Notre Dame, Paris *83*B3
Nottingham (county) *65*D-E3
Nottingham (town) *65*E4
Novara *89*A2
Nova Scotia
1650–1763 *77* 1783 *78*F1
1783–1912 *92*F2
Novaya Zemlya *58*D1
Novgorod (town) *44*F1, *72*B3
Novgorod, Republic of
1370 *44*F1–2
1462–1605 72B-C3
Novi *85*A2
Noyon *49*B3, *62*D2
Nubia *2*A-B5
Numantia
(*mod.* Cerro de Garray) *25*B2
Numidia, during Punic Wars *25*D5
44 B.C. *28*B-C4
A.D. 117 *29*B4
Nuremberg *38*C2, *67*C4
Nursia *35*E2
Nyasa, Lake *96*D5
Nyasaland *see* Malawi
Nyslott *70*E2
Nystad *76*E1

O

Oaxaca *56*B1
Ob (river) *42*C1
Oceanus Atlanticus
(Atlantic Ocean) *29*A1–2
Oceanus Britannicus *28*A-B1
Oder (river) *67*D-E2–3
Odessa *86*E3
Oeta, Mt. *14*B2
Ofen (Buda) *84*D5
Ohio (river) *78*D3
Ohio (state) *92*D3
Oise (river) *99*B3
Oka (river) *72*D3
Okinawa *106*B5
Oklahoma *92*C4
Öland
1370 *44*D3 1660 *70*B4
Olbia, Sardinia *25*E3
Olbia, on Black Sea *11*E1
Oldenburg, 1648 *67*B2
1815 *87*B2 1871 *91*B2
Old Karleby *70*D2
Old Sarum *86*B2
Old Spanish Trail *59*A-C3
Oliva *81*E2
Olmütz *82*E4
Oloron *49*A5
Olympia *14*B3, *18*
Olympus, Mt. *14*B1
Olynthus *14*C1
Omaha *92*C3
Oman
814 *33*F3 1914 *97*B3–4
Ombos 2B3
Ombrone (river) *35*D2
Omdurman *96*D4
Onega (river) *72*C2
Onega, Lake *72*C3
Ontario, Lake *59*D3, *78*E2
Oporto *39*A4, *55*A5, *86*A4
Oradea Mare (Grosswardein) *49*F3
Oran *32*A5
Orange (river) *95*A-C1–2
Orange (town) *43*C4, *69*E4
Orange, Principality of *69*E4
Orange Free State, *95*C1–2, *96*D6
Orbetello *85*B3
Orchomenus *15*B5
Örebro *70*B3
Oregon *92*A2
Oregon City *59*A3

Oregon Trail *59*B-C3
Öreting *37*C1
Orissa *80*E-F3
Orkney Is.
c. 900 *37*B1 1370 *44*A1
1914–18 *98*B1 1968 *107*B2
Orléanais *69*D-E2
Orléans (province) *51*C-D4
Orléans (town) *37*B3, *43*B3
Ormuz *42*B4, *58*D3
Orontes (river) *41*C2–4
Ortospana (*mod.* Kabul) *22*F2
Orvieto *45*D3
Osaka *97*F2
Oseberg *37*C1
Ösel, 1100 *39*E1
1370 *44*E2 1660 *70*D3
1725 *72*A3 1914–18 *98*D1
Oslo *44*C1, *103*C1
Osnabrück *44*B4, *67*B2
Osnabrück, Bishopric of
1648 *67*B2
Osrhoene (Roman province) *29*E4
Ossa, Mt. *14*B1
Ossero *49*E5
Ostend *61*A3
Österbotten *70*D2
Ostia *35*D3
Ostmark *38*D3
Ostrogoths *32*E2
Ostrogoths, Kingdom of the
526 *32*C-D3–5
Ostrolenka *91*E2
Otchakov *73*E3
Otranto *76*E5
Ottawa (river) *78*E1
Ottawa Indians *59*C-D3
Ottoman Empire, 1355 *53*C5
1355–1680 *60*
1556 *57*D-F3–5
1701 *71*E-F2–5
1721 *76*E-F4–6
1812 *86*D-F3–5
1815 *87*C4
See also Turkey
Oudenarde *71*C2
Oudh
1858 *80*E2 1914 *97*C3
Overijssel *61*E2
Oxford *43*B2, *65*D4
Oxus (river) *22*E2

P

Pacific Ocean, during Second
World War, *105*, *106*
Pacific Railway
Chicago-San Francisco *92*A-D3
Montreal-Vancouver *92*A-E1–2
Paderborn *36*C4
Paderborn, Bishopric of
1648 *67*C3 1756–63 *82*B3

Padua *43*C3, *45*D2
Padus (*mod.* Po, river) *25*E1
Paestum (Posidonia) *23*D2
Pakistan *108*C-D2
Palaeolithic sites *1*
Palaestra, Olympia *18*A1–2
Palais Bourbon, Paris *83*A2
Palais de Justice, Paris *83*B2(5)

Palais du Luxembourg, Paris *83*B3
Palais Royal, Paris *83*B2
Palatina, Rome *30*C3(4)
Palatinate, *c.* 1630 *64*B-C5–6
1648 *67*B4 1815 *87*B3
1871 *91*B4
Palatinate, Upper
c. 1630 *64*D5–6 1648 *67*D4
Palatine, Rome *30*D2
Palencia *43*A4
Palenque *56*B1
Palermo *43*D5
Palestine
44 B.C. *28*F4 A.D. 117 *29*D4
1919–35 *101*D2
1942–45 *104*E6
See also Israel
Palestrina *45*E4
Palma *11*B2, *43*B5
Palmyra *29*D4
Palos *55*A6, *58*C3
Palukut (Fellujah) *8*B3
Pamiers *49*B5
Pamir *97*C2
Pamphylia *20*F4
Roman province *29*D4
Pamplona *55*C4
Panama (state) *88*E1
Panama (town) *56*D2
Pannonia, A.D. 117 *29*C2
Pannonia, March of, 814 *33*B3
Panormus (*mod.* Palermo) *16*B2
Pantelleria *101*B2
Pantheon, Acropolis,
Athens *13*, *17*E4
Pantheon, Paris *83*B4
Papal States
(States of the Church)
756–817 *35*
814 *33*B3 1230 *40*C2–3
1454 *45*D-E3–4
1556 *57*C3–4 1701 *71*D4
1721 *76*D5
c. 1800 *85*C2–3
1815 *87*C4
1860–70 *90*C3–4
Paphlagonia, 189 B.C. *26*B-C1
Paphos *11*F3
Para *88*F2
Paraetonium
(*mod.* Mersa Matruh) *22*A3
Paraguay *88*E3
Parana (river) *88*E-F3–4
Paris *39*C3, *43*C2
1789 (detail) *83*
Parliament, Houses of
London *66*B6
Parma *23*B1, *45*C2
Parma, Duchy of, 1721 *76*D4
1803 *85*B2 1815 *87*C4
1859–60 *89*B2, *90*B3
Parnassus, Mt. *14*B2, *15*A5
Paros *14*D3
Parthenon, old *13*
in classical times *17*C-D4
Parthenopean Republic
1799 *85*C-E3–4
Parthia *10*D-E3
Parthian Kingdom
(Regnum Parthorum) 44 B.C. *28*F3
A.D. 117 *29*E-F3–4
Pasargadae *10*D4
Passau *57*D2, *82*D5
Passau, Bishopric of, 1648 *67*D4
Passchendaele *99*A1
Patagonia *58*B5
1832 *88*E4–5
Patara *26*A3
Patavium (*mod.* Padua) *23*C1
Patay *51*C4
Patmos *14*E3
Patna *97*C4
Patrimonium Petri
c. 750 *35*D-E2–3
c. 900 *37*C4
Pavia *43*C3, *45*B2
Peace (river) *59*B2
Pearl Harbor *105*E2
Pécs (Fünfkirchen) *49*F4
Peenemünde *64*E4
Pegu *97*D4
Peipus, Lake *70*E3
Peking *42*E2, *97*E2
Pelion, Mt. *14*B2
Pella *22*A1
Pelopium, Olympia *18*B2
Peloponnesian War *21*
Peloponnesus *14*B3
Pelusium *2*B1
Pembroke *65*C4
Peneus (river) *14*A-B1–2
Penner (river) *80*E4
Pennsylvania
1783 *78*E2 1861–65 *92*E3
Pensacola *78*D4
Peparethos *14*C2
Pépin the Short's gift
to Papal Chair, 756 *35*
Perevolotchna *73*E2
Pergamum *26*A2, *28*D3
Pergamum, Kingdom of
218–189 B.C. *26*
Périgord *62*C4
Périgueux *49*B4
Pernambuco *75*C4, *88*F2
Pernau *44*E2, *73*C1
Peronne *62*D2, *99*A2
Persepolis *22*D2
Persia
500 B.C. *10*D-E4
300 B.C. *22*D4 1914 *97*B2–3
1914–18 *98*F4 1919–35 *101*E2
1939–41 *103*E3
See also Iran
Persian Empire
c. 500 B.C. *10*, *20*
400 B.C. *24*
Persian Gulf *97*A-B3
Persian wars *20*
Peru, 1533 *56*D4
c. 1600 *57*B4–5
1750 *75*B4 1914 *88*E2–3

Perugia *43*D4, *45*D3
Perusia (*mod.* Perugia) *23*C2
Pesaro *45*D3
Pest *39*E4, *60*B1
Peterborough *43*B1
Petersburg *92*F5
Peter the Great
conquests of, 1682–1725 *72*
Petrograd (*mod.* Leningrad) *98*D1
Petsamo *103*D1
Phaestus *12*C
Phalasarna *12*A
Phar *49*E5
Pharsalus *14*B2, *28*D3
Phidias's workshop
Olympia *18*A-B2
Philadelphia, Asia Minor *53*C5
Philadelphia, U.S.A. *78*E2
Philae *2*B4
Philip Augustus (Crusade) *40*B2
Philippeum, Olympia *18*B1
Philippeville *69*E1
Philippi *14*D1, *28*D3
Philippines, *c.* 1600 *58*F3
1750 *75*E3
1914 *97*F4
1941–42 *105*B2
1942–45 *106*B5
1968 *108*E-F2–3
Philippopolis (*mod.* Plovdiv) *60*C2
Philistines, 860 B.C. *9*D4
Phocaea *14*E2
Phocis *14*B2, *15*A-B5
Phoenicia, 860 B.C. *9*E1–2
500 B.C. *10*B3
Phoenician colonies *11*
Phoenix Is. *105*E3, *106*E6
Phrygia (Galatia) *21*F2, *22*B2
Roman province *28*E3
Piacenza *43*C3, *89*B2
Piave (river) *89*D1
Picardy, 1429 *51*D3
1453 *50*B5
Picenum *23*C2
Picts *32*B1
Piedmont, 1800 *85*A1–2
1859 *89*A1–2, *90*A-B3
Pieve di Cadore *45*D1
Pillars of Hercules
see Columnae Herculis
Pillau *70*C4, *100*E1
Pillnitz *81*D4
Pilsen (*mod.* Plzen) *64*D5, *104*C5
Pindus Mts. *14*A-B2
Pinsk *74*C5
Piombino (state)
1454 *45*C3
1801 *85*B2–3
Piombino (town) *85*B2
Piraeus *15*C6
Pirano *45*E1
Pirna *82*D3
Pisa *23*B1, *43*C4, *45*C3
Pisidia
600 B.C. *7*A5
189 B.C. *26*B3
44 B.C. *28*E3
A.D. 117 *29*D4
Pisino *49*E4
Pistoia *35*D1

Pitesti *73*D3
Pithecussa (*mod.* Ischia) *23*C2
Pithom *10*B4
Pitigliano *45*C3
Pittsburgh *78*E2, *92*E3
Pizarro and Almagro, expedition
in South America, 1532–37 *58*B4–5
Place de la Révolution (Concorde)
Paris *83*A2(1)
Place des Victoires, Paris *83*B2
Placentia *23*B1
Place Vendôme, Paris *83*A1(2)
Plassey *79*A4, *80*F2
Plataea *15*C5
Platte (river) *59*B-C3
Plessis *51*C4
Plevna *93*C2
Plombières-les-Bains *91*B5
Plymouth *65*C5
Po (river) *11*C1, *89*A-D2
Podolia, 1793 *84*E-F4
Poissy *62*C2
Poitiers *33*A3, *43*B3
Poitou
1100 *39*B3
1180–1453 *50*
1429 *51*B5
1562–92 *62*B3
Pola *45*E2
Poland, 1100 *39*D-E2–3
1340–86 *74*
1370 *44*D-E4–5
1556 *57*D-E1–2
1660 *70*B-E4–5
1700 *73*C-D1–2
1701 *71*E-F1–2
1721 *76*D-F2–3
1756–63 *82*E-F1–4
1772, 1793, 1795
(three partitions) *84*
1815 *87*C2
1914–18 *100*E3
1919–35 *101*C1
1939–41 *103*C2
1942–45 *104*C-D4–5
1968 *107*C3
Poles *37*D3
Polis *15*A5
'Polish corridor' *102*E4
Pollentia (*mod.* Piacenza) *32*C4
Polo, Marco, route of
1271–95 *58*E3
Polotsk *44*F3
Poltava *73*E2
Polyrrhenia *12*A
Pomerania
1100 *39*D2
1865 *91*C-D2
Pomerania, Farther
c. 1630 *64*E4
1648 *81*D2
1756–63 *82*D-E1
Pomerania, Hither
c. 1630 *64*D-E4
1648 *67*D1–2
1720 *81*D2
1756–63 *82*D1
Pomerania, Swedish *81*C2
Pomerelia *67*E1–2

Pompeii *23*D2
Pondichéry *79*C2, A5, *80*E4
Pontecorvo (state)
1812 *86*D5 1860 *90*C-D4
Pontecorvo (town) *85*C3
Pont Neuf, Paris *83*B2
Pont Royal, Paris *83*A2
Pontus, 189 B.C. *26*C1
44 B.C. *28*F3 A.D. 117 *29*D3
Pontus Euxinus (Black Sea) *28*E-F2
Popes, adherents of the, during
Great Schism, 1378–1417 *47*
Poplar, London *66*E6
Popocatepetl, Mt. *59*B5
Populonia *35*C2
Porta Caelimontana, Rome *30*E3
Porta Capena, Rome *30*D3
Porta Collina, Rome *30*E1
Porta Esquilina, Rome *30*E2
Porta Naevia, Rome *30*D3
Port Arthur *97*E2
Porta Salutaris, Rome *30*D2
Port Elizabeth *95*C2
Porticus Neronis Margaritaria
Rome *31*C-D6
Portland, England *76*B3
Portland, Oregon *92*A2
Port Royal, France *69*D2
Port Royal, Paris *83*B4
Port Said *96*D3
Port St Simeon *41*C2
Portugal, *c.* 1100 *39*A5, *54*A2
1180 *54*D2–3 1476 *55*A5–6
1556 *57*A4 1701 *71*A4–5
1721 *76*A5–6 1812 *86*A4–5
1815 *87*A4
1914–18 *98*A3–4
1919–35 *101*A2
1939–41 *103*A3
1942–45 *104*A5
1968 *107*A4–5
Portuguese colonies, 1750 *75*
Portuguese Guinea
1914 *96*A4
1968 *108*A3
Portuguese West Africa *see* Angola
Portus Gesoriacus
(*mod.* Boulogne) *27*E1
Portus Namnetum
(*mod.* Nantes) *27*D2
Poseidon, Temple of, Delphi *19*B5
Posen (Poznan) *81*D3, *84*D3
Posen (province), 1865 *91*D2
Posidium (*mod.* Al Mina) *11*F3
Posidonia (Paestum) *21*B2
Potidaea *14*C1
Potomac (river) *78*E3
Potosi *56*E5
Potsdam *82*D2
Poznan *84*D3
Praeneste *23*C2
Praesus *12*D
Prague *43*D2, *82*D4
Prasiae *15*D6
Prato *45*C3
Pressburg (Bratislava)
*39*D3, *43*D3, *71*E3
Prestebakke *86*C1
Preston *65*D3
Pretoria *95*C1
Priene *26*A3
Pripet (river) *84*E-F3
Pripet marshes *72*B4, *100*F3
Pritzwalk *44*C4
Prophthasia *22*E3
Propylaea, Acropolis
Athens *13*, *17*A4
Provence *39*C4, *62*E5
Providence *59*D3
Prussia, 1100 *39*E2
1370 *44*E3 1415–1797 *81*
1660 *70*C-D4–5
1700 *73*C2 1721 *76*E2
1756–63 *82* 1812 *86*D2
1815 *87*B-C2 1865–66 *91*
Prut (river) *39*F3
Prytaneum, Olympia *18*B1
Przemysl *100*F4
Pskov *101*C1
Ptolemy III, Gate of *4*
Pueblo Indians *59*A-B4
Puerto Rico *56*E1, *77*B4
Punic Wars, 264–146 B.C. *25*
Punjab
1858 *80*D1 1914 *97*C3
Punt *2*B5
Purus (river) *56*E4
Pusan *97*F2
Puteoli (*mod.* Pozzuoli) *23*C2
Pydna *14*B1
Pylus *14*B3
Pyramids, at Giza *3*
Pyramus (river) *41*C1
Pyrenaei Montes (Pyrenees) *27*D-E4

Q

Qatna *6*C2
Quai d'Orsay, Paris *83*A2
Quebec *78*F1, *92*E2
Queen Charlotte Sound *59*A2
Quimper *49*A3
Quirinal *30*D1
Quito
*56*D3, *88*D2

Raab (Györ) *49*E3
Raab (river) *76*D-E4
Ragusa (*mod.* Dubrovnik)
1100 *39*E5 1230 *40*D3
1265 *52*A1 1701 *71*E4
1721 *76*E5
Rajputana
1858 *80*D2 1914 *97*C3
Rameses II, Mortuary temple of *5*
Rameses II, Temple of *4*
Rameses III, Mortuary temple of *5*
Rameses III, Temple of *4*
Rameses IV, Mortuary temple of *5*
Ramillies *71*C2
Rangoon *97*D4
Rapallo *102*D5
Ras Shamra (Ugarit) *6*C2
Rastatt *76*C3
Ratzeburg *49*D1
Rauriel *27*F2
Rava *74*A5
Ravenna *23*C1, *38*C4, *43*D4
Ravensberg, 1614 *81*B3
Raymond of Toulouse (Crusade) *40*A2
Reading *65*D4
Red (river) *92*C4
Red Russia, 1772 *84*E4
Red Sea *33*D-E4–5
Regensburg *43*D2, *67*D4
Reggio, Calabria *85*D4
Reggio, Modena *45*C2
Regia, Rome *31*C6(8)
Regnum Bospori (Roman province)
A.D. 117 *29*D2
Regnum Parthorum, 44 B.C. *28*F3
A.D. 117 *29*E-F3–4
Reichenau *38*B3
Religious situation in Europe
1560 *63*
Remagen *104*B5
Rennes *49*B3
Reno (river) *35*D1
Rense *64*C5
Resino *49*F5
Rethel *51*D-E3, *61*C5
Réunion *108*C5
Reval *44*E1, *70*D3
Reykjanes *37*A1
Rhaetia *28*C2
Roman province, A.D. 117 *29*B2
Rhegium
(*mod.* Reggio di Calabria) *16*D2
Rheims *39*C3, *43*C2
Rheinsberg *82*D2
Rhenus (*mod.* Rhine, river) *27*F1
Rhine (river) *38*A1
Rhine, Confederation of the
1254 *44* 1812 *86*C2–3
Rhineland, 1936 *102*C4
Rhine Province, 1865 *91*B3–4
Rhodanus
(*mod.* Rhône, river) *27*F3–4
Rhodae *11*B2
Rhode Island
1783 *78*F2 1861–65 *92*E2
Rhodes, *c.* 1400 B.C. *6*A2
c. 500 B.C. *20*E5
under Alexander the Great *22*B2
189 B.C. *26*A3
(Rhodus) 44 B.C. *28*E4
526 *32*E5 814 *33*C4
1100 *39*F6 1265 *52*C2
1355 *53*C6 1556 *57*E5
1812 *86*E5 1878 *93*D3
1912–13 *94*D6 1914–18 *98*D5
Rhodesia
1914 *96*D5 1968 *108*B4–5
Rhytium *12*C
Ribe *43*C1, *70*A4
Richard the Lionheart's fleet *40*
Richelieu *69*D3
Richmond, England *51*B1
Richmond, Virginia *78*E3, *92*F5
Rievaulx *43*B1
Riga *44*E2, *70*D4
Rijswijk *68*B3
Rimini *23*C1, *45*D2
Rio de Janeiro *58*B5, *88*F3
Rio de la Plata *58*B5
Rio de Oro
c. 1600 *58*C3 1914 *96*A3
Rio Grande (river) *59*B4, *92*B-C4–5
Rio Muni, 1914 *96*C4
Rio Negro (river) *88*E2
Ripon *76*B2
Risør *70*A3
Rivoli *85*B1
Roanoke (river) *92*F5
Robert of Flanders (Crusade) *40*B1
Robert of Normandy (Crusade) *40*A1
Rochefort *76*B4
Rochester *49*B2
Rocroi *69*E1
Rodez *69*E4
Rodriguez I. *108*C5
Roer (river) *61*E3–4
Roermond *68*C4
Roldal *70*A3
Roma and Augustus, Temple of
Acropolis, Athens *17*D4
Romagna, 1454 *45*D2
1859–60 *89*C-D2, *90*C3
Roman Catholic Church
expansion *c.* 1200 *43*
Roman Catholics in Europe, 1560 *62*
Roman Empire, A.D. 117 *29*
Romania
1878 *93*C1 1912–13 *94*C4
1914–18 *98*D3 1919–35 *101*C2
1939–41 *103*C3
1942–45 *104*D5
1968 *107*C-D4
Roman Republic, 44 B.C. *28*
1798–99 *85*C2–3
Roma Quadrata *30*D3
Rome *23*C2, *32*C4, *43*D4, *45*D4
(detail) *c.* 100 B.C. *30*
(detail) at the time of
the emperors *31*

Romulus, Temple of, Rome *31*C6(12)
Roncaglia *39*C4
Roncesvalles *33*A3, *36*A6
Røros *70*B2
Rosendal *70*A3
Rosetta *2*A1
Rosheim *69*F2
Roskilde *43*C1, *70*A4
Rossbach *82*C3
Ross River *59*B2
Rostock *43*C1, *44*C4
Rostra, Rome *31*B6(2)
Rothenburg *64*C6, *67*C4
Rotomagus (*mod.* Rouen) *27*E2
Rotterdam *61*C3
Rottweil *67*C5
Rouen *43*B2, *51*C3
Roussillon *69*E5
Rovno *100*F4
Ruanda-Urundi
see Rwanda and Burundi
Rubico (river) *23*C1
Rüdesheim *39*C3
Rue de Sève, Paris *83*A3
Rue St Denis, Paris *83*B2
Rue St Honoré, Paris *83*A-B1–2
Rue St Jacques, Paris *83*B3
Rue St Martin, Paris *83*B2
Rügen
1370 *44*C4 1648 *67*D1
1660 *70*B4 1721 *76*D2
1756–63 *82*D1 1865 *91*C1
Rügenwalde *44*D3, *81*D2
Ruhr (river) *68*C4
Ruhr Area *102*C4
Rumelia
1721 *76*F5 1812 *86*E4
Rusaddir (*mod.* Melilla) *25*B5
Russia, 900 *37*D2
1300–1825 *72* 1721 *76*E-F1–3
c. 1750 *75*D-F1–2
1800–1914 (in Asia) *97*
1812 *86*D-F1–2
1815 *87*C-D1–2
1871 *91*E-F1–3
1914–18 *98*D-F1–3
See also Soviet Union
Russian Principalities, 1100 *39*
Ruthenia *102*E4
Rütli *48*C5
Rwanda *108*B4
Ryukyu Is.
1914 *97*F3
1942–45 *106*B5

S

Saale (river) *44*C5
Saar
1935 *102*C4 1968 *107*B3
Saarbrücken *91*B4
Sabini *23*C2
Sacramento *59*A3, *92*A3
Sadowa *91*D4
Sagres *55*A6
Saguntum (*mod.* Sagunto) *25*C3
Sahara Desert *96*B3
St Andrews *65*E1
St Asaph *49*A1
St Augustine *78*E4
St Bernard *48*B6
St Bernard, Great *85*A1
St Bernard, Little *25*D1
St Bertrand *49*B5
St Brieuc *49*A3
Saint Cloud *86*B3
St Davids *49*A1
Saint Denis *43*B2, *51*C4
Sainte Chapelle, Paris *83*B2(5)
Saintes *49*B4
St Flour *49*B4
St Gallen *43*C3, *48*D5
Saint Geneviève (Pantheon)
Paris *83*B4
St Germain *62*C2
Saint Germain des Prés
Paris *83*B3
St Gildas de Ruis *43*B3
St Gotthard *48*C6
St Helena
c. 1750 *75*C4
1945 *108*A4
St Lawrence (river) *59*D3, *78*E-F1
St Lawrence, Gulf of *78*F1
St Louis *59*C3, *78*D3, *92*D3
St Malo *49*A3
St Mihiel *99*C4
St Omer *61*A4
St Paul, Minnesota *92*C2
St Paul's, London *66*C6
St Petersburg (Leningrad)
*72*B3, *76*E1, *101*C1
St Pol de Léon *49*A3
St Pons *49*B5
St Quentin *61*B5, *62*D2
St Roche, Paris *83*B2(4)
St Thomas *75*B3
St Victor, Paris *83*C4
Saipan *106*C5
Sais *2*A1
Sakhalin, 1914 *97*F1
1941–45 *105*C1, *106*C4
Sakjegözü *6*C2
Sakkara *2*A1
Salado (river) *56*E5
Salamanca *43*A4, *55*B5
Salamis (island) *15*C6
Salamis (town) *15*C6
Salef (river) *40*F4, *41*A2
Salerno *34*B2, *43*D4
Salerno, Principality of *38*D5

Salisbury *43*B2, *65*D4
Salla *103*C1
Salona (Salonae, Spalato, *mod.* Split) *29*C3, *34*B2
Salonika *76*E5, *93*B2, *94*B6, *98*D4
Salt Lake City *92*B3
Salvador *56*B2
Salzburg (town) *39*D3
Salzburg, Archbishopric of
1648 *67*D5 1701 *71*D3
1721 *76*D4
Samara (*mod.* Kuibyshev) *97*B1
Samaria *9*E3
Samarkand *22*E2, *42*C3
Samarobriva (*mod.* Amiens) *27*E1
Samarra *8*B3, *33*D3
Sambre (river) *68*B5
Samnium *23*C-D2
Samoa *105*E3, *106*E6
Samos *20*D4
Samosata *29*D3
Samothrace *14*D1
San (river) *84*E4
Sand Creek *59*B3
San Diego *59*A3
San Francisco *59*A3, *92*A3
Sangarius (*mod.* Sakarya, river) *20*F1–2
Sanlucar *55*B6
San Marino *107*C4
San Miguel *56*C3
San Miniato *45*C3
San Remo *102*C5
San Salvador *58*B3
Sans Souci *82*D2
San Stefano *93*D2
Santa Fe *59*B3
Santa Fe Trail *59*B-C3
Santander *57*A3, *102*A5
Santiago, Chile *56*D6, *88*E4
Santiago, Cuba *56*D1
Santiago de Compostela Spain *43*A4, *55*A4
Santo Domingo *56*E1
Santos *88*F3
San Yuste *57*A4
Saône (river) *69*E3
Sarai *42*B2
Sarajevo *94*A5
Saratoga *78*E2
Sarawak, 1914 *97*E5
Sardes *20*E3
Sardinia, 264 B.C. *23*A-B2–3
during Punic Wars *25*D-E3
44 B.C. *28*C3 A.D. 117 *29*B3
526 *32*C4–5 *c.* 774 *34*A2–3
814 *33*B4 *c.* 900 *37*C5
1100 *39*C5 1230 *40*B3
1556 *57*C4 1701 *71*D5
1721 *76*D5–6
c. 1800 *85*A-B3–4
1812 *86*C5 1815 *87*B4
1859–60 *90* 1914–18 *98*
1919–35 *101*B2 1968 *107*B5
Sardinia, Kingdom of, 1798 *85*
1812 *86*C5 1815 *87*B3–5

1859 *89*A1–2 1859–60 *90*
Sarkars *79*A4–5
Sarlat *49*B5
Sarmatia *28*E-F1
Särna, 1660 *70*B3
Saro (river) *26*C3
Saros, Gulf of *15*C6
Saskatchewan, North (river) *59*B-C2
Saskatchewan, South (river) *59*B2–3
Sassanid Kingdom, 814 *33*E3
Saturn, Temple of, Rome *31*B6(1)
Saudi Arabia *107*F5, *108*C2
Sava (river) *39*D-E4
Savannah (river) *78*D-E4
Savannah (town) *59*D4, *78*E4
Saverne *69*F2
Savigny *43*B2
Savona *49*C5, *86*C4
Savoy, 1454 *45*A1
1701 *71*C3–4 1721 *76*C4
1800 *85*A1 1859–60 *90*A3
Saxon duchies, 1648 *67*C3
Saxons *32*C2
Saxony, Duchy of, 814 *33*B2
936 *38*B-C1 1100 *39*D2
Saxony, Electorate of, 1630 *64*D5
1648 *67*D3 1721 *76*D3
1756–63 *82*C-D3
Saxony, Kingdom of,
1812 *86*C-D3
1871 *91*C-D3–4
Scania
1370 *44*C3 1660 *70*B4
Scapa Flow *98*B1
Schaffhausen *48*C5
Scheldt (river) *61*B4
Schism, the Great, 1378–1417 *47*
Schleswig (town) *64*C4
Schleswig, Duchy of
1370 *44*C3 1648 *67*C1
1660 *70*A4 1866 *91*B-C1
Schlüsselburg (Nöteborg) *72*C3
Schmalkalden *57*C2
Schönbrunn *82*D5
Schönhausen *91*C2
Schweidnitz *82*E3
Schweinfurt *67*C4, *104*C5
Schwerin *44*C4
Schwiebus *81*D3
Schwyz (canton) *48*C5
Schwyz (town) *48*C5
Scone *76*B2
Scotland
c. 900 *37*B2 *c.* 1100 *39*B1
c. 1650 *65*C-D1–2
1721 *76*B2
Scots *32*A1
Scutari *93*D2
Scyllacium *16*E2
Scyllaeum *16*D2
Scyros *14*D2
Scythians *22*B1
Seattle *92*A1
Sebenico *49*E5
Seckau *49*E4

Second World War
in Europe, 1939–41 *103*
in Europe, 1942–45 *104*
in the Far East, 1941–42 *105*
in the Far East, 1944–45 *106*
Sedan *69*E1
Sedgemoor *65*D4
Séez *49*B3
Segesta *16*A2
Segovia *29*A3, *55*C5
Seine (river) *51*C-D3–4, *83*
Seleucia, on the Salef *41*A2
Seleucia, on the Tigris *22*C3
Seleucid Kingdom, 189 B.C. *26*
Selinus (*mod.* Selinunte) *16*A3
Seljuk Empire *40*F3
Selkirk *59*C3
Semgallen, 1795 *84*E1
Seminole Indians *59*C4
Semne *2*A4
Sempach *48*C5
Sena (*mod.* Siena) *25*E2
Seneffe *68*B5
Senegal (river) *96*A4
Senegal (state), 1750 *75*C3
1914 *96*A4 1968 *108*A3
Senj *49*E5
Senlis *49*B3
Sens *43*B3, *51*D4
Seoul *97*F2
Septimius Severus, Arch of
Rome *31*D5(3)
Sequana (*mod.* Seine, river) *27*E2
Serbia, 814 *33*B3
1100 *39*E4–5 1230 *40*D3
1265 *52*A1 1355 *53*A4–5
1565 *57*D3 1701 *71*E4
1721 *76*E4–5 1812 *86*D4
1878 *93*B2 1912–13 *94*B5
1914–18 *98*D4 1919–35 *101*C2
Serbs *32*D4
Seriphos *14*D3
Serkland (Muslim dominions)
*37*A-B5, F4
Servian wall *30*
Seti II, Temple of *4*
Sevastopol *93*E1
Seven days' battle
(during American Civil War) *92*F5
Seven years' War, 1756–63 *82*
Seville *43*A5, *55*B6
Sèvres *102*C4
Shanghai *97*E3, *105*B2
Shantung, 1914 *97*E2
Shawnee Indians *59*C4
Sheffield *65*D3
Shensi *97*E2–3
Sherwood Forest *39*B2
Shetland Is., *c.* 900 *37*B1
1370 *44*A1 1721 *76*C1
1914–18 *98*B1 1968 *107*B1
Shiloh *92*D4
Shimonoseki *97*F2
Shipka Pass *93*C2
Shiraz *33*E3
Shrewsbury *65*D4

Shuruppak *8*C5
Siam, 1914 *97*D-E4–5
See also Thailand
Siam, Gulf of *97*D-E5
Siberia *97*C-D1
Sicily, Greek and Carthaginian
colonization *16*
during Peloponnesian War
*21*A-B3–4
264 B.C. *23*C-D4
during Punic Wars *25*E-F4
44 B.C. *28*C4 A.D. 117 *29*B3
526 *32*C5 *c.* 775 *34*B3
814 *33*B4 *c.* 900 *37*C5
end of 10th and middle of
12th century *38*D6
1100 *39*D6 1230 *40*C4
1556 *57*D5 1701 *71*D5
1714–35 *76*D6
1800 *85*C-D4–5
1812 *86*D5
1860 *90*C-D5–6
1914–18 *98*C4 1919–35 *101*B2
1968 *107*C5
Sicinos *14*D4
Sicyon *15*B6
Side *26*B3
Sidon *41*B4
Siegen *62*E1
Siegfried Line, 1914–18 *99*
Siena (town) *38*C4, *43*C4, *45*C3
Siena, Republic of, 1454 *45*C3
Sierra Leone
1914 *96*A4 1968 *108*A3
Sikiløy (Sicily) *37*C5
Silesia, 1556 *57*D2
1648 *67*E3 1721 *76*D-E3
1742 *81*D-E3–4
1756–63 *82*E3
1865 *91*D-E3·4
Silk route *1*D-E2
Silsilis *2*B3
Simbirsk *97*B1
Simplon *85*A1
Sinai Peninsula *2*B2
Sind, 814 *33*F2
1858 *80*D2 1914 *97*B3
Singapore *97*E6, *105*A3, *108*E2
Sinigaglia *45*E3
Sinkiang *97*C-D2
Sinope *26*C1, *37*E4
Sinus Arabicus (Red Sea) *29*D5
Sinus Persicus (Persian Gulf) *29*F5
Sioux Indians *59*C3
Siphnos *14*D3
Sippar *8*B4
Sittace *24*E6
Sitten *49*C4
Siwah, Oasis of *22*A3
Skaggerak *44*C2
1914–18 *98*C1–2
Skålholt *37*A1
Skanör *44*C3
Skien *70*A3
Slave (river) *59*B2
Slavonia

1812 *86*D4 1912–13 *94*A4
Slavonic peoples *32*D2
Slovakia
1939 *102*E4
1942–45 *104*C5
Slovaks *33*C2, *37*D3
Slovenes *34*B1
Slovenia, 1812 *86*D4
Sluys *61*B3
Småland *70*B4
Smorgon *73*D1
Smyrna *20*D3, *60*C3
Snake (river) *59*B3
Socotra *97*A4
Söderköping *70*C3
Sodom *9*E5
Soest *44*B5
Sofia *52*B1, *94*B5
Sogdiana *22*E2
Soissons *51*D4
Solferino *89*C2
Soli *11*F3
Solomon Is.
1941–42 *105*D3
1942–45 *106*D6
Solothurn *48*B5
Solus (*mod.* Solunto) *16*B2
Solway Firth *65*C3
Somalia *108*C3
Somaliland, French *108*C3
Somerset *65*D4
Somme (river) *61*A5, *99*A2
Soor *81*D4
Sophene, A.D. 117 *29*D3
Soracte *38*C5
Sorbonne, Paris *83*B3
Soubise, Paris *83*C2
Sound, The *44*C3
South Africa
1899–1910 *95* 1968 *108*B5
South America, *c.* 1600 *58*B4–5
1750 *75*B-C4–5
1810–1914 *88*
South Carolina
1783 *78*E4 1861–65 *92*E4
South China Sea *97*E5
South Dakota, 1889 *92*C2
South Dobruja, 1939–41 *103*D3
Southern States of America
1861–65 *92*
South Georgia *58*C5
South Korea *108*E1
South Vietnam *108*E3
Southwark, London *66*C6
Southwest Africa *108*B5
Southwold *76*C3
South Yemen, Republic of *108*C2–3
Soviet Union, 1919–35 *101*D-E1–2
1939–41 *103*D-E1–3
1942–45 *104*D-E4–5
1968 *107*
Spain, 900–1180 *54*
1476 *55*
1556 *57*A-B3–4
1701 *71*A-B4–5
1815 *87*A4–5

1914–18 *98*B3–4
1919–35 *101*A2
1936–39 *102*A-B5–6
1939–41 *103*A3
1942–45 *104*A5
1968 *107*A4–5
Spalato (*mod.* Split) *39*D5
Spanish Caliphate
c. 900 *37*A-B4–5, *54*A-B1
1037 *54*D-E1
Spanish Civil War, 1936–39 *102*
Spanish Colonies, 1750 *75*
Spanish Emirate *33*A4
Spanish Guinea *108*B3
Spanish March, 814 *33*A3
843 *36*
Spanish Morocco, 1936 *102*A6
Spanish-Portuguese demarcation lines after treaties of Tordesillas (1494) and Zaragoza (1529) *58*
Spanish Sahara *108*A2
Spanish Succession, War of the *71*
Spanish territories in northwest Europe, end of 16th century *2*
Sparta *14*B3
Speyer *38*B2, *43*C2
Speyer, Bishopric of, 1648 *67*B-C4
Sphacteria *14*B3, *21*D4
Sphinx at Giza *3*
Spion Cop *95*C1
Spoleto *38*D4
Spoleto, Duchy of, 962 *38*D4–5
Spree (river) *81*D3
Springfield *92*D3
Spy *1*A1
Stade *44*C4
Stagno *49*F5
Stalingrad (*mod.* Volgograd) *101*E1, *104*E5
Stalino (*mod.* Donetsk) *104*E5
Stamford *39*B2
Stångebro *70*B4
Stanley, expedition of, 1871 *96*
Stanleyville (*mod.* Kisangani) *96*D5
Stans *48*C5
Stargard *44*D4
States of the Church
see Papal States
Stavanger *76*C1
Stavern *70*A3
Stavoren *68*C2
Steenkerke *68*B5
Steinheim *1*A2
Steinkjer *103*C1
Steinviksholm *70*B2
Stendal *44*C4
Stepney, London *66*D6
Stettin *44*C4, *64*E4, *70*B5, *81*D2
Stirling *65*C2
Stockholm *44*D1, *70*C3
Stolberg *61*E4
Storhammer (*mod.* Hamar) *70*B3
Stralsund *44*C4, *64*D4, *70*B4, *73*B2, *76*D2
Stralsund, Peace of, 1370 *44*

Strasbourg *38*B2, *43*C3
Strasbourg, Bishopric of
1648 *67*B5
Stratford *65*D4
Stresa *102*C5
Stuttgart *67*C4
Stymphalus *15*A6
Styria, Duchy of, 1556 *57*D3
1648 *67*D E5 1701 *71*D3
c. 1800 *85*D1 1871 *91*D5
Subiaco *35*E3
Suburana, Rome *30*D3(1)
Sucre *88*E3
Sudan *108*B3
Sudetenland, 1938 *102*D-E4
Sudrøyene (Hebrides), *c.* 900 *37*B1
Suevi, Kingdom of the, 526 *32*A3
Suez *96*D3
Suez Canal *96*D3
Suffolk *51*C2
Sully *69*E2
Sumatra
c. 1600 *58*E4 *c.* 1750 *75*E4
1914 *97*D-E5–6 1941–42 *105*A3
1942–45 *106* A6
1968 *108*E3
Sumer *8*C5
Sundgau, 1648 *69*F2
Sundsvall *70*C2
Suomussalmi *103*C1
Superior, Lake *59*C3, *78*D1
Surat *79*C2, *80*D3
Surinam *see* Dutch Guiana
Surrey *65*E4
Susa *10*D4, *22*D3
Susiana *22*D3
Sussex *51*C3
Sutton Hoo *32*B2
Svalbard *58*C1
Sveaborg *86*D1
Sverdlovsk *97*C1
Swabia, 936 *38*B3
1100 *39*C3 *c.* 1630 *64*C6
Swanscombe *1*A1
Swaziland
1900 *95*D1 1968 *108*B5

Sweden
1370 *44*D1–2 1560–1660 *70*
1648 (territories in
Holy Roman Empire) *67*
expansion in 17th century *70*
1700 *73*B-D1
1721 *76*D-E1–2
1812 *86*D1–2
1815 *87*C1
1914–18 *98*C1
1919–35 *101*B-C1
1939–41 *103*C1–2
1942–45 *104*C4
1968 *107*C1–2
Switzerland, 1315–1536 (Swiss
Confederation) *48*
1701 *71*C-D3 1721 *76*C-D4
1800 *85*A-B1 1815 *87*B3
1914–18 *98*C3
1919–35 *101*B2
1968 *107*B4
Sybaris *16*E1
Sybrita *12*B
Syene (*mod.* Aswan) *2*B3
Symaithus (river) *16*C3
Syphax, Kingdom of *25*
Syracuse *16*D3, *23*D4
Syria
860 B.C. *9*F2 600 B.C. *7*B5
under Alexander the Great *22*B3
189 B.C. *26*C4
Roman province 44 B.C. *28*F4
A.D. 117 *29*D4 814 *33*D4
1140 *41* *c.* 1500 *60*D4
1919–35 *101*D2
1939–41 *103*D-E3
1942–45 *104*E6
1968 *107*E5, *108*B-C2
Syrian Desert *6*C-D3
Syros *14*D3
Syrtis Major (*mod.* Gulf of Sidra)
*11*D4, *28*C-D5
Syrtis Minor (*mod.* Gulf of Gabès)
*11*C4, *28*C4
Systerbäck *70*E3
Szechwan *97*D-E3

T

Tabor, Mt. *9*E3, *41*B5
Tabriz *42*B2, *60*E3
Tagus (river) *25*A3, *55*A-C5
Talavera *86*A4
Tallin *107*C2
Tamerlane, Empire of, 1405 *42*
most important campaigns of *42*
Tammerfors *101*C1
Tampa *59*C4
Tanagra *14*C2, *15*C5
Tanais *11*F1
Tananarive (Antananarivo) *96*E6
Tanganyika *108*B-C4

Tanganyika, Lake *96*D5
Tangier *33*A4, *55*B6, *98*A4, *102*A6,
*107*A5
Tanis *2*A1
Tannenberg *74*A4, *100*E2
Tanzania (Tanganyika and Zanzibar)
*108*B-C4
Taranto *38*E5
Taras (Tarentum, *mod.* Taranto)
*11*D2, *21*B2, *23*E2
Tarawa *106*D6
Tarentum (Taras, *mod.* Taranto) *23*E2
Tarentum, Gulf of *21*B-C2

Tarifa *32*A5
Tarpeian Rock, Rome *31*A6
Tarquinii *23*B2
Tarraco (*mod.* Tarragona) *25*C3
Tarraconensis *29*A3
Tarragona *62*C5
Tarsus *26*C3, *28*F3
Tartary *58*D2
Tashkent *97*C2
Tasmania *58*F5
Taunton *65*C5
Tauromenium (*mod.* Taormina)
*16*D2, *25*F4
Tauris (Crimea) *11*E1
Taurus Mts. *60*D4
Tavistock *43*B2
Taxila *22*F3
Tay (river) *65*E1
Taygetus Mts. *14*B3
Tegernsee *43*D3
Teheran *97*B2
Tehuantepec *56*A1
Tell-el-Amarna *2*A2
Tempe, Vale of *14*B1
Temple Tower, Paris *83*C2
Templum Sacrae Urbis, Rome
*31*C6(6)
Tenedos *14*E1
Tennessee (river) *78*D3
Tennessee (state) *92*D4
Tenochtitlan, Mexico *56*A1
Tenos *14*D3
Ten Thousand, Retreat of the
401–399 B.C. *24*
Teotihuacan *56*A1
Terek (river) *72*D5
Terracina *23*C2, *35*E3
Terschelling *61*D1
Teruel *102*B5
Teschen (Tesin) *46*D5
Teschen, Principality of *67*E4
Tesin (Teschen) *102*E4
Tetuan *102*A6
Teutoburgian Forest *29*B1
Teutonic Order, The, 1370 *44*E1–4
14th and 15th centuries *74*
Teutons *29*B-C1
Texas *92*B-C4–5
Texel *61*C1
Thailand, 1941–42 *105*A2
1942–45 *106*A5
1968 *108*E2–3
See also Siam
Thames (river) *66*
Thamugadi (*mod.* Timgad) *29*B4
Thapsacus *24*C5
Thapsus (*mod.* Rass Dimas) *28*C4
Thasos *14*D1
Théâtre Français, Paris *83*B3(7)
Theatrum Pompeii, Rome *30*C2
Thebes (Luxor-Karnak) *2*B3, *29*D5
(Necropolis) *5*
Thebes, Greece *14*C2, *15*C5
Theiss (Tisza, river) *39*E3
Theocoleum, Olympia *18*A2
Theodosia (*mod.* Feodosiya) *11*F1

Thera *14*D4
Thermopylae *14*B2
Thérouanne *49*B2
Thespiae *15*B5
Thessalonica
(*mod.* Thessaloniki or Salonika)
*14*C1, *39*E5, *43*E4, *53*B5
Thessaly
during Peloponnesian War *21*D2
1265 *52*A2 1878 *93*B3
1881, 1912–13 *94*B6
Thingvellir *37*A1
Thompson, routes of *59*B-C2–3
Thorn *44*D4
Thrace
under Alexander the Great *22*A-B1
44 B.C. *28*D-E3
A.D. 117 *29*C3 1912–13 *94*C5
Thracia *11*D-E2
Thracian Sea *14*C-D1
Thurgau *48*D5
Thurii *16*E1
Thuringia, 843 *36*D4
936 *38*C2 *c.* 1630 *64*D5
Thuringians, 526 *32*C2
Thuringian States, 1871 *91*C3–4
Thysdrus (*mod.* El Djem) *29*B4
Tiber (river) *30*B2, *45*D3–4
Tiberias *41*B5
Tibet, *c.* 1300 *42*C-D4
1914 *97*C-D3
Ticino (river) *89*A2
Ticinus (*mod.* Ticino, river) *25*D1
Tientsin *97*E2
Tierra del Fuego *88*E5
Tiflis (*mod.* Tbilisi) *33*D2, *42*B2
Tigris (river) *8*B-C1–5
Tilsit *70*D4
Timbuktu *96*B4
Timor, 1750 *75*E4
1914 *97*F6 1941–42 *105*B3
1942–45 *106*B6 1968 *108*F4
Tingis (*mod.* Tangier) *25*A5
Tinian *106*C5
Tipasa (*mod.* Tefessad) *11*B3
Tippecanoe *59*C3
Tirana *102*E5
Tirka *8*A2
Tiryns *14*B3, *15*B6
Titicaca, Lake *56*E4
Titus, Arch of, Rome *31*D6(13)
Tlaxcala *56*A1
Tlemcen *33*A4
Tobolsk *97*C1
Tobruk *104*D6
Tocantins (river) *88*F2
Togo, 1914 *96*B4 1968 *108*A3
Tokyo *97*F2, *105*C2
Toledo *43*A4, *55*C5
Toletum (*mod.* Toledo) *29*A3
Tolosa (*mod.* Toulouse) *27*E4
Toltec civilization *56*A1
Tomar *55*A5
Tombigbee (river) *78*D4
Tomi *29*D3
Tonga *105*E3, *106*E6

Tongoland, *c.* 1900 *95*D1
Tonkin, 1914 *97*D-E4
Tønning *73*A2
Tønsberg *44*C1
Tor Bay *65*D5
Tordesillas *55*B5
Torgau *82*D3, *104*C5
Torniå *70*D1
Toronto *92*D2
Torres Vedras *86*A4
Tortosa, Spain *37*B4, *55*D5
Tortosa, Syria *41*B3
Toul *49*C3, *62*E2
Toulon *62*E5
Toulouse *39*B4, *43*B4
Toulouse, County of, 1100 *39*B-C4
Tournai *68*A5
Tours *43*B3, *51*C4
Toverud *86*C1
Tower of London *66*C6
Towton *51*C1
Trachenberg *86*D3
Trafalgar *86*A5
Trajan, Forum of, Rome *31*B4–5
Trajan, Temple of, Rome *31*A4
Trangen *86*C1
Tranquebar *79*C2, *80*E5
Transjordan, 1919–35 *101*D2
Trans-Siberian Railway *97*B-F1
Transvaal, 1899–1910 *95*C-D1
Transylvania
1100 *39*E4 1701 *71*F3
1721 *76*E-F4 1812 *86*E3–4
1912–13 *94*B-C4
1919–35 *101*C2
Trapezus (*mod.* Trabzon) *11*F2, *24*D4
Trasimenus
(*mod.* Trasimeno, Lake) *25*E2
Trau *49*E5
Travancore *80*E5
Trebia (*mod.* Trebbia, river) *25*D1
Trebinje *49*F5
Trebizond, Empire of, 1230 *40*F2
1265 *52*E2 1355 *53*E5
Trégnier *49*A3
Trent *45*C1
Trent, Bishopric of, 1648 *67*C6
Trenton *78*E2
Trevi *35*E2
Treviso *43*D3
Tribur *38*B2
Trichinopoly *79*A5, *80*E5
Trier *38*A2, *43*C2, *67*B4
Trier, Archbishopric of, 1648 *67*B4
Trieste *76*D4, *85*C1
Trifels *38*B2
Trim *49*A1
Trincomalee *79*C2, A5, *80*E5
Trinidad *88*E1
Trinil *1*F5
Tripoli (town), North Africa
*33*B4, *96*C3, *104*C6
Tripoli (state), North Africa
1680 *60*A5
1812 *86*C-D6 1914 *96*C3
Tripoli, Syria *41*B4

Tripoli, County of, Syria
1140 *41*C3 1265 *52*E3
Trondhjem (county), 1660 *70*A-B2
Trondhjem (town) *70*B2
Troppau *86*D3, *91*D4
Troppau, Principality of, 1648 *67*E4
Troy (Ilium) *14*E1
Troy, U.S.A. *59*D3
Troyes *51*D4
Trujillo *56*D3, *88*E2
Tsaritsyn (*mod.* Volgograd) *101*E1
Tsushima *97*F2
Tsushima, Strait of *97*F2
Tübingen *43*C3, *91*B5
Tucuman *56*E5
Tuileries, Les, Paris *83*A-B2
Tula *72*C4
Tule Lake *59*A3
Tulle *49*B4
Tulln *76*D4
Tumbes *56*C3
Tune *37*C1
Tunis (town) *33*B4, *57*C5, *85*B5, *104*B6
Tunis (state)
814 *33*B4 1556 *57*C5
c. 1800 *85*B5 1812 *86*C6
1881–1914 *96*C3
1914–18 *98*C5 1919–35 *101*B2
1939–41 *103*A3 1942–45 *104*B6
See also Tunisia
Tunisia *107*B5, *108*B2
See also Tunis
Turan *33*F2
Turenne *69*D4
Turin *43*C3, *71*C3
Turkestan *42*C3
Turkey
1878 (in Balkans) *93*B-E2–3
1912–13 (in Balkans) *94*C-E5–6
1914 *97*A1–4
1914–18 *98*D-F4–5
1919–35 *101*D2
1939–41 *103*D-E3
1942–45 *104*D-E6
1968 *107*D-E4–5
See also Ottoman Empire
Turkish invasions into Europe *60*
Turkmenistan, 1914 *97*B2
Turnberry *65*C2
Tuscany, 962 *38*C4
1701 *71*D4 1721 *76*D5
c. 1800 *85*B-C2
1815 *87*C4
1859–60 *90*B-C3–4
Tusculum *35*E3
Tutankhamon
Mortuary temple of *5*
Tutankhamon, Grave of *5*
Tuthmosis III, Mortuary temple of *5*
Gate of *4*
Tuthmosis IV, Mortuary temple of *5*
Tuxpan *56*A1
Two Sicilies, Kingdom of the
1815 *87*C4–5
1859–60 *90*C-E4–6

Tyana – Tyre

Tyana *24*B5
Tyndaris *16*C2
Tyras (*mod.* Akkerman) *11*E1
Tyras (*mod.* Dniester, river) *11*D-E1
Tyre (*mod.* Sur)
1400 B.C. *6*B2 860 B.C. *9*E2
c. 600 B.C. 7A6

Tyre (cont.) – Tyrrhenian Sea

c. 1140 *41*B4
Tyrol
1648 *67*C5 1721 *76*D4
c. 1800 *85*B1 1815 *87*C3
1859 *89*C1 1919–35 *101*B2
Tyrone *65*B3
Tyrrhenian Sea *23*B-C2–3

U

Ubangi – United Provinces

Ubangi (river) *96*C-D4
Uganda
1914 *96*D4–5 1968 *108*B3
Ugarit (Ras Shamra) *6*C2
Uglitch *72*C3
Ujiji *96*D5
Ukraine (Little Russia), 1796 *72*B4
Uleåborg *70*D2
Ulm *43*C3, *67*C5
Ulster
1429 *51*A1 *c.* 1650 *65*B5
Umbria *23*C1
Umeå *70*C2
Umma *8*C2
United Provinces
1579 *61* 1648 *68*
1701 *71*C1–2 1721 *76*C3
1756–63 *82*A-B2
See also Netherlands and Holland

United States of America – Uxmal

United States of America
1783 *78* 1783–1912 *92*
Unstrut *38*C2
Unterwalden *48*C5
Upper Volta *108*A3
Uppland *70*C3
Uppsala *70*C3
Ur *8*C5
Ural (river) *42*B2
Urbino *35*E1, *45*D3
Uri *48*C6
Uruguay, 1914 *88*E4
Uruk (Erech, Warka) *8*C5
Utah, 1896 *92*B3
Utica (*mod.* Bordj Bou Chateur) *25*E4
Utrecht *39*C2, *61*D2
Utrecht, Bishopric of, 1579 *61*D2
Uxellodunum *27*E4
Uxmal *56*B1

V

Vaal – Varna

Vaal (river) *95*C1
Vafio *14*B3
Valais *48*B-C6
Valence *43*C3, *62*D4
Valencia *43*B5, *55*D5
Valentia (*mod.* Valencia) *29*A3
Valladolid *43*A4, *55*B5
Vallombrosa *35*D2, *43*D4
Vallum Antonini
(Antonine Wall) *29*A1
Vallum Hadriani
(Hadrian's Wall) *29*B1
Valois *51*D3
Valparaiso *56*D6
Vancouver *92*A1
Vandals
Kingdom of the, 526 *32*B-C4–5
migrations *32*
Vandalusia (*mod.* Andalusia) *32*A5
Väner, Lake *44*C2
Vang *37*C1
Vannes *49*A3
Vardar (river) *39*E5
Vardohus (county) *70*B-C1
Varennes *86*C3
Varna *53*C4, *60*C2

Vasa – Venice, Republic of

Vasa *70*D2
Vassy *62*D2
Västerås *70*B3
Västerbotten *70*C-D1–2
Vasvár *76*E4
Vätter, Lake *44*D2
Vaud *48*A6
Vauxhall, London *66*B6
Vecht (river) *68*C2
Veii (*mod.* Veio) *23*C2
Venaissin, 1429 *51*D-E6
Vendée *86*B3
Vendôme *62*C3
Venetia, 264 B.C. *23*B-C1
during Punic Wars *25*E1
1797–1805 *85*C1
1859 *89*C-E1–2
1866 *90*C3
See also Venice, Republic of
Venetian territory in the Balkans
1265 *52* 1355 *53*
Venezuela, 1914 *88*E1
Venice *33*B3, *38*C3, *43*D3, *45*D2,
*90*C3
Venice, Republic of
1100 *39*D4 1230 *40*

1454 *45*C-E1 1556 *57*
1701 *71*D-E3–4
1721 *76*D-E4–5
Venlo *61*E3
Ventimiglia *49*D5
Venus and Roma, Temple of Rome *31*D6
Vera Cruz *56*B1
Vercellae (*mod.* Vercelli) *28*C2
Verden *49*D1, *64*C4
Verden, Bishopric of, 1648 *67*C2
Verdun *38*A2, *99*C3
Verdun, Partition of, 843 *36*
Vereeniging *95*C1
Vermandois *50*B1
Vermont *92*E2
Verona (town) *23*B1, *45*C1
Verona (province) *38*C3
Vervins *62*D2
Vesontio (*mod.* Besançon) *27*F3
Vespasian, Forum of, Rome *31*C5
Vespucci, Amerigo route of, 1501 *58*B5
Vesta, Temple of, Rome *31*C6(9)
Vestal Virgins, House of Rome *31*C6
Vestbygda *58*B2
Vesuvius, Mt. *23*D2
Veszprem *49*F3
Veurne *69*E1
Vézelay *43*C3
Via Aemilia *23*B1
Via Aemilia Scauri *22*A-B1
Via Appia *23*D2
(Rome) *30*D-E3
Via Aurelia *23*B2
(Rome) *30*B-C2–3
Via Campana *30*B-C3
Via Flaminia *23*C2
(Rome) *30*C1
Via Latina, Rome *30*E3
Via Nova, Rome *31*C6
Via Sacra, Rome *30*D-E2–3, *31*C-D6
Via Salaria *23*C2
(Rome) *30*E1
Viatka (river) *72*D-E3
Via Valeria *23*C2
Viborg, Denmark *70*A4
Viborg, Finland *70*E3, *72*B3, *76*E1, *103*D1
Vicenza *45*D1
Vichy *103*B2
Vicksburg *92*D4
Victoria Falls *96*D6
Victoria, Lake *96*D5
Vicus Jugarius, Rome *31*A6
Vienna *38*D3, *43*D3, *60*B1
Vienna, Congress of, 1815 *87*
Vienne (river) *51*C5
Vienne (town) *36*C5, *49*C4
Vigo *102*A5
Viking raids, 800–1000 *37*
Villach *57*D3
Villafranca *89*C2
Villaviciosa *71*B4
Vilna (Vilnyus) *73*D1, *74*C4, *100*F1, *107*C2
Vilnyus (Vilna) *107*C2
Viminal, Rome *30*D-E1–2
Vinci *45*C3
Vindobona (*mod.* Vienna) *29*C2
Vinland *58*B3
Virginia, *c.* 1600 *58*B3
1650 *77*A2 1750 *75*B3
1783 *78*E3 1861–65 *92*E3
Visby *44*D2, *70*C4
Visigoths *32*
Visigoths, Kingdom of the 526 *32*A-B4
Vistula (Weichsel, river) *29*C2, *84*D2–4
Vitebsk *86*E2
Viterbo *57*C4
Vitoria *86*B4
Vitry *69*E2
Viviers *49*C5
Vizagapatam *79*C2, *80*E3
Vladivostok *97*F2
Vlieland *61*C1
Volcano Is. *106*C5
Volga (river) *72*C-D3–4
Volgograd *107*E2
Volhynia, 1793 *84*E-F3
Volkhov (river) *70*E3
Volkhov (town) *70*E3
Volsci *23*C2
Volterra *35*C2
Vorarlberg, 1648 *67*C5
Voronesh *104*E4
Vosegus Mons (Vosges Mts.) *27*F2
Vosges Mts. *99*D4–5
Vulci *23*B2

W

Waal (river) *68*C3
Wabash (river) *78*D2–3
Wagram *86*D3
Waiblingen *39*C3
Waitzen *49*F3
Wake I. *105*D2, *106*D5
Walcheren I. *61*B3
Wales, 526 *32*B2
1100 *39*B2 1429 *51*B2
Wallachia
c. 1500 *60*C2 1556 *57*E3
1701 *71*F3 1721 *76*E-F4
1812 *86*E4 1878 *93*C1
Walvis Bay, *c.* 1900 *95*A1
Walworth, London *66*C6
Warburg *44*C5

Warka *8*C5
Warsaw *73*C2, *74*B5, *103*C2, *104*C5
Warsaw, Grand Duchy of
1812 *86*D2–3
Warta (river) *82*E2
Wartburg *39*D3
Warwick (county) *51*B-C2
Warwick (town) *51*B2
Washington (state), 1889 *92*A1–2
Washington (town) *92*E3, F4
Waterford *37*B2
Waterloo *86*C3
Wearmouth *43*B1
Weichsel *see* Vistula
Weihaiwei *97*E2
Weimar *64*D5, *102*D4
Weinsberg *39*C3
Weissenburg *91*B4
Wellington, expedition to Spain
1808–9 *86*
Wells, England *49*A2
Wells, U.S.A. *59*C3
Wenden *70*D4
Wendland *36*D4
Werben *64*D4
Weser (river) *81*B2–4
Wessex, 526 *32*B2
Western Dvina (river) *70*D-E4
Western Front, 1914–18 *99*
Western Powers, 1939 *103*
West Frankish Kingdom
c. 900 *37*B3–4
West Frisian Is. *68*B-C1
West Indies, *c.* 1600 *58*A-B3
West Irian
(formerly Dutch New Guinea)
*108*F3
Westminster, London *66*B6
Westminster Abbey, London *66*B6
Westmorland *65*D3
Westphalia
c. 1630 *64*C5 1648 *67*B3
1812 *86*C2 1865 *91*B3
West Prussia
13th and 14th centuries *74*A4
1756–63 *82*E1 1772 *81*E2
1865 *91*E2
1919–35 *101*C1
West Turkestan, 1914 *97*B-C2

West Virginia *92*D-E3
West Wales *36*A4
Wetzlar *44*B5, *67*C3
Wexford *65*B4
Whitby *32*B1
Whitechapel, London *66*D6
Whitehall, London *66*C6
White Mountain *64*E5
White Russia, 1772 *84*F2
White Sea *72*C2
Wieliczka *74*B5
Wiener-Neustadt *49*E3
Wiesbaden *102*D4
Wight, Isle of *39*B3, *65*D5
Wilderness *92*F4
Wildhaus *48*D5
Wilhelmshöhe *91*B3
Wilhelmsthal *82*C3
Willendorf *1*A2
Wiltshire *51*B3
Winchester *43*B2, *49*B2
Windau *44*E2
Windsor *51*C2
Winnipeg, Lake *59*C3
Winterthur *48*D5
Wisconsin (river) *78*D1–2
Wisconsin (state) *92*C-D2
Wismar *70*A5, *82*C1
Wittenberg *57*C2, *64*D5
Witwatersrand *95*C1
Wolfenbüttel *64*C5
Wollgast *81*D2
Worcester (county) *51*B2
Worcester (town) *39*B2, *65*D4
Worms *38*B2, *43*C2, *67*C4
Wörth *91*B4
Wounded Knee *59*B3
Wroxeter *36*B4
Württemberg *38*B2
Württemberg, Duchy of
1648 *67*C4–5
Württemberg, Kingdom of
1812 *86*C3 1815 *87*B-C3
1871 *91*B-C4–5
Würzburg *43*C2
Würzburg, Bishopric of
1648 *67*C4
Wüsterhausen *81*D3
Wyoming *92*B2–3

X

Xerxes' Canal
*20*C1
Xerxes' expedition against Greece
480 B.C. *20*

Y

Yalta *104*E5
Yanaon *80*E4, *97*C4

Yangtse-kiang (river) *97*D-E3
Yarmouth *44*A4

Yarmuk (river) *9*F3, *33*D4
Yellow Sea *42*E-F3
Yemen
814 *33*E5 1968 *108*C2
Yenan *97*E3, *105*A1, *106*A4
Yenisei (river) *42*D1
Yokohama *97*F2
York *43*B1, *44*A3, *65*D3
York Factory *59*C2
Yorkshire *51*C1

Yorktown *78*E3
Ypres *61*A4, *99*A1
Yser (river) *99*A1
Yucatan *56*B1
Yugoslavia
1919–35 *101*C2
1939–41 *103*C3
1942–45 *104*C5
1968 *107*C4
Yukon (river) *59*B1

Z

Zab, Little (river) *8*B-C1–2
Zab, Great (river) *8*B1
Zacynthos (*mod.* Zante) *14*A3
Zagreb *101*C2
Zaiton *42*E4
Zama *25*E5
Zambezi (river) *96*D5
Zambia (formerly Northern Rhodesia) *108*B4
Zante *71*E5
Zanzibar *96*E5
See also Tanzania
Zara *39*D4, *85*D2, *102*D5
Zaragoza *43*B4, *55*D5
Zealand *91*C1
Zeeland *61*B3
Zeitz, March of *38*C2

Zela *26*C2
Zenta *71*E3
Zerbst *64*D5
Zeus, Temple of
Acropolis, Athens *17*D4
Zincirli *6*C2
Zipangu (Japan) *58*F3
Zorndorf *82*D2
Zug *48*C5
Zuider Zee *61*D2
Zululand, *c.* 1900 *95*D1
Zürich *48*C5
Zweibrücken *69*F2
Zweibrücken, Principality of *82*B4
Zwiefalten *36*D5
Zwing-Uri *48*C6
Zwolle *44*B4, *61*E2